Healing Public Schools

The Winning Prescription to Cure Their Chronic Illness

Leon M. Lessinger
Allen E. Salowe

scarecrow
education

The Scarecrow Press, Inc.
A Scarecrow Education Book
Lanham, Maryland, and London
2001

SCARECROW PRESS, INC.
A Scarecrow Education Book

Published in the United States of America
by Scarecrow Press, Inc.
4720 Boston Way, Lanham, Maryland 20706
www.scarecroweducation.com

4 Pleydell Gardens, Folkestone
Kent CT20 2DN, England

British Library Cataloguing in Publication Information Available

Library of Congress Cataloging-in-Publication Data

Lessinger, Leon M.
    Healing public schools : the winning prescription to cure their chronic illness / Leon M.
Lessinger, Allen E. Salowe.
        p. cm.
    Includes bibliographical references.
    ISBN 0-8108-3968-7 (alk. paper)—ISBN 0-8108-3969-5 (pbk. : alk. paper)
    1. School improvement programs—United States. 2. Education—Standards—United
States. I. Salowe, Allen E. II. Title.

LB2822.82 .L46 2001
371.01'0973—dc21

00-067969

⊗™ The paper used in this publication meets the minimum requirements of
American National Standard for Information Sciences—Permanence of
Paper for Printed Library Materials, ANSI/NISO Z39.48-1992.
Manufactured in the United States of America.

Contents

Acknowledgments

Jay Wilson, a J. P. Morgan vice president, reviewed an early monograph on this subject, *Coopetition: Cooperative Competition, How to Gain and Keep Wealth in the New American Economy* (1995). His notes led to a more results-focused book.

Our earlier book, *Game Time: The Educator's Playbook for the New Global Economy* (Lessinger and Salowe 1997), was aimed at the professional audience of educators and stakeholders with the power to influence better school performance. They can promote the action steps necessary to achieve continuous school improvement, if they so choose.

Healing Public Schools is aimed at a wider audience. It is targeted to the grass roots of the American population in hopes of mobilizing support for widespread action to improve classroom teaching reliability. Its messages were periodically tested. Especially valuable were roundtable sessions with educators and CEOs of large and small Florida businesses. Meetings sponsored by Enterprise Florida, a public–private business consortium, included the Florida Jobs and Education Partnership and the Florida Department of Education.

Our thanks to those who helped improve the finished work, but they are in no way responsible for any of its shortcomings.

Foreword

America has a problem—and it is a big one.

For all our innovation and creativity; for all that we are the driver of the global economy; for all that we have been and continue to be to ourselves and to the world, we have one big problem.

As a country, we are complacent. Nowhere is that more apparent than in our educational system.

I am not an educator by trade, although I teach both MBA and professional extension courses. My focus on education is based on my business and organizational experience in every sector and throughout this country for the last twenty years.

The constant? In every organization, we see the impact of the problems in the educational system.

It doesn't matter that for twenty years—since the "Why Johnny Can't Read" uproar—we have seen educational systems at every level and in every community make new claims to how they would change the situation. Johnny can read and he will—no matter what it takes.

What it has taken over these past years has put a toll on everyone involved in every aspect of education: the educators trying to find a way to bring higher learning—and more importantly, a love for learning—into the classroom; the administrators all dealing with constant change in a system that seems to result in the same outcome—too many Johnnys still can't read; the parents desperate to ensure that their children will be able to succeed in their learning and fit comfortably into this new economy; the children, who suffer through an almost ongoing lab course of experiments in everything from changing methodologies to ever-increasing and unrealistic standards to be met.

The constant? With all that change, nothing has fundamentally changed. The precepts upon which teaching is performed and school districts are administered have stayed fundamentally the same through thick and thin, change after change, new program after new program.

Every one of those programs was to provide the right answer—this time. Yet, ultimately, no one has truly addressed the issues that need to be addressed to ensure that Johnny will read, write, compute and, more than anything else, think. Johnny has to learn how to think.

The Challenge

The problem with education and educators, as with most large organizations, is that they are entrenched. In many ways, the educational system is the best example of the complacency of this country. We rest on our laurels even as we say we are going to do things differently.

These problems are further exacerbated by the political climate in which decisions are being made. The educators who become politicos— no matter how well trained, well thought, and well intentioned—become victims of the system. Education may be *funded* by the government but should not be *managed* by the government.

As with any specialized industry, education should be monitored and overseen by those who truly specialize in the field. It is an area of expertise as much as it is a field of endeavor.

Moreover, those who house the educational organization at every level have a passion for and a belief in what they do. They are truly committed to fulfilling the needs of the students—of assisting in the creation of thinking, sentient beings who will be valuable, contributing adults. They should be allowed to work to their passion, innovate and create within their classrooms, yet always work within a system that is designed to succeed—as well as to create success for its "customers," the students.

Educators are well aware that the output of their system is the input into society. We all see the results of education as it stands today, and it is not acceptable for individuals or for society. In fact, unless and until we directly address the fundamentals of the system, we are dooming our society to a future of being an also-ran. We may believe our press at the moment—but moments pass and we will be working from a seriously disadvantaged position in the not-too-distant future.

Signs, Portents, and Industry History

Those who work in industry are already seeing the signs and portents of things to come. Organizations have to provide far more extensive training in basic skills than ever before. The technology industry, while still recruiting in this country, spends untold millions recruiting in what are considered third-world countries for qualified candidates. Worse yet, they are finding more and more candidates in those countries than they do in our own.

Yet we have had the answer to all these questions and challenges for many years. Our complacency has kept us from acting as we need to act.

In the late 1970s, America realized that it had a problem with Japan. Suddenly, it seemed, the Japanese had cornered our markets in both automobiles and consumer electronics. We were at war. We were under siege. We were not prepared.

Yet for anyone who had been paying attention, it was clear since the 1950s that the Japanese were actively and conscientiously working toward creating marketable products. They knew their products had to be both competitive and attractive to the American audience.

Where they did not have the foresight to innovate new products, they licensed or bought our technology. Where they already had the products, they focused on creating the highest quality they could so that their products could be easily differentiated from ours.

"Made in Japan" quickly moved from an insult to an expression of the highest regard.

Still, we were unprepared.

Our solution? We mobilized. We learned what the Japanese had done and how to apply it to our way of doing business. We adopted and adapted their systems and turned them into our own. We created a quality-improvement system and methodology that continues to keep our organizations competitive to this day.

The lessons to be learned from this bit of history are many and varied—and all apply to education as it now stands.

We are at a crossroads—not only for education, but for our country. It is our responsibility to ensure that we look at the fundamentals of how we perform the business of education to ensure that the products and services we create are of the highest order.

"Made in America" should be a point of pride, and what we must make in this country—first and foremost—is the highest-caliber citizen and societal contributor possible.

That can be achieved, in part, by bringing *quality* precepts into the educational system. There are no surprises here. We have all been aware for a very long time that the problem exists. The only question has been, what must we really do about it to ensure that it is fixed—and fixed for the long term.

Opportunities Abound

There is no better time than now to adopt a quality focus and system in education. Whether it is because we simply want to solve a long-standing problem or because we have a strong and true vision for the future doesn't matter. The fact is, we do have a problem, it does have a workable solution, and we must have a vision for the future if we are to have a future of our own making.

We are also in the luxurious position of having our answers clearly—and successfully—mapped out for us. This country has over twenty years of experience in the whys and how of quality. We know how to do it and we know how to do it well. Better yet, we even know what the most common mistakes are and how to recognize and avoid them.

We have the answers. Now the only question is, do we have the wherewithal?

By nature, I am an optimist. I believe that we can do anything we set our minds to. More important, as a country, we have the ability to band together and create miracles—fast and furious.

Well, the chips are down. This situation works in our favor because we all can see the problem. It is no longer someone else's issue; it has become the country's issue.

Private industry is escalating its work with schools in their areas. Parents and teachers are banding together to better identify how the children's learning problems can be solved. Schools are trying and trying again to get it right.

All of which means that the passion for success in creating the educational system we all want and need exists. We have to harness that passion and all the energy being put into changing the current system and focus on truly affecting the fundamental system. We must question and challenge—again and again. We must look at how our educational organizations are operating and determine why they are as they are and what needs to be done to make them as we need and want them to be.

We need to use a system already successfully implemented in this country and throughout the world, and turn around the educational system just as we would any ailing organization. The talent is there. The will is there. The method is there.

And so, like any organization working assiduously to create strategic and tactical success, we must channel our energies into making the educational system one of which we can all be proud. That way, no matter where Johnny might live, which school he or she attends, or what he or she wants to be when grown up, we are all sure that the dreams of the child will be facilitated by the adult with grace, skill, and ability—a tribute to him or herself, the country, and society as a whole.

LESLIE L. KOSSOFF

Prologue

Why now, more than ever, do parents, educators, and businesspersons need to pay attention to and use the prescriptions laid bare in *Healing Public Schools*?

Here are three compelling reasons:

1. Unlike many approaches to solving the well-publicized problems of public education, our prescription for improvement is built on the fact that most Americans want to reform the existing public schools, not support schemes for abandoning or excessively tinkering with them.

2. In line with what the most accurate polling results tell us, we directly address the most urgent question on people's minds, "How do we go about improving and strengthening the existing public schools?" *Healing Public Schools* offers a prescription—tested know-how that everyone can understand and use.

3. *Healing Public Schools* addresses what we now know is the single most distressing challenge in all public schools: the unreliability in the quality of classroom teaching from one classroom to another, from semester to semester, and from school year to school year. We directly address this tyranny of chance and show how it can be overcome.

Much has been written about public school performance. It is as though a chronic illness has overtaken one of the world's great education systems and it is now laid up sick in bed. What is needed is a straightforward set of treatments to explain the *why* and the *actions* necessary to heal these ailments. The goal of these treatments is to help school classrooms work reliably through quality improvement. The Malcolm Baldrige National Quality Award Criteria for Education and ISO 9000 Education Standards are part of the ingredients in the elixir to get public schools back on their feet. *Healing Public Schools: The Winning Prescription to Cure Their Chronic Illness* is our prescription.

A forerunner to this book, *Game Time: The Educator's Playbook for the New Global Economy* (Lessinger and Salowe 1997), received positive reviews from educators and business leaders alike. For example:

- The National Association for Industry–Education Cooperation (NAIEC) January 1998 Newsletter lauded the book's collaborative planning recommendations.
- Dr. Roger Kaufman, Office of Needs Assessment and Planning, Florida State University, summed it up this way: "If education is the key to our future, this book is the key to education. Use it."
- Dan Lavely, senior vice president of the Connecticut Development Authority, challenged educators: "Your role is to help your students to develop real skills to make real contributions in the real world. If you don't understand what that means, get another job."
- Dr. William Kiefer, who directed the nation's first successful ISO school certification in the Lancaster (Pa.) School District, wrote: "*Game Time* captures a new vision for public education. It uses the fundamental tenets of the Baldrige Quality Award and ISO 9000."
- Bob Alten, director of accountability for the St. Johns County (Fla.) School District concluded that: "this fascinating and practical work promotes ideas which launch action."

The time is now to take education one step further. The persuasive reasons for reading and applying the insights from *Healing Public Schools* are summarized below.

What the American People Care about When Asked

"The notion that the public is dissatisfied with its public schools is based on myth instead of fact," says the 2000 Phi Delta Kappa/Gallup poll summary. "Respondents continue to indicate a high level of satisfaction with their local schools, a level of satisfaction that this year approaches its all-time high among the parents whose children attend those schools" (Rose and Gallup 2000).

Supporters of the public schools found other promising news. The report showed a "turning away from high-stakes testing; the leveling off and the downward trend in support for choice involving private or church-related schools; the fact that lack of financial support has jumped into first place as the biggest problem; the preference for balance in the curriculum over a focus on "the basics"; and the clear support for public schools that is evident throughout the poll."

Here is the first clue to where we are going with *Healing Public Schools*. From the Gallup summary again, "Public satisfaction is also evident in the fact that 59% of Americans believe that reforming the existing system of public schools, rather than seeking an alternative system, is the best way to bring about school improvement."

Setting aside the popular political arguments of the day, our bottom line is supported by the results of the Gallup researchers: "When given the specific choice, 75% [of respondents] would improve and strengthen existing public schools while just 22% would opt for vouchers, the alternative most frequently mentioned by public school critics."

Financial resources will always be limited, but zeal for school improvement will continue unabated. This leaves the unanswered question as simply: How do we go about improving and strengthening the existing public schools? *Healing Public Schools* answers the nagging "how" question.

Healing Public Schools is squarely in the same camp with the Gallup report, which states: "Today's accountability efforts are directed toward the schools' role in improving achievement. The parents have a greater effect than the schools, teachers, or students themselves on student achievement." The report goes on to clarify the public's inertia, concluding that "these findings may go a long way toward explaining why the public does not seem inclined to blame the public schools when students have difficulty achieving satisfactory levels of learning."

We strongly disagree with any conclusion that encourages letting the public schools "off the hook." *Healing Public Schools* argues that it is precisely because the public schools do not currently have reliable quality systems in place that the public schools do not and cannot hold themselves to the higher standards of performance mandated by their states. This is a major underlying reason for the poor student achievement, poor student behavior, and inadequate school leadership so often noted in discussions of public education.

For example, with limited human and financial resources, the movement for charter schools—along with vouchers, a leading choice for many reformers—may in fact further distract us from concentrating on solving the school-improvement equation. Most parents have neither read nor heard about such schools. Most parents surveyed oppose freeing charter school operations from state regulations, especially in matters related to curriculum. The public strongly believes that charter school must be accountable to state standards in the same way other public schools are accountable.

When all else fails, the public and its political leaders, only (sometimes really "front-running followers") watch where polls lead them, then turn to the quick fix. Money is now named as the number one problem. Topping the school-improvement agenda is lack of financial support followed by lack of discipline, overcrowding, violence, and drugs.

Healing Public Schools sets forth what many authorities believe schools are for. We mirror what the public defines as the purposes of the public schools and what it expects from these schools. Gallup reports that "the public sees the most important purposes [of the public schools] as preparing students to become responsible citizens and helping people to become economically self-sufficient. These are purposes that are frequently mentioned as reasons why public schools were first created."

Faced with difficult choices, the public chooses public schools providing a balanced education over solely teaching the basic subjects. Moreover, seeking a more pragmatic view of purpose, "The public chooses preparing students for college or work over preparing them for effective citizenship" (Rose and Gallup 2000). It grades extracurricular activities as supplements to academic subjects.

A majority of the public believes that all students have the ability to attain high levels of learning. "The most important finding in this area is the strong public consensus that most students achieve only a small part of their full academic potential in school" (Rose and Gallup 2000).

Healing Public Schools places testing in the context of teach what you say you are going to teach, and then measure it. Increased emphasis on the use of standardized tests is not supported by Gallup's findings. The public sees class work and homework as significantly more important than tests in measuring student achievement. They would not use standardized tests to determine what students have learned, but to determine the kind of instruction they need.

The public strongly affirms the principle of local control.

- They would like to see less federal influence.
- They would like to see the state government have somewhat less influence.

- They view local boards of education as having the right amount or too little say in decisions that affect the local schools.
- They seem reasonably satisfied with the role of principals and superintendents.
- They are less ambivalent about the role of local teacher unions.
- They would like to see more decisions made by students, parents, and teachers.

We take issue with this mixed bag. These principles may have worked well in simpler times, but now there is need to update and more sharply focus our goals.

Healing Public Schools goes head to head on the need to prepare students for twenty-first-century, world-class job competition. It seeks to energize the nation to no longer accept lagging U.S. educational results when compared with other industrialized nations of the world. The U.S. may lead the globe in guns, ships, planes, food production, a strong economy, and standard of living, but America's public schools simply do not stack up very well when it comes to preparing its students to effectively compete in a new information-driven economic world. How we gain school improvement while holding fast to our American values of local school control underpins our story.

THE WINNING PRESCRIPTION: THE HOW QUESTION

The subtitle of *Healing Public Schools* reads: *The Winning Prescription to Cure Their Chronic Illness*. We chose the term *prescription* after careful thought. It may seem obvious in talking about healing to think of a prescription. Most people have observed their doctor writing an order for some needed medicine or treatment. We use the word *prescription* in that same sense. In fact, this book is a kind of written order for a treatment.

A prescription is also a formula directing the preparation of something. Our book describes a prescription for healing sick schooling — that is, a formula for helping solve the major problems that stand in the way of effective education for all students.

The winning prescription in *Healing Public Schools* is made up of two formulas: ISO 9000 education standards and the Malcolm Baldrige

National Quality Award education standards. The blending of these two powerful "stimulants" results in an unexcelled quality tonic for what most ails public schools.

The ISO Formula. The next time you buy a package of photographic film, look carefully at the fine print. You'll notice, perhaps for the first time, the film speed classification ISO on the box. That identification assures you that the film meets international standards of quality and that it will fit and work the same in all cameras that take that size film, regardless of where the film is made.

With that experience in mind, and the new awareness, you will be amazed to find the ISO term on many products and on flags and banners flying over companies. The ATM card you use to access the cash you need to buy the film is also built on the ISO standard.

If you go to Lancaster, Pennsylvania, and pass by a school or the school district's offices, you'll see a large, conspicuously placed banner announcing *ISO Registered.* Several other school systems in our country are in the pipeline for registration. The public schools of Lancaster are the first in the U.S. to be officially registered as ISO certified.

Why is this newsworthy? Why is it important for a product like photographic film or a provider of a service like a school to be ISO registered? Why are thousands of American companies now or in line to become ISO registered?

The Term ISO. *ISO* is a Greek word best translated as *harmonize.* When something is harmonious, the parts come together pleasingly or appropriately. We think of harmony properly when we think of music. The word *rapport*—a relationship of mutual trust or emotional affinity—is another kind of harmony or suitable blending, this time among people. If all the workers who make a product or deliver a service are in harmony, the likelihood of the product or service being of top quality is certainly increased. When used in connection with product or service provider standards, the word *ISO* suggests a formula for bringing harmony to the people systems that have been organized to produce the products or deliver the services.

The International Organization for Standardization, headquartered in Geneva, Switzerland, took as its name the Greek word *ISO,* meaning *equal.* The true parents of ISO are the members of the European Union (EU). The countries of the EU, in trying desperately to improve their marketplace prowess after World War II, found that they were severely handicapped in working together to produce quality products. They often had differences in their ways of measuring standards and in assuring customers of the quality of their products. They needed to have common standards for the people processes that reliably produce quality products. The first ISO standards were aimed at manufacturing product assurance. That box of ISO-certified photo film we buy today results from that series of standards.

Companies adopting and meeting the ISO standards found two impressive classes of benefits: the recognition that they were ISO certified improved their competitive position in the world marketplace, and the costs of producing their products went down while the reputation of the product's quality went up.

ISO Service Provider Standards Are Widespread.   At this writing, at least 100,000 companies worldwide have been registered as compliant with the ISO standard. Current estimates are that there will be 200,000 U.S. ISO registrations, including the auto industry equivalent, QS 9000, in the near future.

ISO for Schools and Colleges.   In 1987, ISO issued the first version of ISO 9000 standards directly aimed at service enterprises like schools. Having seen the power of ISO in improving the reliability of the quality of product manufacturing with its dramatic shrinking of waste, it was natural to look for similar results in the service sector. Happily, this has happened.

ISO Accomplishments.   Based on what actually happened to companies that succeeded in becoming ISO registered, companies can claim that they have quality-assured processes in place and customers can believe that the products and services they produce meet specifications and perform reliably.

The basic assumption—now demonstrated in the marketplace—that underlies ISO standards is this: a reliable quality-assurance process helps satisfy customer needs by reducing specification failures while the product or service is being built and/or delivered.

This simple idea has proven so impressive that companies in 110 countries around the world now use ISO standards. Great Britain has pioneered the use of ISO standards for schools and colleges. Nations as widely disparate as Singapore, Israel, and Saudi Arabia have followed suit with their school systems. The United States is joining.

ISO Philosophy.   The two basic goals of ISO are to satisfy customers by (1) providing a level of quality for products and services and

(2) to reduce waste and failure. The standards reflect the hard-earned knowledge that (a) it is in the processes that are used to make a product or deliver a service that quality is shaped and (b) that a standard set of guidelines helps leaders and staff look carefully at their processes and *continually* improve them.

ISO turns the familiar "The proof of the pudding is in the eating" to "The proof that the pudding will be eaten lies in the reliability of the quality processes that make it."

The Record of ISO in Schools and Colleges. Education enterprises have found that ISO makes possible for them to *warrant* that they have:

* established a quality-assured management system
* reduced costs that make their services efficient
* made it possible for suppliers to give them better-quality products and services
* an educational system that meets recognized world-class standards.

How ISO Works in Public Schools and Teachers Colleges. Companies in pursuit of reliability in the quality of their products and services know that the basic process for doing their work centers on the repeated use of the cycle: Plan-Do-Check-Act. The repeated use of this cycle is the noble road to continuous improvement.

ISO standards ask schools to look carefully at their uses of this basic PDCA Cycle and provide written documents that:

* show what you propose
* show the actual results
* measure the differences between the proposal and the results
* modify the plan and start over to improve the process

ISO Local School Control. In completing the ISO review process with independent examiners (required for world-class registration), the local school writes its own quality manuals, plans to meet its specific needs, articulates procedures to accomplish its goals, and lays out work instructions geared to its capabilities and student population. These required records, together with independent on-site inspections, give ISO registrars the necessary evidence of fulfillment at the local school level.

Examples of ISO Standards in Action in Schools.   ISO carefully defines all terms for maximum ease of communication.

Definitions: For the purposes of the American National Standard, the definitions given in ANSI/ISO/ASQC A8402 and the following definitions apply.

Instruction: The process of planning and providing the time, order, place, materials, and guidance required for students to meet the instructional specification. Although there are philosophical and practical differences between training and education, they do not affect the quality system and are not differentiated in Z1.11. *Instruction* is used to cover both education and training.

Instruction Specification: Written information, made available to students about a program or course, should include, but not be limited to, the following:

a. title of program or course
b. credit, diploma, degree, or certificate
c. time required
d. intended outcomes/training goals
e. student entry skill and knowledge
f. performance objectives and standards
g. major concepts and content
h. classroom, laboratory, or shop activities
i. measures of student competence; e.g., written examinations or instructor observations.

Entry-level Skills: Skills and knowledge the students have acquired prior to the instruction in order to complete instruction successfully.

ISO suggested actions necessary for reliable quality: Conduct a needs assessment and analysis (sometimes referred to as "performance systems analysis" or "needs analysis"). The needs assessment should be conducted to identify potential or actual performance needs that may have been created, in part by the absence of or inadequate instruction, to determine:

a. how instruction can provide skills that help to meet needs
b. how future opportunities can be identified and how needs can be met

c. specific measures to determine instruction effectiveness
d. if skills to be taught match initially identified needs. (This type of summative evaluation is referred to as *Level 3 and 4 evaluations* in training literature.) These studies provide information used in the instruction review process.

ISO requires verification of customer rights (4.6.4 Verification of purchased product): An instruction suppliers' official announcements, applications, and other descriptive information should state the right, whenever educational and training institutions afford the customer the right, to verify at the instruction site the suitability of the facilities, the suitability of the academic and technical staff, and conditions for the delivery of the instruction.

The Malcolm Baldrige National Quality Award (MBNQA) Criteria

In the 1980s, it was widely recognized that America's ability to compete as a nation increasingly depended on the quality of our products and services. We must therefore have high-quality and reliable systems for manufacturing and providing services. The American people saw some handwriting on the wall, stating: "If we do not produce well, we will not live well."

How could we get our enterprises to improve, given the well-known American appetite for independence and self-reliance? Certainly, an order from government would be foolhardy. The answer turned out to be a competitive prestigious national quality award containing the known quality criteria, to be awarded by the president of the United States.

President Ronald Reagan signed the Malcolm Baldrige National Quality Award into law in 1987—the same year that ISO launched the quality standards for service providers. It was named for the popular Secretary of Commerce who died that year. Since then, the award has altered and improved how business is done. The Baldrige is now generally respected as one of the keys to the continued success of U.S. businesses both at home and worldwide. It highlights customer satisfaction, workforce empowerment, and increased productivity. The award has come to symbolize America's commitment to excellence.

A still-small, but growing, number of local school districts use the Baldrige prize criteria as a quality stimulus. More than forty states (forty-four at last count) now have their own quality award programs based on Baldrige criteria. In the Baldrige model, educators find a system that: (a) focuses on the customer; (b) aligns internal processes with customer satisfaction; (c) puts everybody in the organization to work on shared goals; (d) facilitates long-term continuous improvement; (e) demands management by fact; (f) promotes prevention rather than reaction; (g) looks for ways to be a more flexible and responsive organization; (h) seeks opportunities for partnerships; and (i) values results.

The Baldrige Quality Award Criteria. The categories of the Baldrige criteria are generic and can be used by any organization, public or private. Applying the Baldrige quality principles to an organization has been shown to improve the organization's overall competency, quality of service and products, customer satisfaction, and profitability. Seven principles are addressed in detail.

- Leadership. Looks at how leadership is exercised throughout the organization, and is the basis for and the way key decisions are made, communicated, and carried out at all levels. Leaders should constantly reinforce the organization's mission, vision, values, and high expectations.
- Strategic Planning. Refers to how the organization sets strategic direction, determines action plans, and translates them into performance and results.
- Customer Focus and Satisfaction. Relates to how the organization determines the requirements and expectations of its customers, enhances those relationships, and measures satisfaction.
- Information and Analysis. Data about customers, processes, and results are repeatedly used to make fact-based decisions and to improve individual and organizational performance.
- Human Resource Development and Management. Employees who are led, trained, and rewarded to act instinctively on behalf of the customer create value by designing, executing, and improving processes.
- Process Management. Looks at how key processes are designed, effectively managed, and improved. By carefully analyzing internal processes, the organization can eliminate unnecessary steps,

errors, and timing barriers that slow responsiveness or reduce value to the customer.

- Results. Provides a "results" focus for all processes and process improvement activities. When measures in key processes are aligned with customer satisfaction measures, managing internal processes should yield high levels of customer satisfaction.

ISO and Baldrige: Putting the Winning Prescription into Action

Organizations use the ISO standard as a means to establish a strong quality system en route to entering a corporate, state, or national award, such as the Malcolm Baldrige National Quality Award (MBNQA) or any one of over forty state quality awards. ISO itself is not an award, and no scores are reported for its performance. Any organization that satisfies the self-imposed requirements, as established in the standards, can become registered to ISO.

Many CEOs of companies reported starting down the road to ISO registration after they hear a presentation on the Baldrige Award held each year in Washington, D.C. Those literally passionate with the quality of their services see value in striving for MBNQA. Rather than immediately targeting a Baldrige application, many choose ISO registration as a first-step strategic business investment. They clearly see the distinct promise of ISO as a way to formalize their organization's quality structures and use independent third-party verification—similar to the familiar accounting audit verification—of their quality systems. They also recognize that registration dramatically demonstrates their service quality to their current clients and serves as powerful criteria for future client satisfaction.

Healing Public Schools sees a school ISO program as the foundation for other quality-related initiatives. Most states currently have quality initiatives in place, and most, if not all, based on the Baldrige. Because there is some overlap and reinforcement between the requirements of ISO and the Baldrige, an effective ISO program may serve as an initial, practical, and user-friendly step toward a Baldrige-based state program. Successful quality practitioners see similarities among the different quality tools and techniques. As a result, local schools are able to parlay the strengths and achievements established in one program into building an improved program.

Pocket-Sized Prescription under ISO/Baldrige for Education

* Say what you are going to do; write it down: Document your processes.
* Do what you say you're going to do: Follow your own procedures.
* Measure what you said you'd do: Use complete and accurate records.
* Make changes for improvement: Apply continuous improvement.

ADDRESSING THE TYRANNY OF CHANCE IN PUBLIC EDUCATION

Healing Public Schools is the first book to address the central question on every parent's mind when they send their child off to school, "Will my child get a good teacher this time?" On the first day of school, parents wonder about the teacher that their child will get *this* school year. They know from personal experience that what that teacher can do for the child in that classroom is the most important factor in their child's success that term. And they know intuitively that, currently, it is chance whether the teacher this time will be a good one.

Parents have always known that it really matters which teachers their children get. That is why those parents with the time and skills to do so work very hard to ensure that, by hook or by crook, *their* kids are assigned to the best teachers. That is also a major reason why the children of less "school-smart" parents are often left with the most ineffective teachers.

The naked truth is this: in the matter of the reliable quality of classroom teaching, schools operate under a tyranny of chance. At the same time, teacher quality is on the national agenda as never before.

One serious error is still being made in discussions about getting highly qualified teachers into America's classrooms. It is an error that precludes any real solution to this most crucial solution to education's needs. What is missing is, in fact, the Achilles' heel of teacher quality and effectiveness in the classroom. The missing part is recognizing the supreme importance of the reliable quality of the system that leads, manages, and administers the school and school system in which the teaching takes place.

Major lessons learned from the quality revolution now infused into American business and industry are either unknown or ignored in discussions about teacher and teaching quality. The chance of getting a good teacher into *every* classroom can only be warranted in a system specifically designed and managed to achieve reliable classroom teaching quality. It is clear that, without such a system, only the tyranny of chance can rule. Further, putting a qualified teacher into an unreliable system only serves to raise the likelihood that the teacher will not stay long or be severely blocked in reaching his or her full potential.

The prescription in *Healing Public Schools* sets out the formulas for achieving improvements in the people systems of public schools. If properly and continuously applied, it can come to eliminate the destructive effects on students and stakeholders that flow from the present tyranny of chance in classroom teaching.

CHAPTER 1

What's Ailing Our Public Schools?

If a doctor who practiced surgery one hundred years ago were to enter today's modern operating room, he would scarcely know where to begin. Every stage of the operating room process and the equipment used is totally different. If a teacher who taught school one hundred years ago were to walk into today's classroom, she would know exactly where to begin. She would find the blackboard, chalk, papers, pencils, subjects, and methods little changed from the past.

Health care is a metaphor we use to reflect needed changes. To heal the long-term chronic illnesses that afflict the public schools calls for virtually the same steps as treating a person's sickness. Like a skilled physician, we need to screen, carefully listen to and observe the patient, test our hypotheses, follow up with a diagnosis, recommend and administer treatments, observe the results of our actions, and adjust, if necessary, the course of treatment. We plan to follow this path to guide the reader toward helping local schools get better.

Immediately following Russia's launching its Sputnik space shot in 1957, a historically unparalleled series of events, reports, and forums convinced stakeholders in American education of the need to improve our elementary and secondary schools. As we passed the end of the twentieth century, improving public schools was seen as essential for the nation to grapple with the grave social, economic, and political problems facing it in the new century.

State legislatures rushed to pass hundreds of statutes aimed at improving their schools. Existing school systems were challenged from every direction. Schools, like business and government, needed to be transformed if America was to survive and prosper in the twenty-first century.

At the very moment when the nation needed a highly skilled workforce to prevent further losses in international trade, commerce, science, and technology, public school systems fell further behind in their basic job of preparing students for entry into the new workforce. Millions of Americans, some already high school graduates, were classified as functionally illiterate by even the simplest literacy measures. Businesses and the military spend tens of millions of dollars each year to deliver remedial schooling in basic skills for their newest employees and enlistees. American schools are failing far too many of its students, along with their future employers and the nation as a whole.

A BRIEF HISTORY OF CALLS FOR CHANGE IN EDUCATION

From its earliest days, a central aim of U.S. education has been to help the individual fulfill his or her capacities to become a thinking person, one who has learned how to learn. This process was understood to run from immaturity to maturity, from dependence to independence. Developing the self-instructing learner, who knows how to organize and guide his or her own learning experiences, is not a new goal.

In 1873, Herbert Spencer wrote, "in education, the process of self-development should be encouraged to the fullest extent. Children should be led to make their own investigations, and to draw their own inferences. They should be *told* as little as possible, and induced to *discover* as much as possible. Humanity has progressed solely by self-instruction; and . . . to achieve best results, each mind must progress somewhat after the same fashion." (from *Education: Intellectual, Moral, and Physical*)

Along the way, reformers made serious attempts to improve the public schools. This was long before computer-assisted and managed learning. In the 1920s, Mary Ward, a supervisor of arithmetic in the San Francisco State Normal School (now San Francisco State University), suggested to her students that they prepare learning materials so that their pupils could proceed at their own rate. She found, for example, that the number of days needed by each child to master the "high-second-grade arithmetic" ranged from less than five to as many as sixty-five days.

Her university president, Frederic Burke, became excited about her instructional exercises for existing textbooks. Later, many of these exercises were used instead of texts. Individual instruction was widely used in the elementary school attached to the Normal School. A few prominent school systems took up the practice, but it could not be sustained. Individualized instruction was overcome by the culture of schooling, which continues to this day.

President Burke presented a serious indictment of the traditional classroom system used in schools when he stated:

> The class system has been modeled upon the military system. It is constructed upon the assumption that a group of minds can be marshaled and controlled in growth in exactly the same manner that a military officer marshals and directs the bodily movements of a company of soldiers. In solid unbreakable phalanx the class is supposed to move through the grades, keeping in locked step. This locked step is set by the "average" pupil—an algebraic myth born of inanimate figures and an addled pedagogy. (Burke 1927, cited in Dale 1967)

Since World War II, the history of education is full of examples of proposed changes. At the outset, these were taken up with great enthusiasm, but this lasted for only a brief period of time. They failed to take root or become part of the mainstream of educational practice.

Typically, these "innovations" involved a small number of interested parties. Many were temporarily subsidized by substantial outside funding. Quietly, they faded away after affecting only a few schools or students. Wry comments from an educator with even limited on-the-job experience summed it up this way: "this too shall pass" and "here we go again," suggesting that many educators viewed educational change as something to be endured.

This may help to explain why many educators react to demands for educational change with the spirit of lukewarm milk. They usually reply that the major problem in education is the frequency of change. In many cases, educational faddism is confused with change.

When a call for change is understood as something distinctly different, it soon becomes clear that schools have changed very little since their inception in the 1800s. Significant changes in education, when they have occurred, have mostly been responses to legal or societal issues. Desegregation and collective bargaining are just two examples.

American educators have relentlessly pursued new programs, texts, and methods in order to improve educational processes. Most often, they have not brought these into widespread use. Observers note a predictable pattern of shifts every few years, similar to the fleetingly familiar educational fads of the past. The predictable shifting of emphases caused many educators to display a nonchalant attitude when recent mandates for change were issued.

THIS TIME IS REALLY DIFFERENT

During the early 1980s, educators experienced a wave of demands for reform that meant that teachers and administrators needed to do more of what they had been doing, only do it better. The existing educational system was to be fine-tuned. It required more testing of teachers and students. Demands grew for higher standards for graduation and teacher certification. There was need for a more closely defined curriculum. School boards and staff began making more careful selection of textbooks. The call for more school accountability was finally beginning to be heard.

Coalitions of concerned citizens organized themselves. Parents, educators, elected officials, business and industry leaders, and private citizens all offered up quick solutions to fix broken schools. Fixing education was still viewed primarily as a people, not a system, problem. The existing educational system would improve if people were just smarter and worked a lot harder.

By the mid-1980s, it became clearer that these approaches were aimed at fixing a badly fragmented system. Improvements prescribed from the top down were not and did not significantly change the situation. Demanding that educators do more of the same or do the same things better did not—and could not—produce the desired results.

To fix broken and badly fragmented schools required changing the system. It meant putting "Humpty Dumpty" back together again. But the American educational system, which was originally designed to meet the agricultural age and later retrofitted to meet the needs of the Industrial Age, was now hopelessly out of date. It was ill prepared and woefully unable to meet the needs of an Information Age society.

The Student as Customer

We know that product and service quality rest on two pillars: *fitness for use* and *customer satisfaction*. Hitting the mark on customer "needs" and providing customer "fulfillment" build customer loyalty over time. Loyalty is even more important than satisfaction. Loyalty relates directly to meeting or even exceeding user expectations.

It is useful to look at what makes up the customer/supplier model. In this model, the supplier provides inputs that are processed and remade into outputs that are used by the customers.

- In the first stage, the internal customer (be it a coworker, employee, or teammate) receives the output of an internal supplier (another coworker, employee, or teammate). In the next step, value is added to the output by refining (building upon or improving) it in some way. In the third stage of the process, they now become the suppliers back to the internal customers. At the last stage, the external customer is the final purchaser or user of the finished product or service.
- Satisfied and loyal customers generate a continuing need for the product or service. This allows that organization to stay in business. It provides paying jobs for members of that organization. Quality is achieved only when everyone in the organization is focused on the same purpose.
- Innovations contribute to the organization's mission of providing a quality product or service to help the customer lead a better life. Innovations are best introduced after (1) careful research, (2) the value to the customers is established, (3) the costs are determined, and (4) the employees are trained in the use of the innovation.
- Improvement is not a one-time effort or project. It means a step-by-step improvement to a quality product or creating a new product. Improvement is not achieved by focusing solely on results, it is achieved by focusing on improving the systems that create the results. It is improvements to the system that yield the most lasting results.

In this event, improvement boils down to two things. First, using tools along with the right mind-set to identify and solve problems and second, to further the process of continuous improvement thinking, to gather and use data.

Many educators soon find that when quality principles are adapted and applied in the classroom, they successfully influence the entire school environment.

- Educators instinctively recognize that customers are the people they serve. These include students, parents, future employers, and other educators.
- Educators appreciate customer needs for high-quality schooling that can help the student live as productive citizens in a changing world.
- It is not difficult for educators to accept that the customer decides what quality is and not the producer. After all, educators are in the business of making judgments about the quality of work produced by others.

Educators can easily visualize schools as a system made up of many interrelated subsystems and further, that school subsystems need to be focused on a common goal. They can see education as an input/output process that takes what is supplied, adds value to it, and then sends it on to the next step in the process. With almost no exception, the concepts associated with producing quality, such as *Kaizen* (Japanese continuous improvement) and quality thinking, apply equally to education.

However, the terms *product* and *service* are exceptions and they are important exceptions. The terms *product* and *service,* as used in the for-profit sector setting, do not always seem applicable in public education.

- In business, the term *product* generally defines the "something" physical that is produced, for example, a lamp.
- The term *service* is often associated with the attitudes shown while delivering or maintaining the product, such as those of helpful clerks or auto repair mechanics.
- The quality of a product seems to generate more attention than the quality of the service. For example, a customer might buy a good car even if the service were not outstanding.
- The quality of service is more apparent when the car breaks down or the air conditioner stops working on a hot July afternoon.
- The product is tangible. Customer service appears to be an intangible.

However, educators do not think of product or service in this way. Educators argue convincingly that:

- The product that the school produces is learning, a change in human behavior.

- The product, the change in behavior, generally cannot be credited to a single event or factor.
- The learning experiences, meaning the instructional activities provided, are the service, and these are more easily documented.
- The service, therefore, appears to be more tangible than the product.

Educators ask, "Is quality determined by the product (the changes in the behavior) and, if so, which ones? Or is quality determined by judging the learning opportunities (the service) and, if so, which ones?" Deciding what to judge or what is important, the product or the service, is a major source of confusion, and stands as an obstacle to school reform.

The Industrial Age distinction between product and service makes no sense whatsoever in the new knowledge economy. *All* work is service. In the new economy, *everyone* in the organization serves the customer. Not everyone deals with the external customer, but everyone in the organization serves the customer. Think again of the person who receives the work of the internal supplier and adds value. At the end of the process, quality is determined by the customer's opinion of the value received. The only opinion that really counts is the customer's opinion.

> The customer's entire experience determines his (or her) perception of quality. That perception is affected by the organization's "product," processes, and practices as they compare to the customer's expectations. Quality is the measure of the customer's satisfaction with the entire experience. (Albrecht 1992, 14)

Lessons from Business Help Construct a New Educational Culture

There is an old cliché: "The more things change, the more they stay the same." Drake and Roe (1986, 176–177) note the following aspects of the school learning processes that prevailed in the 1880s in the United States. They still seem applicable to most schools, even today.

When looked at closely, we see that schools at the turn of the twenty-first century are little changed from those operating near the end of the nineteenth century, with the exception of the size and number of schools. Public school systems are organized and operated in fifty separate states. This says much about the entrenched culture and the role tradition plays in education.

LEARNING PROCESSES IN U.S. SCHOOLS (CIRCA 1880)

1. Classes are, for the most part, graded rather than ungraded.
2. Students are taught each subject by a single teacher, rather than by a team or series of teachers.
3. Class periods are of a uniform duration, such as forty to sixty minutes.
4. The school year consists of approximately 180 days.
5. The formal school is held spring, winter, and fall, and closed during the summer months.
6. Academic subjects are given an equal amount of time throughout the school year, no matter what the subject.
7. The academic courses in the school curriculum are essentially the same from one school to another.
8. The student is expected to complete four years of high school before graduation.
9. All classes begin at the beginning of the semester or school year and end at the end of the semester or school year.
10. The formal school day begins at a certain time for students and ends at certain times for students.
11. Students generally remain in school for twelve to thirteen years.
12. An evaluation system, usually letter grading, is provided for pupils that compares them with the group rather than themselves.
13. Most schools have some semblance of a college preparatory, vocational education, and general education track system for students.
14. The school building and the classroom are where formal education takes place.
15. Schools have a superintendent, a principal, and a teacher hierarchy.
16. All schools have a board of education and are part of a state system.

As a government-directed institution, the public school is particularly resistant to change. Public education represents stability in an otherwise chaotic world. Significant changes are occurring around the globe, both in politics and economics. The church and other basic institutions are in turmoil. Human relationships, especially the family, have given way to change. Many people may be reluctant to see their schools change because schools appear to be one of the few anchors in a very stormy sea, perhaps one they can romanticize from their own school experience. The words of American humorist Will Rogers still ring true. "Schools ain't what they used to be and never was," he quipped.

People know that change must occur to meet the needs of society. Accepting this need rationally does not mean that the change is accepted for any real decision making. Acceptance is a function of feeling and emotion.

People are attached to the culture of education by virtue of their common schooling experiences. We have old school ties and root for our high school or college team. Unconsciously, even the old school colors are part of our favorite wardrobe. We debate traditional rivalries through old age. We are invited to the annual homecoming game. Changing the culture of education causes people, both educators and the public, to experience some loss.

This brings a story from school board days to mind. Allen had endless discussions among his board members and staff on how to get the parents more involved with their youngsters' schools and teachers.

Staff and administration held some very strong (mostly negative) feelings about the merits of this involvement and seemed to pay only lip service to the suggestions. Board members felt equally strong that ways needed to be found to more involve the parents in the education of their children.

The upshot of many discussions was the realization that school and teachers create a form of intimidation upon students that never really quite rubs off as an adult. Many parents display the same innate shyness today as they did as a student when they come in to meet their youngster's teacher. They are even asked to sit at their kid's desk, which today appears like a miniature for a six-foot-tall father or adult mother.

It is the job of the teacher and the building principal to put the parents at ease, to make them feel truly welcome, to invite them to contact the teacher or principal on their own busy work schedules, and to treat the parents with the same enthusiasm they would show if these were guests that were invited into their home.

In a commonsense way, organizational culture is defined as "the shared understandings people have about the way their organization works and about how they work in their organization." Consciously or unconsciously, as people work in an organization, they come to internalize how things are done in the organization. They learn about the acceptable standards for behavior, how to treat one another, what the organization really values, and what the rules are for getting the job done. These shared understandings hold the organization together. They give it a distinct identity. It is what is meant by the phrase "that's the way we do things around here."

The nature of culture in an organization is portrayed well by Sashkin and Kiser (1993) in their collaborative work with Richard Williams:

> Culture is the cumulative perception of how the organization treats people and how people expect to treat one another. It is based on *consistent and persistent management action*, as seen by employees, vendors, and customers.

In searching for America's best run companies, Peters and Waterman (1982) found that culture was closely tied to the success of excellent companies. They noted that the stronger the corporate culture, and the more the culture was directed toward valuing the customer, the fewer policy manuals, organization charts, detailed rules, and procedures were needed. With clearly defined guiding values, people throughout the organization knew what they were supposed to do in almost every situation.

In these companies, there were heroes and heroines and a strong prevailing mythology. On the walls hung pictures of the founders, and the trophy case displayed the softball and bowling awards. An identifiable corporate culture was strong in each of these excellent companies. Prospective employees even made decisions as to whether or not they would consider working for such an enterprise based upon their understanding of its culture and its match with their own values and beliefs.

THE MISSION OF THE SCHOOL IN THE INFORMATION AGE

Briefly and succinctly, the mission and job to be done by the quality school in the twenty-first century can be looked at as follows:

Learning and earning are now inseparable.
> A quality educational system is an absolute essential to the economic, political, and social welfare of the United States.

It's now time to think and work smarter.
> Demanding that people work harder or do more of what has always been done in the way it has always been done cannot produce needed changes or results.

We need to stop driving down the road with our eyes on the rear-view mirror.
> The current system is structured and organized to meet the needs of an age and society that no longer exists.

The social and economic transition is well under way; the school system must catch up.
> The system must be restructured to meet the needs of a society already in a transition to an enriched cognitive economy and an information age.

Make "this is the way we've always done it around here" famous last words.
> The new culture consists of common understandings about the rules, roles, and relationships between and among employees and stakeholders.

Businesses, parents, citizens, and educators demand better schools.
> Educators cannot make the needed changes in public schools alone. The "public" nature of the school makes all citizens a legitimate partner to change.

Change must be persistently ground out.
> The changes needed in education require long-term commitment to improvement. There is no quick fix.

"It's the economy, stupid"—Slogan of the 1992 Clinton–Gore campaign.

There is agreement about the purposes of public school in one area. There is a consensus that students need employable skills for the new economy.

We need schools to meet the needs of a cognitive-rich Information Age economy.

School leaders and policymakers must commit to the transformation of education and understand what this fully means—or it will not occur.

Leave no stone unturned.

Every aspect of the educational process and system must be studied and reconsidered in light of new and different societal expectations.

We must spell out the purposes and outcomes of public education at the national, state, and local levels. There must be a shared understanding among educators and their constituents about the goals and outcomes of the school process. Baldrige and ISO 9000 processes bring together all the interested parties as participants.

Facing this challenge may boggle the mind of many educators. After more than two decades of almost unrelenting criticism and pressure, many educators are skeptical, disillusioned, and just plain worn down. It is understandably threatening to some educators to suggest that they now set out to change the system in which they have succeeded both as students themselves and as professionals.

DEMING'S FRAMEWORK FOR IMPROVING SCHOOLS

Having demonstrated its effectiveness for half a century, W. Edwards Deming's quality management principles serve us well in learning how to apply Baldrige/ISO 9000 criteria to public schools. Dr. Deming himself provided the following guideposts:

Constancy of Purpose:
- Meeting or exceeding customer needs commits the total organization.
- Everyone in the organization looks for continuous improvement of products and services, research and education, and innovation.

- Constancy of purpose helps everyone work together to move the organization, school, or school district in a single direction with a long-term focus.

Continuous Improvement:
- The total organization commits to ongoing improvement.
- It looks for refinement of products, services, and processes as the means of satisfying the customer.
- The status quo is *never* good enough. All processes are under study at all times.
- Improvement occurs through both step-by-step change and through carefully evaluated innovation.

Comprehensive Perspective:
- The organization is viewed as a system of interconnected components.
- Constancy of purpose is achieved when all the components of the system work toward the same aim. This is system optimization.
- All share responsibility for the final product or service.

Customer-Driven Service:
- Quality improvement involves finding out what the customer wants and satisfying that customer time and again.
- Determining the needs and desires of the customer is an ongoing effort because customer needs and desires change with time.
- Systems are designed to deliver what the customer wants without hassle.

School and District Culture:
- The shared understandings that people in the school and district have about how things work in the district are its culture.
- Culture represents the basic mind-set, attitudes, and values of the community.

Counting for Quality:
- Everyone in the school analyzes, understands, and solves quality-improvement problems using statistical methods and problem-solving processes.

• Use of the most important tools—brainpower and rational thinking—needs to be encouraged.
• Decisions are made based on data and not based on opinions, assumptions, and habits.

Decentralized Decision Making:
• Quality-improvement decision making is decentralized within the total system to empower those closest to the point of improvement.
• An integral part of decentralization is internal communication.
• Roles, responsibilities, and relationships are affected by decentralization.

Collegial Leadership:
• Barriers between people and departments are eliminated.
• Teamwork and cooperation is encouraged so that employees can focus on the purpose of quality improvement.
• Knowledge, resources, ideas, and solutions are pooled to solve problems.

ANOTHER ANGLE ON THE NEED FOR SCHOOL QUALITY

As many have said in different ways, the demographic, economic, social, and cultural realities of the twenty-first century require a new and different system of education.

Once American schools led the way. They were the engines of upward mobility in America and the doorway to economic success. They readied individuals to go on to serve our society. A century ago, America had the best-educated workforce in the world. Americans were first to exploit the technologies of Europe, just as Japan and other Asian nations have with the West during the last half of the twentieth century. With the exception of graduate schools emphasizing such areas as math, science, and business, American education currently lags badly behind other developed nations.

In many respects, American schools have been victims of their own success even as our schools have brought about a deep respect for education among our citizens. No people prize and admire education more than do Americans. It is the sum and substance of the American dream, but the better educated Americans became, the more was expected of education. By expecting too much, disappointment was inevitable. Our schools, in fact, did successfully produce a nation of workers and citizens sufficiently educated for the demands of an earlier day.

Today, America's thorniest social problem is not unemployment but too many *unemployables*. "The gap between haves and have-nots is increasingly a chasm between 'knows' and 'know-nots'" writes former *Harvard Business Review* editor Bernard Avishai in *The Wall Street Journal* (July 29, 1996).

The modern economy requires broadly and deeply educated workers who can effectively communicate with coworkers and customers. They need both verbal and writing skills. Workers need to know how to solve problems and innovate. They need to be able to think critically and analytically. They must meet the public and deal with complex electronic technologies. These workers must be alert, presentable, and have a well-developed "work ethic." And, vitally, these workers need to be prepared to continue learning over their entire working lives.

Each year, American business is forced to hire more than one million entry-level workers who cannot read, write, or count. The cost of training such workers recently exceeded $200 billion each year. No longer can we afford to write off the children who have not learned to read or write—yet today's high schools are graduating 700,000 functionally illiterate young people each year, and still another 700,000 drop out of high school each year.

Imagine any surviving enterprise that says that it cannot compete because the world around it has changed. Enterprises that fail to change are enterprises that fail. So it is with the public schools. Of necessity, the public schools must take into account social and cultural trends, just as they must incorporate changes in the nature of work.

Without an educated workforce, American business cannot hope to compete in a global economy. American business cares about education because business must. The reason is not rooted in humanity or self-sacrifice. It takes educated workers to achieve the required economic return on investment and to reach the "bottom line." People create the wealth of the new economy. Educated people create more wealth faster.

American education is falling behind faster for the simplest of reasons. The public schools are fundamentally out of step with the larger social and economic realities of the global economy. Public schools, like all government enterprises, are slow to change. They have not kept up with the changing economic and social landscape in America.

The problem is stark. Too many students lack even the minimum skills needed to meet the demands of the current economy, let alone those of the future. A torrent of business studies report that as many as 60 percent of high school graduates cannot handle an entry-level job.

A growing number of American companies report they are experiencing problems. As manufacturing processes have become more automated and other business procedures have advanced, the level of reading, writing, and mathematical skills needed in the workplace has also risen. Too many worker deficiencies in these skills are proving to be a barrier to companies introducing new techniques and competitive strategies.

WHY IS TRADITIONAL EDUCATION OUT OF STEP?

The product of twentieth-century Industrial Age schooling creates weak learners.

- They become overly dependent on their teachers. They lack confidence in their ability to function independently and lack skills held by others who know how to learn.
- They can merely parrot back correct answers, but are unable to properly tackle problems.
- They do not understand the principles involved in their answers. They frequently revert to personal, naive concepts after leaving the classroom setting.
- They are passive, often bored, inattentive, and uninvolved in their own learning.

In the explosively successful Industrial Age economy, it was hard to make the case that something was wrong with the traditional teaching model. In industrial workplaces, tasks were also narrowly defined. Workers were neither expected nor encouraged to be versatile.

All that has changed. Today, operating a new U.S. Army tank is considerably more complex than in World War II or Korea. Patton's vintage tank was all mechanical and low tech, in comparison to running the control system of an electronically controlled Desert Storm tank. The educational practices that put the control completely in the hands of the teachers fit neatly with the top-down command structure of the typical industrial workplace and less complex military machine.

In the old established pattern, teachers could pour knowledge into essentially passive students. Meanwhile, on the job, higher-level employees were expected to receive and pass on orders while lower-level workers were expected merely to follow the orders.

Just as traditional learning emphasized strengthening the bond between stimuli and correct responses, workers in the Industrial Age workplace were only expected to handle well-defined, nonambiguous situations. Workers were trained to have a limited number of responses to a limited number of possible circumstances. Specialized support personnel and supervisors were there to handle more difficult or unusual events. In the context of that standard workplace, increasing skill meant simply increasing the number of stimuli for which the individual knows the correct responses.

Public schools emphasize getting the right answer. There is little attention given to having students learn from mistakes and develop alternative ways to solve problems and prevent mistakes. In the traditional workplace, there is a strikingly similar process. There is greater emphasis on completing the task than on understanding what is being done.

Even the traditional view of quality control matches the educational neglect of learning from mistakes. Errors, when they occur, are repaired at the end of the production line. Quality control does not get built into the way the work is done. There is no emphasis on understanding the process where improvements are more likely with repetition. As a result, workers fail to learn from their mistakes. Products and processes are not improved.

It is probably no coincidence that the failure to expect workers to understand much about the context in which they work is matched so closely by traditional classroom teaching. Both assume knowledge should be learned independently of the context in which it will be used. Both school learning and the traditional workplace assume context is not important. Tasks are well defined and routine.

But fast-moving, information-driven enterprises find it far too expensive to continue production and service processes that depend on low-cost, low-skilled workers who wait to be told what to do. Knowledge

workers need a broad understanding of the systems in which they operate. More importantly, workers need a conceptual grasp of what they are
doing. Only that kind of understanding permits them to carry out tasks
or solve problems that they have not previously encountered.

WHAT SCHOOLS NEED TO DO NOW

American workers are now held to a higher standard of excellence and
accountability than previously required. This means schools must do a
far better job of teaching basic skills. Verbal, mathematical, and scientific literacy must also be achieved. Students must come away with the
capacity to reason logically.

Secondly, a society dominated by knowledge workers makes ever
more exacting demands for social performance and responsibility. After
all, these are the folks who will run our society some day. They need political and philosophical savvy to carry out this role. To this end, they
need a solid moral and technical education. Students need to know
where our notions of right and wrong, good and evil, liberty and slav-
ery, come from.

As a worker in an Information Age organization, the elementary
skills of effectiveness include (1) the ability to present ideas orally and
in writing, briefly, simply, clearly; (2) the ability to work with people;
and (3) the capacity to shape and direct one's own work. The worker
needs to understand the contributions he or she can make and how those
contributions relate to their career goals. The schools must produce students who are technologically literate in the sense of their having a good
understanding of the way the world around us turns.

Internship programs need to become a regular part of the secondary
school program. Employers can assist in training the people they will
need in the future. Students gain understanding of what they want, as
well as how they do, in life.

In elementary school, greater attention needs to be paid to teaching
management of the self. This is the responsibility everyone has for con-
structively participating in group endeavors, whether as a citizen or as
an employee on whom others depend.

It's time to discard the notion, and it was never really true anyway,
that schools can teach students everything students will need to know

through life. More so than ever, learning is a lifelong process of keeping abreast of change. Thus, the most pressing task is teaching people how to learn. This sense of learner achievement is crucial. Schools must focus on the strengths and talents of learners so the students may excel in whatever it is they do well.

There is a model that explains how economies and societies evolve. It shows that new knowledge leads directly to new technology. In turn, this causes changes in the basic ways in which people create and share wealth. These changes in the economic life of people lead to social and political forces. This ultimately creates new views of reality. This model can be used to explain the economic, social, and political changes our country is experiencing. It also explains the current predicament of educators.

Organizational transformation is a key part of the new business language and will soon find standard usage in public schools. It differs from *organizational development*, a once-stylish term. The new emphasis is on the process used by the school organization to develop itself, rather than facilitating change by outside intervention. The past practices that used to increase productivity and effectiveness are no longer adequate. Leaner staffing, simpler structures, getting closer to the customer, encouraging autonomy and entrepreneurship, and the rest of the prescriptions for excellence require active employee collaboration.

Today, how our country organizes and delivers formal education in our public schools matches surprisingly well with the basic requirements of the U.S. economy and how people earn a living. But the context of earning has changed. The learning institutions, which have matched themselves to previous settings, are experiencing serious mismatching and disconnection. That is precisely what has happened to public schooling in America.

CHAPTER 2

Classroom Teaching Suffers Its Pain in Silence

Most of us dread visiting the doctor's office. Too many of us suffer in silence while our illnesses progress, or worse yet, even more serious disease develops. From long experience, we know that the sooner the doctor catches a serious malady, such as heart disease, diabetes, or cancer, the better the chance that the patient can survive.

Doctors act as though a symptom is the direct effect of the disease on the person. It's as though the symptom is the voice of the disease coming through the patient's mouth. But the physician's understanding of the symptoms is quite different from the patient's, and this is a source of frustration to both. The doctor must look further for the interconnected set of the patient's meaning and link it to the doctor's world of medical meanings. In this manner, the symptoms help us properly define the causes and the extent of the illness.

Former ambassador to Russia Robert Strauss liked to start his presentations this way: "Before I begin," he said, "I have something to say." Before you get deeper into this book, we want to make several points:

Our title, *Healing Public Schools: A Winning Prescription to Cure Their Chronic Illness,* is chosen to set the stage for proven ways to ensure reliable quality in classroom teaching. The concept of winning also helps us show related quality examples from the world of business, where the prescription has already been proven effective. These examples are tools for the reader to gain more appreciation of quality system management. Talking about trends in global business helps us drive home some powerful ideas. Readers need to demand reliable teaching quality in their local school classrooms today.

The authors are optimists by design; we are practical guys who seek real answers. We apply useful tools to achieve solutions. We do not accept excuses to long-standing and seemingly intractable problems. We convey real-world experiences that have been proven in other settings, including schools. We make the argument that knowing how to use the right tools ensures reliability in every classroom.

The central theme is *reliable quality in classroom teaching time, all the time*. In this sense, *reliability* simply means what you can count on getting every time, not just occasionally, or from time to time. Words like *dependable* and *durable* also fit the definition of reliability. Reliable quality in classroom teaching is what we should expect for every child.

Our book is also intended as a thoughtful guide to *praxis. Praxis* is not a common term, but it is an important element in changing strategy. It is the only term that means an inventory of what works reliably in a professional field. There is praxis in medicine and in management, to mention just two. There is praxis in education, but it is not currently a central feature of regular teaching practice. As we go along, we shall illustrate some of its major elements.

OUR PROPOSITION

Every term at every school, parents wonder about the teacher that their child will get *this* time. From personal experience, parents know that what that teacher can do for their child in that classroom is the most important factor in their child's success that term. Parents have always sensed that it really does matter which teachers their children get. School staff members typically reject these notions of parents. When parents ask for their children to be assigned to a particular teacher, or to be moved out of a class of another teacher, they are met with an assurance something like this: "Your child will learn what he or she needs to learn from any of our teachers."

Careful research now available from Tennessee, Texas, Massachusetts, and Alabama shows conclusively that parents have been right all along (Sanders and Rivers 1998). They may not always know which teachers are really the best, but they are absolutely right in believing that their child will learn a lot and be more attracted to learning from some teachers, and learn only a little or be entirely turned off to school from others. This can be true even though the two teachers can be in classrooms of the same grade level or subject and be side by side.

There is now widespread acceptance of the fact that the teacher is the single most important school-based element in student learning, as well as in helping students gain a positive attitude toward schooling. That fact agrees with every parent's common sense as well as the best research.

There is strong evidence that we can produce the qualified teachers by combining

- high entry standards;
- rich incentives, generous scholarships, and loan forgiveness for highly able professionals who want to teach where they are desperately needed;
- accountability that rewards colleges for the number of top students that enter teaching; and
- nontraditional, yet still rigorous, routes into the teaching profession.

THE ACHILLES' HEEL OF RELIABLE TEACHER QUALITY

There remains a serious error still being made in all the discussions about getting highly qualified teachers into America's classrooms. It is an error that stands in the path of any real solution to this crucial problem of education's needs. The missing part is recognizing the supreme importance of the reliable quality of the system that leads, manages, and administers the school and school system in which the teaching takes place.

Major lessons learned from the quality revolution, now increasingly a part of American business and industry, are either unknown or totally ignored in discussions about teacher and teaching quality. The chance of getting a good teacher into *every* classroom can only be warranted in a system specifically designed and managed to achieve reliable classroom teaching quality. It is clear that without such a system only the tyranny of chance can rule. Further, putting a qualified teacher into an unreliable system only serves to raise the likelihood that the teacher will not stay long or will be greatly hindered in reaching his or her full potential.

Heed these findings. Following two years of intense study and discussion, the prestigious National Commission on Teaching and America's

Future concluded in a 1998 report that the reform of elementary and secondary education depends first and foremost on restructuring its foundation—the teaching profession. The commission said:

> It is now clear that most schools and teachers cannot produce the kind of learning the new reforms demand—not because they do not want to, but because they do not know how, and the systems they work in do not support them in doing so.
>
> When it comes to widespread change, we have behaved as though mandates could, like magic wands, transform schools. But successful programs cannot be replicated in schools where staffs lack the know-how and resources to bring them to life. Wonderful curriculum ideas fall flat in classrooms where they are not understood or supported by the rest of the school. And increased graduation and testing requirements create only greater failure if teachers do not know how to reach students.

This book concentrates on the most proven management tools for building reliable quality school teaching. We describe through a winning prescription the tools for maintaining quality over time. With these tools, there is no longer the need for the "dance of the lemons," the phrase school administrators use when they have to distribute their poorer teachers each term into teaching spots where parent criticism is likely to be the least.

With the winning prescription, a leadership and management style takes over. It produces steadily improving student achievement. With it are fewer failures, less need for remediation, more dedicated and satisfied teachers, and vastly happier parents. How is this seeming miracle pulled off?

From every stage of the schooling process, information is fed to the other stages. This includes statistical data that everyone, including students and their parents, can easily understand. Administrators and teachers learn from each other. All learn from stakeholders and suppliers. Across all levels there is teamwork. "Private turf" is a thing of the past.

WHAT'S HAPPENING NOW?

To those who study school systems, elementary school classrooms are remarkably similar. It is in this setting that the school forms the foundation for a needed lifetime of learning. The students and teachers work in the familiar "egg-crate" structure of individual classrooms. Twenty to thirty students spend nearly the whole day with one teacher who delivers instruction in all subjects. The students are assigned to a single grade by age. Most are promoted annually, but not as a group. Students and teachers meet one another all over again each year, and both spend considerable time becoming acquainted. They learn to get along together and sometimes review previous work.

This is pretty much the same teaching picture everywhere. There have been many efforts to promote alternatives. These include multiage grading, continuous progress, team teaching, and subject matter specialization, but these changes are not in common practice; rather, the traditional classroom looks something like this:

- Students are grouped for reading and math, beginning in the first grade.
- Students who are believed to have similar levels of ability sit and work apart from others.
- A small group of students works with the teacher while everyone else does seatwork. There are three such groups in most classrooms.
- Reading instruction consists of the teacher working with one group after the other.
- When the entire class seems to be working as a whole, members of each group are given different levels of work.

Students are well aware of ability grouping and the status differences that it makes necessary. Students in lower groups get less demanding and more routine work. Teachers erroneously refer to this practice as "individualizing instruction." They report that it helps them to manage their work. In doing so:

- teachers use a mixture of seatwork; students may work alone on a written assignment, work in small groups, and in whole-class instruction.
- seatwork dominates up to 70 percent of class time. Whole-class instruction includes lectures or recitations related to seatwork.
- subjects are broken up into separate domains. Spelling is taught independent of reading and writing. Writing is unattached to reading. Grammar is presented as distinct from either reading or writing.

- knowledge is segmented within subjects. Children study lists of spelling words, sheets of places to be identified, pages of individual math problems, and the like.

Schoolbooks and other instructional materials support this "bits-and-pieces" subject matter presentation management. Texts in reading, language arts, spelling, and math present knowledge in this fragmented manner. Most worksheets for individual seatwork follow this pattern.

Teachers and students treat knowledge as fixed and given by authorities. Teachers question and students respond. Teachers lecture and students listen. After studying more than a thousand classrooms, John Goodlad concluded, "explaining and lecturing were the most common activities" (Goodlad 1984, 106).

Teachers search for "right answers," which students offer up in single words, numbers, or short phrases. Ongoing discussion is uncommon. Students infrequently talk with one another as part of the instruction.

INSTRUCTIONAL DIFFERENCES SUGGESTING UNRELIABILITY

American public schools have fewer elements of common purpose. They have less common curricula, assessment, and teacher education than most other nations. Our schools are politically decentralized. The market plays a large role. Even the state, which by law governs public schools, plays only a modest role in U.S. education.

Americans are divided about educational purpose and content. Publishers, school systems, schools, and teachers have greater freedom here than in many other systems. Texts are in classroom use everywhere, but their content differs considerably. Math textbooks, for example, often give the same topics different treatments, one covering topics that others ignore. Tests often cover topics differently, and different texts lead to different student achievement results.

The curriculum that teachers offer varies, despite similar educational ground rules. Teachers present arithmetic in conventional ways but differ in how they cover the topic. Such differences occur even when teachers use the same textbook. Teachers' habits and decisions are the most important factors in classroom instruction. They are not guided by a clear system of common purpose and content, despite curriculum guides and state mandates. Classrooms can best be described as "an individualistic sort of scattered, academically relaxed tradition."

Teachers' work is guided by "folklore" practices. Their independent classroom decisions govern what they cover and how they cover it. Teachers' work lacks any defined, clear and common view, or professional definition of good practice.

Between the mid-1960s and mid-1970s, large-scale studies of schooling held that schools made little difference in student achievement. James Coleman and Christopher Jencks argued that what counted for education was the educational resources that students brought to school, not the school's resources. They reasoned that students, whose families and communities had many social and cultural advantages, arrived in class with plenty of educational resources. Therefore, these students found it pretty easy to make good use of what schools offered. On average, they did relatively well on various measures of academic achievement. Students whose families and communities had fewer social and cultural advantages, however, arrived with fewer educational resources. These students found it difficult to make good use of what schools offer. They did poorly on tests and on other measures of academic achievement.

Since the mid-1970s, studies show that *both* schools' and students' resources count, but in more complex ways than earlier suggested. How schools mobilize their educational resources is as important as the resources that children bring to school.

Teacher actions and beliefs are crucially important to student performance.

Some teachers have coherent strategies for instruction. They use lessons, books, and other resources in ways consistent with those strategies. They believe that their students can learn and that they have a large responsibility to help. They have definite objectives, which instruction is organized to achieve. Lessons are thought out, organized, and paced.

These teachers regularly check to determine how well students are doing, whether some need more work, and the like. They may use the same conventional methods. They may use the same sorts of tests, worksheets, texts, and seatwork described earlier, but they use them as part of a well-crafted strategy to improve children's learning. And it works.

In contrast, other teachers lack a consistent strategy for instruction. They use resources in scattered and badly chosen ways. They have vague objectives. Their lessons are not well thought out and are disorganized. Classroom work is poorly paced. Teachers do not regularly check to see how students are doing. If they do check, they do not make many midcourse corrections to assist student responses.

John Goodlad reported that more than half of the elementary students in his major study of education said that they "did not know what they were supposed to do in class" (Goodlad 1984, 114).

Teachers of this sort do not apply themselves to creating educationally fruitful connections with students. Many seem to act as though they believe their only responsibility is to "present the material" and to let students get it if they can. When such teachers work with children from disadvantaged circumstances, the effects can be very harmful. These teachers often act as though they believe that students can handle only watered-down instruction.

There is growing evidence that some of a school's characteristics greatly influence instructional results. In healthy schools, faculty and students share a common vision of the purposes of instruction and commitment to success. Teachers have a commitment to help students succeed. In such schools, there is teamwork. They use what works, have lots of contact between teachers and students in class and outside, and develop high morale. Healthy schools run along with communities in which students and teachers show responsibility for their own actions and for the common good.

Other schools are fragmented. Teachers, staff, and students lack a common vision of instructional purposes. They have little common commitment to success. There is little teamwork. There is little use of tested, good teaching practices, little contact among teachers and students outside of class, and lower morale.

Typically, students in "together" schools do better than students in "fragmented" schools.

Today, few would deny that the educational resources that students bring with them are crucially important. Many children from socially and economically advantaged homes arrive in school able to read and even write. They find it easy to do well with the instruction that schools offer, even if it is routine and dull, or makes little obvious sense to an outsider. Many students from much less advantaged circumstances come to school with more modest educational resources. Though still often bright and curious, many have not learned to read or to write at home. They often receive little help with schoolwork. They may lack breakfast or a quiet space in which to read or do homework.

Some students who grow up in such difficult circumstances arrive in school with little motivation to succeed. They walk into the school-house already alienated or openly hostile. Many researchers argue that these circumstances are neither the sole nor even the chief cause of poor school achievement. A prime reason may be the fact that the schools lack know-how. If students from disadvantaged homes come to school poorly prepared to take advantage of conventional instruction, most schools and teachers are equally and woefully ill prepared to help these students.

The students do not know how to deal with adults and conventional schoolwork. The teachers do not know how to organize books, lessons, and conventional school resources to take advantage of the curiosity and intelligence that most students first bring to school. This mutual incapacity is crippling for many students. It is eventually defeating for many teachers.

So-called ability grouping further complicates all of this. Students in lower groups tend to get thinner, slower, and less rich instruction. They have fewer opportunities to learn, and they learn less. The most disadvantaged students tend to be placed in the lowest groups with others like themselves, and this is particularly troubling. Students are learning resources for each other as well as for themselves. Therefore, less advantaged students not only get thin instruction but also fewer social resources of education.

There is no apparent hateful intent. Connection between the extensive unevenness in American society and school routines is explanation enough. The typical result is a growing disparity in school achievement. Indeed, the longer students from disadvantaged circumstances stay in school, the farther they fall behind their more advantaged peers. The situation is a dreadful one. Present estimates are that roughly 40 percent of America's children are "educationally disadvantaged."

Analysts now think differently about educational resources. Rather than fixing attention on materials, facilities, and teacher degrees, researchers now focus on the ethical commitments, knowledge, and skills that guide teachers' use of materials and facilities. They focus on the way teachers are led and managed to achieve success for all students.

The experts have broadened the idea of educational assets to include various qualifications of schools and classrooms. Key assets include leadership, shared goals, collegiality, and organizing instruction. These are features of the winning prescription. There is a shift in professional interest away from customary beliefs about family status, teacher qualifications, and school facilities. Research has come to concentrate on instructional practices, organizational arrangements, and the knowledge and skills of schools and school organizations. This is exciting because it offers hope and clues to practical solutions rather than blaming, hand wringing, and pessimism.

This new perspective defines resources in terms of their influence on results. This leads directly to the promise of the winning prescription. The prescription does not deny the importance of school materials, facilities, and formal teacher qualifications. It puts them in a total framework that emphasizes effective processes—what is used and how well teachers use them.

Because of this new perspective, we can look at school improvement in more productive ways. For example, the national movement to improve "basic skills" that began in the 1970s paid off for poor and disadvantaged students everywhere that school staff and stakeholders paid attention to its contents. The movement promoted a high-performance curriculum for all students. It focused on minimum competency tests, the principles that support effective schools, and Direct Instruction—an elementary student reading program.

Direct Instruction challenges the prevailing orthodoxy of many professors of education, which purports that only teaching approaches that build on child-centered learning should be tolerated. That bias is so strong and its effects so pervasive in schools that a further word about the praise by teacher educators of "spontaneous, non-teacher directed learning" is warranted.

There is a consensus among leading educators that school achievement can improve significantly where (1) students and teachers know the standards, (2) exams are aligned to the standards, (3) curriculum is aligned to the standards, (4) students receive expert instruction, (5) schools offer as much time and teaching as students need to learn, and (6) "stakes" in student and teacher success are high by holding the system accountable for results. The most significant element centers on the phrase *expert instruction.*

Let's look more closely at what research shows to be "expert instruction" in the teaching of reading. Reading is the most basic and crucial subject in school because it is the foundation for success in all other subjects. In early April 2000, a long-awaited report on beginning reading was released by the National Reading Panel. The panel consisted of leading reading research scientists, representatives of colleges of education, reading teachers, educational administrators, and parents. The panel, mandated by the U.S. Congress in 1997, is to give public schools authoritative guidance on teaching reading.

They examined approximately 100,000 reading research studies published since 1966, and another 15,000 published before then. "For the first time, we now have guidance based on evidence from sound scientific research on how best to teach children to read," the director of the panel said.

The panel found that the research conducted to date strongly supports the concept that explicitly and systematically teaching children to manipulate phonemes significantly improves children's reading and spelling abilities. The evidence for this is so clear-cut that this method should be an important component of classroom reading instruction.

The panel also concluded that the research literature provides solid evidence that phonics instruction produces significant benefits for children from kindergarten through sixth grade, and for children having difficulties learning to read. The greatest improvements in reading were seen from systematic phonics instruction. This type of phonics instruction consists of teaching a planned sequence of phonics elements, rather than highlighting elements as they happen to appear in a text, as is suggested by other reading programs. The evidence was so strong that the panel concluded that systematic phonics instruction is appropriate for routine classroom instruction.

For children with learning disabilities and children who are low achievers, systematic phonics instruction, combined with synthetic phonics instruction, produced the greatest gains. Synthetic phonics instruction consists of teaching students to explicitly convert letters into phonemes and then blend the phonemes to form words.

Remarkably, the panel's findings support the elements of the Direct Instruction program, a program repeatedly found over the last thirty years to be effective. This is hardly surprising given the fact that the vast research on effective schools—schools that produce reliable student success—is amazingly consistent. There is *always* higher student achievement in an orderly and safe classroom that is run in a knowledgeable and businesslike manner using methods that research and field-testing have shown repeatedly to be effective. Direct Instruction is such a program. The Direct Instruction program is, in fact, an exemplar of what is best practice in teaching reading.

It is not too strong to state that it borders on malpractice when a profession substitutes its bias against carefully researched methods. Such manipulation sentences large groups of students to failure and to ultimate economic hardship.

With hindsight, we can see why unequal achievement continues to this day. New resources have been nonstrategic, and are constantly not packaged wisely. The new monies arrive in carefully targeted mandates. They often require spending on something specific, like classroom aides or special project staff or bigger busses. Such decrees often produce strange results. Consider the classroom with the required special staff or services but lacking adequate books and other materials.

Much of the increased money, of course, is also used simply to raise teacher salaries or to hire more teachers. Unhappily, the research does not find a relationship between such expenditures and improved student achievement.

Conclusion? Undoubtedly our earlier portrait of instruction was incomplete. While curriculum, guidance, and instructional materials are mostly similar in elementary schools, they differ in many other ways. Students in low ability groups have fewer chances to learn, and they therefore learn less.

There are significant differences in teachers' and schools' capacities to effectively use the instructional resources they have. Some students from disadvantaged homes have remarkably constructive educational experiences. Many do not.

There is a deceptive sameness about our public school classrooms. There are extremes, of course. At the one extreme are unsafe or damaging classes in which students are out of control, or teachers are incompetent or cruel, or both. Studies in several big cities estimate that about 5 percent of elementary classes fall into this category. Tragically, they enroll more children from poor families.

At the other extreme are unusually well-to-do and uncommon classrooms. Instruction in them is more exacting than usual. Students read a great deal and read in depth. Teachers use textbooks, but are less dependent upon them. The students are involved in exciting projects and make extensive use of the technology that is readily available to them. Students often go after complicated independent or small-team work. Teachers are better educated and continue their studies. Classrooms of this sort are models for other schools to follow. They are found by chance in big cities, and even in their poorest neighborhoods. They are most often found in affluent suburbs.

THE NATURE OF SCHOOL CHANGE THAT FURTHERS THE TYRANNY OF CHANCE

Some teachers in a particular school will make revisions in what they teach, how they teach, and how they understand teaching and learning. Other teachers in the same school will not. Some schools with an energetic principal will decide to try out a new reading text series oriented toward literature and comprehension of text instead of phonics. The principal may have read some materials or taken a course that promoted teaching reading without phonics and emphasizing complex thought and interpretation. Some schoolteachers will continue past practices, others will get on the "bandwagon."

Sometimes, state departments of education embrace some new vision of curriculum and instruction, invite schools to follow suit, and provide workshops as incentives. The adoption is spotty. Little attempt is made to have a uniform adoption.

The "new" approaches may or may not have any foundation in research or have been tested in real school settings. They may be embraced with little effort to see the actual effect on student learning. All this is clearly a prescription for a tyranny of chance.

Case Studies

The cases reported here are real. The names of the teachers have been changed.

Ms. Barnes teaches in a suburb of New York City where a "writing to read" approach has been introduced. She depends heavily on the textbook and materials that supplement it, and her students write stories about what they have read. She reports that her students become more involved with the new approach, and that they "love the materials." The students are more excited by class work than students were before.

Ms. Joan Dowling works in a large city in a West Coast state. She now uses a new "literature-based" program that her district recently adopted in response to new ideas about reading and a revised state policy. She no longer uses any textbook approach to teach reading, but has the class reading several novels. Some of the students have difficulty with basic word recognition. Ms. Dowling has them in a separate group using remedial-type workbooks. They do not participate in the discussions about the literature. Ms. Dowling has also changed the pace and organization of instruction. Her principal told teachers that they are no longer expected to finish the textbook. Teachers were encouraged to create larger and more complex units around particular stories or novels. They did not receive training in how to teach with this new approach.

Ms. Dowling quickly took advantage of this approach, but other teachers did not. For instance, while reading about *Marco Polo,* she asked students to write letters to him, to create freehand maps of Europe tracing his route, and to write daily diary entries from his perspective. The talk in her class also has changed. She asked students more complicated questions and invited them to draw inferences rather than relate facts. Her questions used to be of the one word answer type; now they were more open-ended.

Ms. Stanton follows a still different approach to reading in her deteriorated inner-city school. She has eliminated reading ability groups and thrown away the basal reading text. Most of her instruction now involves the whole class. Like Ms. Barnes and Ms. Dowling, these changes are associated with the district's adoption of a new approach. In Ms. Stanton's school, the approach was the "whole-language" text series.

Interestingly, the three teachers all report that thus far the results are promising. Not one of the three schools requires an evaluation to see if any new method is worthwhile, and not one of their state departments of education has launched a study of the effects of these new teaching efforts on student achievement.

THE FOLLOW-THROUGH STUDY

During Leon Lessinger's term as associate U.S. commissioner for elementary and secondary education in Washington, D.C., a study of all the reading programs available that purported to be effective for student learning was conducted. It was called *the Follow-Through Study.*

Project Follow Through was the largest, most expensive educational experiment ever conducted in our country. Over 10,000 low-income students in 180 communities across the nation were involved in this $500 million project designed to evaluate different approaches to educating economically disadvantaged elementary students.

State, school, and national officials nominated school districts that had high numbers of economically disadvantaged students. Representatives of these school districts chose to participate after hearing presentations from twenty sponsors of different educational classroom teaching approaches. Each participating school district then implemented the selected sponsor's approach in one or more schools.

Each sponsor was required:

- to provide the community with a well-defined, theoretically consistent, and coherent approach that could be adapted to local conditions;
- to provide the continuous technical assistance, training, and guidance necessary for local implementation of the approach;
- to exercise a "quality control" function by consistently monitoring the progress of program implementation;
- to serve as an agent for change, as well as a source of program consistency, by asking the community to retain a consistent focus on the objectives and requirements of the approach, rather than responding in an ad hoc manner to the daily pressures of project operations;
- to insure implementation of a total program, rather than a small fragment, such as reading, with a resulting possibility for a major impact on the child's life; and
- to provide a foundation for comprehending and describing results of evaluation efforts.

The orientation of the sponsors varied from the loosely structured, open-classroom approach to the highly structured, behavioral-analysis approach. To be included in the Follow-Through evaluation, a sponsor had to have more than three active school sites that could be compared to control school sites in the same communities.

Each model was evaluated across four to eight school sites with students who started school in kindergarten or first grade. Each Follow-Through school district identified a non-Follow-Through comparison site for each Follow-Through site. The comparison site acted as a control.

Summary of the Results of Project Follow Through

No matter which analysis is used, and there were several tested evaluation approaches, students who were in the Direct Instruction model made the most gains in all areas when compared to the other models. Popular educational theories suggest that students should interact with their environment in a self-directed manner. The teacher is supposed to primarily be a facilitator and to provide a responsive environment. In contrast, the most successful model, Direct Instruction, featured teacher-led direction and used thoroughly field-tested curricula that teachers were to follow precisely.

Follow-Through models based on self-directed, child-centered reading approaches scored at the bottom of academic and effective achievement. The intellectually oriented approaches produced students who were relatively poor in higher-order thinking skills. Models that emphasized improving students' self-esteem produced students with the poorest self-esteem.

Educational reformers search for models that produce superior outcomes for at-risk and disadvantaged students. The models must allow schools to (a) implement the model across different school settings, (b) use the model across grade levels so that all students can be involved in a rigorous sequence of instruction, and (c) help students feel good about themselves.

The Follow-Through data confirms that Direct Instruction has these features. Most of the other models do not. Direct Instruction works across various sites and types of students (urban blacks, rural populations, and non-English-speaking students). It produces positive achievement benefits in all subject areas—reading, language, math, and spelling. It produces superior results for basic skills and for higher-order cognitive skills in reading and math. When compared to the other Follow-Through models, it produces the strongest positive self-esteem.

For a system of classroom teaching to achieve first place in virtually every measured outcome, the system must be very efficient and use the limited amount of classroom teaching time to reliably produce a higher rate of learning than other models. If the total amount of "learning" produced over a four-year period could be represented for various models, it would show that the amount of learning achieved per unit of time is probably twice as high for the Direct Instruction models as it is for the non-Direct Instruction models.

Perhaps the most disturbing aspect of the Follow-Through results is the persistence of classroom teaching models that are based on what data now confirm is whimsical theory. The teaching of reading models emphasizing the language experience approach that is quite similar in structure and procedures to the whole-language approach performed so poorly on the various measures that it needed to have carried negative implications for later reforms, but it did not.

The notion of the teacher as a facilitator and as a provider of incidental teaching of reading was used by the British infant school model. It was a glaringly bad failure, an outcome that should have carried some weight for the design of later reforms in the United States. It did not. Ironically, it was based on a system that was denounced in England by its Department of Science and Education in 1992. At the same time, states like California, Pennsylvania, Kentucky, Ohio, and others were in full swing in the idiom of "developmentally appropriate practices," which are based on the British system.

Equally disturbing is the fact that while states like California were immersed in whole language and what they defined as "developmentally appropriate practices," there was no serious attempt to find models or practices that really worked from the 1980s through mid-1990s. Quite the contrary; Direct Instruction was abhorred in California and only a few Direct Instruction sites survived. Most of the Direct Instruction programs that did survive in California did so through deceit, pretending to do whole language. At the same time, those schools implementing whole-language reading were causing students to fail at a tragic rate. In fact, because of the crisis in poor results, California has now formally abandoned the whole-language approach to reading.

Possibly the major message of Follow Through is that there seems to be no magic in education. Only by starting at the skill level of students and then having teachers carefully build foundations that support higher order structures achieve gains. It will be interesting to see what happens to the authoritative findings of National Reading Panel mandated by

Congress, cited earlier, and reported as this book is written. Will it again yield no new results similar to Follow Through? Or will it finally be used as regular teaching practice in the nation's schools for producing reliable quality in classroom teaching of reading?

It is helpful in considering the topic of change in classroom teaching to stand back and gain some perspective on the "operators" and "customers" of the nation's school systems. There is, for example, extraordinary support among parents and the public for higher standards and expectations for students. They strongly favor clear guidelines on what students should learn and teachers should teach. They firmly believe that by asking or even demanding more, you get more achievement. They do not believe in passing kids from grade to grade, or even letting them graduate without evidence of achievement. They oppose giving "As for effort."

There are, however, fundamental differences between how educators and the public view the schools and efforts to improve them. Until these views are better aligned, which means until there is real communication between educators and the public, progress is unlikely—if not impossible.

The public values education as much as ever. It strongly supports the goal of racial integration and believes that each child deserves an equal education. But it strongly believes that while the schools can't be blamed for today's problems, they are way off track in addressing them. People suspect that the solution to many of these problems has little to do with more money or smaller classes.

One of their chief concerns is making the schools safe, orderly, and purposeful enough for learning to take place. People see and read about schools in chaos; schools with little sense of order, respect, or discipline; schools where teachers dress or act unprofessionally; schools in which discussions take place that people consider improper for the classroom; and schools increasingly infested with drugs and violence. How, people ask, can learning take place in such a disaster zone? Shouldn't this problem be fixed before any other school improvement is tackled?

Almost nine out of ten Americans believe that dependability and discipline make a real difference in how well students learn. Another major factor is a strong suspicion that educators are promoting fuzzy and experimental teaching techniques at the expense of the basics. People believe these basics to be that children should learn to read, and to learn grammar and spelling before creative writing. They believe that students should learn to add, subtract, multiply, and divide by hand before depending on electronic devices do it for them. For most people, it does not seem cruel or wasteful for students to memorize the fifty state capitals and where they are located.

People are discovering through their own interactions and experiences with young people that those basic skills are seemingly not there. When someone observes a supermarket checkout person who cannot make change, that—to them—is "authentic assessment." It convinces people that the basic skills are not being taught or learned, and they regard those basics not only as important in themselves but also as the foundation for more advanced learning. To promote "higher-order thinking skills" when kids can't read words or make change seems to many parents and the public to be wrongheaded, if not absurd.

Public views on teaching techniques remain pretty traditional, and people are concerned about what they see as educational "fads." They tend to reject extremes of any kind. For example, they support neither corporal punishment nor the use of street language in teaching inner-city kids. There is a perception among many that some teachers are more anxious to be pals with kids than role models. People cite good teachers and an orderly learning environment as the most important factors needed for students to learn.

Not surprisingly, when parents and the public visit reliable quality classes where teachers use a businesslike approach to learning, they are visibly impressed and enthusiastic. They see well-trained teachers conducting lessons in an orderly environment. They see students mastering the basics. They watch, often in amazement, pre-kindergarten and kindergarten children who are often termed "at risk" reading at quality levels much like affluent youngsters in the first and second grades.

PAST, PRESENT, AND PROSPECTIVE

The criteria for change in schools are unclear. Though public schools have changed dramatically in some respects, they have changed little in others. In 1880, students' desks and chairs were bolted down in rows facing front. Discipline was so tight that students needed individual permission for a trip to the bathroom. Students and teachers addressed each other according to rule, and teachers dressed formally. Classrooms slowly grew less rigidly organized through the twentieth century, a development that picked up speed in the 1960s and early 1970s and is now virtually complete.

Teachers now are probably more considerate of student feelings than they were at the turn of the century. Discipline has greatly relaxed. The tone of classrooms is much less formal. The furniture is movable, and it is often moved to accommodate activities. Many elementary students now sit in "cooperative learning" groups of four or five, facing each other. Teachers dress more casually. Students have much more self-rule. They are able to move around more freely to do their work. Most seem able to go to the bathroom when they wish.

In many classrooms, they also enter and leave at their own initiative to attend special classes or other activities. Teachers who describe themselves as stern disciplinarians tolerate noise, side conversations, and mischief that would have been quickly stamped out a generation or two ago. These might seem like trivial changes to adults in the 1990s, but they would seem revolutionary to parents, teachers, and students who were visiting from the 1940s.

Classroom dialogue also has been altered a great deal. In 1900, students and teachers typically worked within a rigid recitation format. Teachers put questions to individual students who were expected to answer on the spot. A great premium was placed on speed and precision, and the entire exercise was conducted at a brisk clip. There was little or no room for students to develop a point, let alone to ask questions or discuss the matter. Students usually had to stand when called on to speak. They were often graded on posture and deportment. Today, recitations are a much-diminished feature of the elementary landscape. When they do occur, they are much less formal.

Additionally, students often manage more of their own instruction. The materials of instruction have changed as well. There are more texts, supplementary works, and trade books for students than there were in the 1950s. These materials are also more diverse in style, format, content, and intended audience than ever before. They are better designed and more attractively presented than anything that was available in the 1950s, let alone in 1900. In addition, new instructional media—television, radio, audiotape, videotape, and computers—are increasingly making their way into classrooms. Some of these open up astonishing instructional possibilities.

But if these changes seem to show promise for reformers today, some other features of instruction have persisted intact for at least a century. The inherited egg-crate, age-graded organization of school life remains intact. So, too, is the snapshot approach to topic definition and content coverage. Concepts of knowledge seem little changed.

Although the recitation has moved away from formality and importance, the bits-and-pieces approach is still dominant. Discourse is much less rigid, and students typically take little intellectual initiative. New and often exciting materials and media are generally used within a long-standing and inherited approach to learning.

Reformers have had great success changing the culture and social organization of classrooms. They have improved the quality of educational materials, but they have not touched the core process features of classroom instruction. Unreliable teaching practices for teaching such basics as reading and math are still dominant.

The Political and Economic Circumstances of Reform

The incentives to work hard in school are now weaker for many students. Many skilled and semiskilled workers have lost jobs in manufacturing. They have been forced to take unskilled work in service industries. Many high school graduates can look forward either to similar prospects or no work at all. Thus, the prospects for further change now seem mixed.

An impressive academic agenda is developing for public education, and ambitious new standards and assessments seem to promise a better and more challenging life in schools. Teaching has begun to change, but it will take extraordinary efforts to sustain and extend the new work. Indeed, it clearly appears that it will take a considerable effort for most schools to simply do a better job of conventional instruction with conventionally advantaged children.

Even more unusual measures are required to do a much better job of conventional instruction in schools that enroll the students that America has traditionally neglected or rejected. Truly astonishing efforts are needed to thoroughly reform instruction for those children.

We recommend the use of two widely accepted standards to treat the apparent pains that come about from the tyranny of chance in classrooms.

First, the criteria of America's most prestigious award for excellence and continual improvement, *The Malcolm Baldrige National Quality Award Criteria in Education,* established by the U.S. Congress, should be applied to every school and school district. Second, the instructional design principles and standards of *ISO 9000–9004,* the international criteria for achieving and maintaining quality performance that is currently in use by several free-world school systems and adopted in over one hundred countries, must be integrated into the mission and operations of the school classroom.

We know we are able to better organize schools and plan for curing the tyranny of chance in the classroom. We know that this chronic illness can be treated and successfully healed, but it takes a determined effort to seize on the advances made and proposed to get qualified teachers. We then need to link those teachers into a system that merits and dedicates itself to the optimal development and use of the talents of such teachers.

CHAPTER 3

Positive Steps to Help Relieve Chronic Pain

It is crucial that we turn attention to the major causes of the illness that afflict the public school. We must gain a solidly grounded understanding of which prescription may work best and how we will eventually proceed to use these courses of treatment. But the typical physician understands pain control poorly. In hospitals, they have pain control units and the relief of pain is often turned over to pain-management specialists.

We must proceed with evaluating alternative treatments that properly match the causes of the illness, not merely the symptoms. A good doctor knows that, first, we must do no harm.

THE CRUELTY OF CHANCE IN EDUCATION

Here's a no-brainer: When reliable teaching methods are encouraged by the system, students succeed. If these are ignored, students fail. It's as simple as that.

We know a great deal about what it takes to create and manage a system to produce reliable quality in classroom teaching, but many reliable quality teaching methods are even ignored. Although many well-researched and effective teaching methods and management systems are available, there are still far too many useless—even damaging—techniques in use. Every parent knows that it is foolish and even dangerous to gamble with his or her youngster's classroom schooling. The classroom is not a gambling casino. It is not the place for a game of chance.

A lack of concern or ignorance of long-proven teaching methods is a surefire prescription for promoting chance. The fallout of chance in the classroom is the student's loss of future opportunities. This loss goes on to negatively affect the student's chances of success in later classes. It may eventually result in the student's loss of potential earning power as an adult. Once on this slippery slope, the student's life may slide downward just as surely as a sled on a snowy day.

This description does not overstate the situation. We also know that this downward spiraling effect is not in the best interests of the general public. In fact, the National Institutes of Health (NIH) has gone so far as to label the nation's reading deficiency "a national health problem."

Tyranny is power used unjustly or cruelly. Chance in education is like an evil despot that threatens our security, scuttles individual prospects for improvement, and encourages cynicism about the future of public education. Several states have put curriculum and student work performance standards into place. They now publicly report achievement test results of those standards, and these have begun to expose serious deficits in achievement. At the same time, the issue of chance in education has emerged as one of the nation's top concerns.

We see the tyranny of chance every fall on the first day of school. Parents and students eagerly await the assignment of new teachers with a touch of anxiety. They are eager because they know how important the teacher is to the success of their student. They are anxious because they are not sure that they can depend upon the school system to guarantee a teacher who can provide quality classroom instruction. They are entrusting to this school system their life's most precious asset.

EVIDENCE OF UNRELIABILITY IN CLASSROOM TEACHING

We have all spent time in school classrooms.[1] Common sense tells us that school classrooms are workplaces that assign teachers to run them properly. Running an orderly, learning-focused, and academically sound workplace is a teacher's most important job.

---

[1]David Berliner is a distinguished educational psychologist. His impressive body of research on teaching both practical and theoretical methods is based on thousands of hours of classroom observation. Two examples of that corpus relating to the evidence of the basic arguments are cited here (Berliner 1979, 1987). More than half of coauthor Leon's nearly fifty-year career in education was spent as a classroom teacher, principal, superintendent, and professor—giving him firsthand experience and observation of classroom teaching. Berliner's insights and observations are comparable with Leon's and form the substance of the evidence presented in what follows.

We find the vast research on effective schools—schools that produce reliable student success—is quite consistent. There is *always* higher student achievement in an orderly and safe classroom that is run in a businesslike manner. Regrettably, many schools do not have systems in place to aid teachers less skilled in classroom management. Let's look at the evidence:

Evidence of Poor Planning

Teachers, like all those in charge of groups of people, are supposed to plan. Plans made by teachers early in the year and followed carefully have a major effect on teaching and learning throughout the school year. Each teacher should have a yearly plan to cover the subject. From this, the teacher makes a semester plan, a monthly plan, and the daily lesson plan. The daily plan is a teacher's framework of how class time is to be used, and a strategy to identify requirements for materials or people support. Studies show too many teachers do not do such planning.

Evidence of Poor Communication

Teachers need to communicate their goals and objectives to the students and their parents. All must know the teacher's expectations, including how the student determines when he or she has been successful. This is a crucial component in quality classroom instruction. The teacher needs to use well-organized lessons and communicate to students high expectations for performance. Both greatly affect student achievement and performance, but too often, the student does not know what the teacher expects. This causes the student to waste time, guess, or be confused about what is expected.

Students pay better attention when the teacher covers the goals and organization of the lesson and then gives clear directions for the student to follow. Both success rate and attention improve when teachers spend time shaping the lesson and giving direction.

By clearly communicating goals and objectives, the teacher is now helping the students plan their learning. By communicating expectations, the teacher sets high but achievable performance goals. In this setting, student performance usually improves. On the other hand, if goals are set low, then performance also usually decreases.

Evidence of Inconsistency

Chief state school officers, superintendents of schools, school board members, and principals generally believe that they know what is taught in their classrooms. They would be astonished to find out how often they do not.

It is instructive to visit classrooms. It is not unusual to find teachers teaching something other than what a state or a district requires. Teachers often select subject content based on what they feel is the subject difficulty for the student. This decision also involves the teacher's own feelings of adequacy to teach it. A competent schoolteacher who enjoys teaching reading or math can do so more ably than one who does not. During the school day, schoolteachers can literally become a law unto themselves. They select what to include or ignore. When teachers take this responsibility with care and align curriculum standards, subject matter and standards are likely to be met. If they do not, the results for student and program success can be disastrous.

Evidence of Discrepancies

The classroom time assigned to particular subject areas is a principle source of student achievement in content areas. This is just as true of good results in music, art, and physical education as it is in science, mathematics, writing, speaking, and reading. As observed in the classroom, studies of teachers show a wide variation in classroom time devoted to subject matter.

Evidence of Labeling

Most teachers have classes with fifteen to thirty students. They need to form work groups to carry out instruction. The grouping decisions are serious judgments that affect student achievement and attitudes toward a subject. Once students are grouped and labeled as *fast, bright, slow,* or *disadvantaged*, the group label can become the basis for the teacher delivering different subject matter in different ways to the students.

The plans and practices that teachers use for high and low groups differ. Research shows that the students judged by teachers to be low performers are then treated as groups, not individuals. They are called on less often to answer questions. They are given less time to answer those questions. They are praised more often for borderline and imperfect answers and treated in other depreciating ways. This kind of treatment influences the students' final performances.

Evidence of Wrong and Unproductive Teaching Methods

Teachers can have students participate in reading circles, seatwork, recitation, and homework. They can lecture or use question and answer techniques. They can approach the teaching of reading through direct instruction or whole-language instruction, for example. There is an inventory of "what works" available, and there is hard evidence that many teachers are unable to compare the costs and benefits of one form of teacher and student activity over another.

The process of choosing how to teach certain objectives and what kind of work the student is to do in class is a major decision. It is very much like the challenge a physician faces in matching treatment to the health problem a patient presents. The process affects student mastery of needed knowledge and skills. There is a lack of teacher knowledge, training, and experience in this basic part of reliable quality teaching. This probably accounts for the reason that many teachers follow only a few familiar classroom activities, even when they are ineffective, and avoid changing routines.

Evidence of Poor Pacing and Succession

Common sense tells us that the rate of speed at which a lesson proceeds is important. Some teachers successfully cover more lessons and more subject content per course than others. The more a teacher effectively covers in a lesson and a term, the more the student can learn. The unevenness in a teacher's coverage of subject matter for similar groups of students is alarming. One teacher may cover twenty practice problems in math, another only five. One teacher adds fifty words to the students' vocabulary, another only fifteen. These differences in student achievement show up on test results. Studies show that the pace of teacher instruction may account for 80 percent of the difference between successful and unsuccessful learning.

How one thing being taught follows another is a vital part of the quality classroom teaching process. The flow of instruction is a crucial process variable. Many teachers lack training and skill in this part of the teaching process.

There are scores of useful books on managing time. Few relate to education or are studied by teachers and administrators. Time is what we pay for with our tax dollars. In collective bargaining contracts with teachers, for example, the minutes of teacher time (time spent working with students) are strictly specified. Time is, in fact, the precious commodity that can be translated into classroom learning. Time must be controlled once it is assigned or it is lost forever. We cannot bring back yesterday. It is easy to lose time if the teacher does not bring about an effective and efficient use of time.

There are many ways time can be lost in the classroom workplace. For example, changeover times—the time between classroom activities (the start-up time and time needed to put things away)—mounts up rapidly. In one classroom study where the school day was the typical 300 minutes, 70 minutes was spent just on passing from one to another activity. This means that almost one-fourth of the instructional day was lost. Children were simply moving from one activity to another—they were not learning subject matter. This waste of time in classrooms is not uncommon.

Simple teacher-led management techniques make a big difference in controlling time. One example comes from the Mabel Wesley Elementary School in Houston, Texas. All teachers write their language arts assignments on the board before the children come into the classroom. The first student into the room starts to work. No one waits until the last student wanders in for oral instruction from the teacher. Savings over the typical classroom of at least six minutes a day are common. This adds about 180 student learning minutes a day. It can provide a half-hour more of instructional time a week, and potentially it adds eighteen hours of classroom instructional time per school year.

Evidence of Poor Management

Problems of discipline occur frequently in class. This causes teacher stress, interferes with classroom teaching time, and breaks the orderliness and flow of classroom life—the pacing, sequencing, and feedback to students for corrective action of classroom lessons.

Discipline problems are rare in classes where the teacher has mastered the "take charge of the workplace" process. The students aren't given time to misbehave. The teacher puts in place quality instruction processes to provide momentum and smoothness. These are the positive effects of their mastery of praxis—the inventory of good practice.

Evidence of Poor Motivation and Evaluation

Student performance can improve with properly applied measurements. When performance is inadequately measured or not measured at all, only chance governs results. When performance is measured and then reported back with teacher-led corrective action, the rate and quality of student performance speeds up. Students become motivated to improve their performance.

Measuring human achievement using performance standards has a long history. We use music recitals; marksmanship tests in the military and police; drivers' license exams; writing examinations; and problem-solving exams in math, science, and social science. To these, we can add contests measuring achievement. These range from body building to hair design, from flower arranging to cake decorating, and requirements for careers from barbers to court reporters.

The advent of standardized tests, true–false questions, paper-and-pencil multiple-choice items as testing devices and machine scoring changed teacher behavior. Before this type of measuring mastery, teachers relied on direct approaches to assessing results. Students wrote essays, were asked to spell words, answer questions, solve problems at the blackboard, and make things work. School board members went into classrooms to have students, selected randomly, audition for them by performing academic tasks. Testing was direct and observable; it was not secondary and done by proxy.

Evidence of Unevenness and Absence of Quality Control

Some teachers use consistent strategies with lessons, books, and other resources. They believe that each of their students can learn and that they have the responsibility to help. They pursue definite objectives around which their classroom instruction is organized. Lessons are well thought out, organized, and paced. Teachers check often to determine how well each student is doing and whether some need more work. They use the results to guide remedial action.

In contrast, too many teachers lack a consistent strategy for instruction. They marshal resources in a scattered fashion. To students, they have vague objectives. Their lessons are not well thought out and, in fact, are disorganized. Classroom work is poorly paced. These teachers do not regularly check to see how students are doing and if they do check, they do not make many midcourse corrections to accommodate student responses.

Teachers of this sort do not exert themselves to make effective educational connections with students. Many act as though they believe that their responsibility is simply to "present the material," and to let students get it if they can. When such teachers work with students from disadvantaged conditions, they often act as though they believe that these students can handle only watered-down instruction.

Evidence of Ignorance and Apathy

There is no shortage of ideas for improving classroom instruction. Stakeholders are flooded with supposedly better curriculum, teaching methods, and materials. When decisions are made, the question "What does the research say really works in the matter of reliable quality classroom teaching?" is seldom heard.

Unhappily, if this question were asked, little reassurance would come from the answer. Very weak research work exists that translates knowledge about learning into effective methods and materials for widespread classroom use. This truth exists despite the fact that in the last three decades American universities, foundations, and governments have spent hundreds of millions of dollars for research on K–12 education (Miller 1999, A17–A18). There are however some noteworthy exceptions to this dismal picture.

In 1998, the American Institutes for Research (AIR), at the direction of the major national groups representing teachers, principals, and school administrators, took a close look at the research behind all federally funded educational programs for disadvantaged children. AIR rated the effectiveness of twenty-four programs on a four-point scale, from "mixed or weak" to "strong." Only three of the twenty-four received a highest rating. The three were Direct Instruction, Success For All, and High Schools That Work.

The report covered a thousand or more schools across the country. Of the eight programs whose research base was marked "weak" or "marginal," three had previously been adopted. Several well-established school programs have still never been subjected to rigorous studies (American Institutes for Research 1999).

The reasons for this are not too hard to figure out. Two stand out. First, education scholars usually avoid research that shows what works in classrooms. They favor studies that simply observe student behavior and teaching techniques. Second, many professional educators ignore existing research. Moreover, they fail to support new research that does not fit their ideological preferences. This mind-set continues to insist that the best kind of learning is the kind that impulsively springs forth from students without specific direction from teachers. This strongly held view reflects the dominant theme in teacher training. That is to say, a learner-centered approach that assumes learning only comes about when the "developmental conditions are right" (Miller 1999, A17–A18).

THE TYRANNY OF CHANCE AND EDUCATIONAL MALPRACTICE SUITS

A brand new kind of legal action is quietly evolving in education. It comes as a response to alleged negligence occurring because of the tyranny of chance. These cases are called *educational malpractice* actions. As in medical malpractice, the term is drawn from negligence on the part of the professional practitioner.

There are two major types of educational malpractice suits—for the handicapped and for incompetent high school graduates. The first issue arises from educational services to be provided for the handicapped. The second is based on the tested lack of ability and skills of high school graduates who have been awarded a bona fide high school diploma.

Section 504 of the 1973 Rehabilitation Act (PL 93-380) and the federal Education for all Handicapped Children Act (PL 94-142) have generated many lawsuits of the first type. Basically, these legal actions are concerned with some aspect of educating the handicapped child. They usually involve failure to treat a student who has some handicapped condition. It includes the failure to diagnose a handicapping condition, a misdiagnosis, or mistreatment of a handicapping condition.

Other suits involve architectural barriers to handicapped pupils. These include a building without elevators, a building with steps and without ramps, a classroom door too narrow for a wheelchair, restroom facilities that do not accommodate a person in a wheelchair, water fountains unsuited to handicapped persons, and generally inaccessible physical facilities. There is considerable litigation in this area, with several important cases recently adjudicated.

The other major type of malpractice suit is the student competency suit. The student, or his or her parents, brings suit against specific teachers or school districts (or even a state) for failing to provide an adequate quality of instruction. The typical case involves a student who has received a high school diploma, yet is unable to acquire a meaningful job because he or she is functionally illiterate. These students allege that holding a high school diploma suggests competency at least adequate to survive in our society, but the pupil with no appreciable reading or writing skills may not be able to survive. The student sues the school district and sometimes the teachers for educational malpractice, claiming that he or she did not receive proper instruction in the fundamentals of education.

Related to competency suits is the trend in education toward minimum competency testing. Many states now require pupils to pass a minimum competency test for the high school diploma. Students who cannot pass the test may sue the school district, alleging that the schools did not provide them with proper instruction for passing the test.

Examples of Specific Competency Suits

Competency-type malpractice suits have the potential for creating the most litigation in this new tort area of education. Once the door opens, an avalanche of litigation will probably follow, with both founded and unfounded actions. If every student who fails to master all of the survival skills of society should bring suit against his school district and its teachers for educational malpractice, the country's courtrooms would be immediately overwhelmed.

The first of the major competency malpractice cases was *Peter W. v. San Francisco Unified School District* (60 C.A. 3d 814, 131 Cal. Rptr. 854, 1976). Peter W. graduated from the San Francisco schools with a high school diploma. A California statute requires that high school graduates read at a level above the eighth grade. Apparently, Peter W. could not survive in society, because he lacked reading or writing ability. He sued the San Francisco Public Schools on five counts.

1. "Negligently and carelessly" failed to apprehend his reading disabilities;
2. "Negligently and carelessly" assigned him to classes in which he could not read "the books and other materials";
3. "Negligently and carelessly" allowed him "to pass and advance from a course or grade level" with knowledge that he had not achieved either its completion or the skills necessary for him to succeed or benefit from subsequent courses;
4. "Negligently and carelessly" assigned him to classes in which the instructors were unqualified or which were not "geared" to his reading level; and
5. "Negligently and carelessly" permitted him to graduate from high school, although he was "unable to read above the eighth-grade level, as required by Education Code 8573 . . . thereby depriving him of additional instruction in reading and other academic skills" (Connors 1981, 149).

Peter W. was seeking two sets of damages. First, he sought general damages because of his "permanent disability and inability to gain meaningful employment." In parallel, he sought specific damages to compensate him for the cost of tutoring to correct the injury that the San Francisco schools had inflicted upon him.

The California Court of Appeals affirmed the superior court's dismissal of the suit against the school district.

Less than two years later, the second important competency malpractice case was decided 3,000 miles away from California. The New York Supreme Court Appellate Division also ruled against a pupil alleging educational malpractice in *Donohue v. Copiague Union Free School District* (407 N.Y.S. 874 2d 64 A.D. 2d 29, 1978). In this case, Edward Donohue sought $5,000,000 in damages, making two allegations. First, his lawyers claimed that the public schools failed to

teach the several and varied subjects to plaintiff, ascertain his learning capacity and ability, and correctly and properly test him for such capacity in order to evaluate his ability to comprehend the subject matters of the various courses and have sufficient understanding and comprehension of subject matters in said courses as to be able to achieve sufficient passing grades in said subject matters, and therefore, qualify for a Certificate of Graduation. (Connors 1981, 150)

Since Donohue did not have basic skills in reading and writing, the suit claimed that the school system breached its "duty of care" because it:

gave to the plaintiff passing grades and/or minimal or failing grades in various subjects; failed to evaluate the plaintiff's mental ability and capacity to comprehend the subjects being taught to him at said school; failed to take proper means and precautions that they reasonably should have taken under the circumstances; failed to take proper means and precautions that they reasonably should have taken under the circumstances; failed to interview, discuss, evaluate and/or psychologically test the plaintiff in order to ascertain his ability to comprehend and understand such subject matter; failed to provide adequate school facilities, teachers, administrators, psychologists, and other personnel trained to take the necessary steps in testing and evaluation processes insofar as the plaintiff is concerned in order to ascertain the learning capacity, intelligence, and intellectual absorption on the part of the plaintiff, failed to hire proper personnel . . .; failed to teach the plaintiff in such a manner so that he could reasonably understand what was necessary under the circumstances so that he could cope with the various subject . . .; failed to properly supervise the plaintiff; [and] failed to advise his parents of the difficulty and necessity to call in psychiatric help. (Connors 1981, 151)

The New York court, using the Peter W. case as precedent, also claimed that public policy does not allow the judiciary to become embroiled in educational affairs.

A teacher dismissal case with implications for the competency malpractice area is *Gilliland v. Board of Education* (365 N.E. 2d 322, 1977). An Illinois school board dismissed a tenured elementary teacher because she had

ruined the students' attitudes toward school, had not established effective student/teacher rapport, constantly harassed students, habitually left her students unattended and gave unreasonable and irregular homework assignments. (Connors 1981, 153)

With more and more states implementing minimal competency tests as prerequisites for receiving a diploma, there is only one thing certain in the future. Pupils' suits to recover damages as a result of educational malpractice have laid the groundwork for more and more attempts.

The Texas Case

A January 7, 2000, decision by a federal district judge in Texas is decisive in this litigation area. The following excerpt from a recent publication presents the case.

> Who should issue driver's licenses to teenagers? Should it be the driving instructors who are responsible for teaching teens to drive? Or should it be an impartial examiner who tests each teen to see if he or she has the skills and knowledge needed to drive? (Clowes 2000, 2)

Most people agree that using an examiner is the better way of making sure that driver's licenses aren't given to teens who can't read traffic signs and don't know the rules of the road.

U.S. District Court Judge Edward C. Prado, in an important and closely watched Texas case, handed down a similarly commonsense decision in January 2000. The case asked: Who should be responsible for issuing high school diplomas? A student's teachers, who may give the student passing grades in all classes? Or the Texas Education Agency (TEA), which may flunk the same student for not possessing a minimum set of academic skills?

Judge Prado gave the nod to the state, not to the teachers. He upheld the right of TEA to make the award of the high school diploma conditional on passing a competency test.

"In spite of projected disparities in passing rates [of different ethnic groups], the TEA determined that objective measures of mastery should be imposed in order to eliminate what it perceived to be inconsistent and possibly subjective teacher evaluations of students," wrote Prado, noting the state agency presented evidence of subjective teacher evaluations. The problem with subjective teacher evaluations, he noted, is that they "can work to disadvantage minority students by allowing inflated grades to mask gaps in learning" (Clowes 2000, 3).

"Texans want a high school diploma to mean something," explained Texas Education Commissioner Jim Nelson (Clowes 2000, 3).

Education officials in several states had anxiously awaited the outcome of this case. Many already have or are developing similar high-stakes graduation tests. Nineteen states have tests required for graduation. At this writing, another eight have plans to put them into place. The court ruling preserves the Texas school accountability system, where the state holds educators accountable for student learning, attendance, and dropout rates.

Texas Governor George W. Bush said he was "really pleased" with the decision and that it confirmed the state's strong education accountability system. He has frequently cited this in his run for the White House (Clowes 2000, 3).

Public school students in the Lone Star state start taking the Texas Assessment of Academic Skills (TAAS) test in the third grade. In the tenth grade, all Texas public school students are given what is called the "exit-level" TAAS exam. They must pass this exam to graduate. The test measures proficiency in reading, writing, and mathematics.

Students who achieve a 70 percent score on the exit-level test—which is based largely on eighth-grade material—are entitled to receive a high school diploma at their twelfth-grade graduation. Students who fail the test are given seven additional chances to take the test before their scheduled graduation date.

The use of the TAAS test to deny high school diplomas was challenged by the Mexican-American Legal Defense and Education Fund (MALDEF). They argued that the test was discriminatory simply because the failure rate for African Americans and Hispanics was higher than for whites. MALDEF claimed the test had "an impermissible adverse impact on minority students in Texas" and also violated their right to due process (Clowes 2000, 4).

A case was brought on behalf of nine students who did not pass the TAAS exit-level examination prior to their scheduled graduation dates. They requested that their respective school districts issue their diplomas. The court denied their request.

MALDEF presented an argument frequently made by apologists for the poor performance of urban public schools—that the state cannot hold students accountable for acquiring any knowledge unless it guarantees that all students are given an equal opportunity to learn. According to MALDEF, it is unfair to penalize minority students by denying them a high school diploma when their school district has not provided them with the same opportunity to learn that white students have. Teacher assessments, not TAAS test results, should be the main criteria for awarding diplomas, argued MALDEF.

Judge Prado rejected this argument. He recognized that minorities were underrepresented in advanced placement courses and in gifted-and-talented programs, and that noncertified teachers disproportionately taught minority students. But he went on to find that:

> The Plaintiffs presented insufficient evidence to support a finding that minority students do not have a reasonable opportunity to learn the material covered in the TAAS examination, whether because of unequal education in the past or the current residual effects of an unequal system. (Clowes 2000, 4)

Prado further went on to say the TAAS test accomplishes exactly what it sets out to accomplish, which is "to provide an objective assessment of whether students have mastered a discrete set of skills and knowledge." Since the state has linked the test to the state curriculum, "the Court finds that all Texas students have an equal opportunity to learn the items presented on the TAAS test, which is the issue before the Court" (Clowes 2000, 4).

While acknowledging "the TAAS test does adversely affect minority students in significant numbers," Prado ruled there was an "educational necessity" for the test. The plaintiffs, he determined, had failed to identify equally effective alternatives. He also concluded there had been no violation of due process rights, since the TEA provided adequate notice of the consequences of the exam and ensured that the exam is strongly correlated to material actually taught in the classroom.

"The system is not perfect, but the Court cannot say that it is unconstitutional," he wrote (Clowes 2000, 4).

THE LIKELY FUTURE

The prospect of more malpractice suits for incompetence due to the tyranny of chance is unacceptable and needless. Very simply, recognizing a cause of action in negligence to recover for "educational malpractice" would eventually require the courts to oversee the administration of a state's public school system. Thus far, courts have held that state public policy recognizes no cause of action for educational malpractice.

However, the New York court also felt that the process of education is a two-step process. First, there must be teaching. Second, there must be learning. The court was not willing to conclude that when a pupil does not learn it is automatically the fault of the teacher. The New York court put it this way. "The failure to learn does not bespeak a failure to teach. It is not alleged that the plaintiff's classmates, who were exposed to the identical classroom instruction, also failed to learn" (Connors 1981, 152).

The court placed a certain amount of the burden of fault on the student himself, and on the parents as well.

> The grades on the plaintiff's periodic report cards gave notice both to his parents and himself that he had failed in two or more subjects, thus meeting the definition of an "underachiever" provided in the regulations of the Commissioner of Education (8 NYCRR 203.1/2). Having this knowledge, the plaintiff could properly have demanded the special testing and evaluation directed by the statute. (Connors 1981, 152)

But since neither the student nor the parents requested special help, the court felt that they could not blame the failure to learn on the school system or its teachers.

There is one vital difference between the *Peter W.* and the *Donohue* decisions. The New York Supreme Court Appellate Division did not completely rule out future education malpractice suits. The court suggested that if more than a single individual suffers injury as a result of educational malpractice, a negligence suit might be successful.

> This determination does not mean that educators are not ethically and legally responsible for providing a meaningful public education for the youth of our State. Quite the contrary, all teachers and other officials of our schools bear an important public trust and may be held to answer for the failure to faithfully perform their duties. It doesn't mean, however, that they may not be sued for damages by an individual student for an alleged failure to reach certain educational objectives. (Connors 1981, 153)

A PERSONAL STORY FROM THE BOARD

Several years ago, Allen Salowe served as school board president in Plainfield, New Jersey. The population characteristics of this suburban city of 50,000 sharply changed after the 1960s urban riots. Up until that time, Plainfield was a typical New York bedroom commuter town located on the Jersey Central Railroad Line. The shot that ended the life of Dr. Martin Luther King ricocheted throughout this normally quiet city.

In the aftermath of the King assassination, a Plainfield policeman was stomped to death right on the street. The New Jersey National Guard moved tanks into the city to quell the riots. Anxiety and stress grew rapidly among Plainfield's citizens of all colors.

The social and economic problems of a city are often seen resulting from such an eruption. Parents rushed to pull their kids out of school. Others put their children in private or parochial schools. Still others placed "For Sale" signs in front of their lovely suburban houses and simply moved elsewhere. Little noticed was the demographic mix of the shifting population. More and more minority families left the high-stress urban areas of Newark, Jersey City, and the Bronx to seek a better quality of life for their children. Plainfield offered the promise of a safer haven to these persons.

It wasn't very long before Plainfield's city services were stretched and strained beyond their limits. This included placing an increasing load on the public schools. In the wake of *Brown v. Board of Education*, the Plainfield school board was already under court order to bus students to achieve racial balance.

Soon the city's political battles reached an impasse. The city council and school board members refused to even speak with one another. They would not even agree to a face-to-face meeting. The leaders could not bring themselves to put the needs of 10,000 schoolchildren first.

In the shadow of this setting, Allen was asked to join the mayor-appointed school board. He was a professional corporate planner. His family had been lifelong Plainfield residents. His first objective was to get a head-on meeting between the warring council and school board members. Council president David Rothberg, a longtime friend, helped Allen pull this peacemaking effort together.

The icebreaking session started to turn the tide toward the needs of Plainfield students. By this time, school population was 93 percent nonwhite. Though there remained little need to continue cross-city bus-ing, the practice continued for another twenty years.

In the heat of this battle, the school board tried concentrating on the needs of these kids. It began to redefine the mission of the school sys-tem. It turned its attention to the quality of teachers and staff who would help the waves of minority families.

During his three tortuous years on the school board, Allen experi-enced weekly what Leon Lessinger, a lifelong educator, came to label as the *tyranny of chance*. Issues brought before the board by parents or interested citizens, as well as direct talks with teachers and administra-tors, appealed to the needs of students. All too often, the words of re-sponse from the professionals seemed hollow and superficial. Behind the smokescreen of staff excuses, the shortcomings of the school district could not produce a reliable student outcome. Only the school profes-sionals seemed satisfied with what was happening.

Another personal story may help light up the dilemma. All of us re-call a favorite teacher. Usually, it is because that teacher had that same feeling toward you. This is the kind of relationship that helps set the stage for a kid wanting to meet his parent's expectations. Putting it an-other way, if your teacher doesn't give a damn about you, then why would you give a damn about school?

At the time, Allen's middle son Kenny was a fifth-grade student in Mr. Ken Bowlby's science class. Each evening, Kenny would come home jabbering enthusiastically about what Mr. Bowlby had done in class that day. He'd tell what he had been taught and why it was an ex-citing class to be in. This teacher has had a lifelong impact on Kenny, who is now a father in his own right.

Two years later, Mr. Bowlby became an issue before Allen's board. Mr. Bowlby's principal complained to the board that this teacher was too "unconventional" in his teaching methods. The administration charged, "Bowlby is too hard to manage. He spends his classroom time explaining science experiments as though he were performing on TV."

Allen shared with fellow board members the positive impact this teacher had already had on his own son. Other parents came to support the teacher and his effectiveness. The superintendent rushed to support the principal in his arguments and complaints. The staff decided they had no interest in renewing this teacher's contract.

Other board members started to raise the bar on questions to the staff. Tell us "in what ways is this teacher ineffective?" one board member asked. "What's wrong with his expressive teaching methods?" asked another. Now on the defense, the superintendent went for his standard justification for action: "This is an operational matter and not a policy matter," he scolded the board. Board members immediately shrank. They lost their energy to defend an innovative teacher. Once again, the school staff placed its concern for the status quo system ahead of the needs of the students. The system was about to successfully drive out one more dedicated and innovative teacher.

One more board story is even more compelling. This same Plainfield superintendent constantly complained that the reasons student and class test performance scores showed continuous decline was the need to accommodate too many children who had moved into the district from other schools.

The board asked staff to do an analysis of selected classroom performance and separate the test scores into two groups: (1) students who had moved into the district, and (2) students who had taken their earlier grades in the Plainfield schools.

The analysis results were eye opening. The students who performed best were those who had moved into the district. The students who did the poorest were those kids who had been schooled in the Plainfield district the longest. In other words, the results were exactly the opposite of what the superintendent claimed. The report showed that the longer a child was schooled in the Plainfield school system, the "dumber" he or she got. Not long after, the superintendent was asked for his resignation.

SOME DISCUSSION TOPICS ABOUT WHAT HAPPENS IN THE CLASSROOM

These discussion topics are directed to school staff. They are presented here as topics of conversation to help the reader pinpoint harmful teaching practices in the local school classroom.

Some years back, Leon Lessinger served as the associate U.S. commissioner for elementary and secondary education. There he worked with Don Stewart, a pioneer in bringing the idea of malpractice in education to the attention of teachers, administrators, and the general public. Through seminars, workshops, and publications, Stewart successfully raised awareness of those key features in classroom practices that result in the tyranny of chance (see especially *Educational Mal-practices*, 1971). Some of this pioneering work is reflected in what follows.

The Primary Purpose of Schooling

The following examples of common classroom teaching practices raise troublesome issues of poor practice or even malpractice in schooling. These discussion topics are *always* focused on the most important reason for schooling: "The primary purpose of schooling is the student's successful achievement of learning standards."

Topic of conversation number 1.   Do school materials and student readiness match? What is the result of having the teacher give the student learning materials, knowing full well that many students cannot be taught from these materials? Can the teacher justify failing the student for not learning something that the teacher already knew beforehand the student would be unable to do?

Topic of conversation number 2.   Does the student's readiness for schoolwork and any remedial efforts match? Too often the school enrolls students from "disadvantaged" groups that are known to have many entrance achievement deficits (cumulative ignorance). Can these students achieve successfully or are they doomed for failure from the start?

Topic of conversation number 3.   Why isn't more time devoted at admission time to helping students define and overcome their skill shortcomings? Here, the concern goes well beyond the loss of potential earning power if failing grades cause the student to be suspended or drop out early. It also deals with the student's loss of self-respect as a result of failure. If gaps remain in the student's preparation, such as low grades or having not taken an earlier course, what are the realistic chances for the student's success in this school?

Topic of conversation number 4.   Can the teacher give the student a list of objectives covering prerequisite material for the new courses, or give the student a test covering this material in order that the student can determine what he/she needs to know? If such a list is not available, what opportunities are there for the student to make up for any lack of prerequisite knowledge or skills? Is there assistance to help the student identify what it is he/she should know to take the course? Can the student try to learn the prerequisite material on his or her own?

Topic of conversation number 5.   Is social promotion a blessing or a curse? Is it responsible for a teacher to allow a student to leave a course or grade level, knowing full well that the student has not achieved the required knowledge, understandings, and skills for the next grade? Would your doctor tell his patient that if they do not get well by January 27 or June 10 that they might as well quit the treatment and stay sick or die?

Topic of conversation number 6.   If the student got a C (D or F) in a course, does the student know what a C is worth in that course? Is it 60 percent, 70 percent, 80 percent, 65 percent, or 75 percent? Does the student know what percentage of the course he or she learned, in order to earn only a C?

Topic of conversation number 7.   Teachers have long known that administrators look upon giving too many A and B grades in classes generally typecasts the teacher as being an "easy" grader. Is it fair to both the student and the teacher alike if the school administration expects the teacher to use a learning situation in which a certain percentage of students must fail or do poorly?

Topic of conversation 8.   How do we close the gap between remedial work and student knowledge? Why are students who take a course for a second time because of a low grade required to take the *entire* course over again, instead of the 20, 30, 40 percent, or more that they did not learn when they took the course the first time? Is this done for school convenience?

Topic of conversation number 9.   Time frames are arbitrary units of measure for most learning. All schools still measure results on the basis of time, such as two years of a language, two years of math, one semester of this, two semesters of that, etc. This practice continues regardless of how much learning has taken place. If learning a course is important, then why aren't students kept in certain courses until such time as they have learned whatever it is they need? Doesn't using time as a measure of achievement, rather than learning, skirt the issue that different students learn the same materials at different rates of speed? In fact, aren't some students ready to leave the course much earlier than others? Aren't they likely to become bored when they have to stay to the end of the course?

Topic of conversation number 10.   Can teaching methods be mistaken for punishment? When a teacher uses a classroom learning activity as a form of punishment, this very quickly convinces the student that this kind of learning activity is always punishment. This practice takes place when students are disciplined by having to write phrases or sentences many times, or to write extra essays, or assigned extra problems to solve. In physical education classes, students are often made to run around the gym or field and/or to perform certain extra exercises. Unknowingly, the teacher can very seriously affect a student's future view of learning because of this archaic and common practice.

Topic of conversation number 11. There is confusion between school accreditation and teaching results. All too often, state and regional associations give official accreditation to a school because of its facilities, the faculty, library, building size, and teacher credentials. Doesn't it seem logical that accreditation needs to take into account whether the necessary learning is taking place within the school?

PRACTICE TEACHING OR A TEACHING PRACTICE?

Most of us are familiar with practice teaching. Many of us probably still recall a day or two when a newly minted teacher came to practice teach in our classroom. But what are we really looking for in the teaching profession?

The core of a real profession consists of using the knowledge and skill of that profession to get expected results. These methods are called *professional practice.* We know these in medicine, in law, and in engineering, to name just three.

We expect a professional practice of law, a professional practice of engineering, and a professional practice of medicine. Can we expect even the appearance of reliability in classroom teaching without training teachers in the good practices of a professional practice of teaching?

Teachers "practice-teach." Teachers are not expected to achieve a professional teaching practice. Teachers are not required to acquire an agreed-upon body of methods and procedures. It is good practice that gets dependable and durable results.

This is not to imply that there are not some teachers who apply good practice diligently and consistently. Indeed, there are a few top-notch examples of good teaching practice in many school districts, but standard operating procedures are known to be effective and become the lifeblood of reliable organizations.

GOOD PRACTICE, POOR PRACTICE, AND MALPRACTICE IN EDUCATION

Good Practice is defined as the professional way, the standard operating procedures, of doing things in the instructional process. Good Practice will reliably produce an intended student learning outcome or result. Good Practice is the legacy of long experience. It is the product of research and development.

Poor Practice, on the other hand, is ways of doing things that have unpredictable or chance results. None of us would care to ride in an airplane that is piloted by a crew that has irregular results. The results we demand include safety and reliability.

Malpractice reflects ways of doing things that generally produce a harmful result or are illegal. When we choose a surgeon we expect that the doctor will do no harm. We should expect no less in schools of school teaching. We demand that the doctor's activities be legal and we anticipate helpful results. Consider some other examples:

- In medicine, it is good practice to sterilize a wound. In law, it is good practice to exercise due process. In engineering, it is good practice to build safety features into a structure.
- In medicine, it is poor practice to routinely use antibiotics. In law, it is poor practice to release privileged information about a pending trial. In engineering, it is poor practice to place a part that will require servicing in an inaccessible place.
- In medicine, it is malpractice to leave a surgical instrument or other harmful materials inside a patient. In law, it is malpractice to force a client to perjure himself. In engineering, it is malpractice to knowingly use a set of materials that does not meet specification.

But in education, there is only the simplest understanding of the notion of good practice, poor practice, and malpractice in the instructional process. In fact, when the classroom door closes, almost any instructional process the teacher uses is protected and free from correction.

Susan Markle shows us how an outrageous failure to achieve a professional teaching practice can be interpreted.

> The idea of a major industrial concern turning out, on a standardized production line, 10 per cent superior products, 20 per cent good products, and 50 per cent average products, with the remainder classed as disposable is so ludicrous in this age of modern technology that it would hardly bear mentioning were it not for the obvious parallel between this outlandish image and the present situation in education. (Markle 1967, 110)

A profession that cannot distinguish among good practice, poor practice, and malpractice is doomed to remain in a primitive state. All persons in such a field will have difficulty proving their professional credibility. There is a major obstacle to improving school effectiveness and the status of educators based on two factors: (1) a lack of educators adopting the known "good practice" as standard operating practice in the classroom, and (2) their adopting a management system that supports high reliability classroom teaching.

THE REALITIES GOOD PRACTICE MUST SATISFY

To begin with, good practice must address the realities of public education. It needs to pull away from some hoped-for procedure that might be touted as being better for schools. Facing up squarely to the realities of public education means that the good practice must be useful to an everyday classroom of students.

Good practice must work in settings where: (1) the teacher has a course of study to follow in a fixed period of time, (2) there is limited time for problem-solving tests, (3) extra adult classroom help is generally not available, (4) student diversity is great, and (5) student achievement must be graded. Nothing short of these criteria will do.

There are two more matters to be considered. Good practice needs to deal with the widespread fact of "cumulative ignorance" and "learned helplessness." These are an outcome of today's teaching mode. Cumulative ignorance is the academic insufficiency to succeed in the next program or learning step. Learned helplessness is the depressed feeling that no matter what one does, it will not be sufficient.

ENDING THE TYRANNY OF CHANCE

The solution to the tyranny of chance in education can be likened to balancing a board on a fulcrum; if one end is chance (the unpredictable management system), the other must be reliability (the dependable and durable management system). The basic solution to the challenge of producing well-prepared students will come about only when we transform our current school systems. Too many schools are dominated by the tyranny of chance and need to become ones that are managed by the processes of high-dependability organizations. Schools we can count on to dependably produce student mastery of curriculum standards need to be accurately assessed. Students need to have accurate measurement of their performance and have it publicly reported. A dependable common home temperature thermostat, not a pair of dice, symbolizes this series of events.

Education's masterful metaphor is the temperature thermostat that each of us probably has in our home. Consider how it works. We set it at the temperature we want for most comfort. Engineers have found that people set it generally between 68 and 72 degrees, but each one of us as individuals can set it any place we want. It meets our individual needs.

After we set it, the device automatically responds to our temperature requirement. If it gets too hot or too cold, that is, if there is a gap between what we want and what is actually happening, the thermostat sends a signal to a "helper"—an air conditioner or heat pump. The helper responds by quickly putting hot or cold air into our room until the standard we have set is met.

The thermostat is a wonderful example of the meaning of reliability. It meets our requirements every time and over an extended period of time. It is dependable and durable. If we examine the thermostat from the perspective of reliable quality teaching in the classroom, we can easily see that it has the following elements.

1. *The setting of standards that the system must meet.* We can choose the particular temperature we want.
2. *An assessment—a test—to see if the standard is being met.* The device measures the actual temperature and compares it with the required standard we have set for the system.

3. *As assistance partner.* The air conditioning or heat pump is connected to supply what is needed if there is a gap between what we have set as a standard and what is actually happening.
4. *Feedback for quality control.* If there is a gap, the device sends a signal for assistance and corrective action takes place. This is the definition of *quality control*—feedback plus corrective action.
5. *Reliable quality.* We can depend on getting the temperature we want every time, all the time.

At the other end of the scale is a pair of dice. Dice represent the tyranny of chance. Sometimes we get what we want, sometimes we don't. Getting what we want or what we need to have is always a gamble. The thermostat, on the other hand, represents the prime example of reliable quality. It does what we want. It meets our expectations.

We hope that, as you travel through this book, it helps you discard the pair of dice as the symbol for getting quality classroom teaching. We look forward to that time when the winning prescription ushers in the reliable symbol for getting quality classroom teaching every time, all the time—the educational thermostat.

We also hope that a parent not sit idly by while a poor school system fails to deliver quality teaching to their child. Insufficient learning demands parents take prompt action to bolster their child's education. Two doctrines emphasize this parental duty; (1) the doctrine of avoidable consequences; results which could have been avoided by prudent conduct, and (2) the concept of willfull blindness; the parent who should have known and could have asked but deliberately chose not to act. Parents should not sit by through the school years only to one day discover that their 18-year-old is functionally illiterate or unable to add two-digit numbers. A parent that suddenly makes this discovery has no one else to blame for a child's lost years.

Finally, "we hope that parents and employers consider taking the positive step of urging their state legislature to enact a statute permitting educational malpractice torts under certain limited conditions, as a way of further holding the educational bureaucracy accountable and responible, just as other professionals are held accountable in courts." [Attorney Robert Standler, January 10, 2000].

CHAPTER 4

Reliable Treatments Help Sick Schools Get Better

In the world's great cities, such as Paris, London, New York, Chicago, San Francisco, and Tokyo, their subway systems tie together the lives of their citizens. An electric third rail powers the trains. It delivers the current necessary to keep this vital transportation network moving. It is our conviction that, in its own way, the energy of the quality-improvement process for a school and its classrooms is reliability.

The main message of the Baldrige and ISO 9000 criteria is *continuous improvement.* Continuous improvement is the overriding issue that determines the success of the winning prescription. By gut feel, the school administrators and teachers know what is meant by continuous improvement. It is easy to describe but tough to implement. It means getting quality thinking into the mind-set of each person, and taking daily steps to achieve some crystal-clear result. Thus, quality thinking becomes second nature.

Most often, efforts at school and business improvement are not continuous. We Americans are problem solvers; we solve a problem, and then we stop and move on to deal with a different problem. Continuous improvement calls for repeating the process of getting better over and over again. It's like mastering the skill of hitting a softball. We repeatedly go over the steps until we can see it in our mind's eye. This process also calls for steadily updating the improvement process itself.

We can picture improvement in two ways: simple and continuous. Using simple improvement, we go after and solve specific problems. With continuous improvement, we tackle and manage ongoing processes for the purpose of heading off specific problems.

The winning prescription asks us to answer two key questions related to continuous improvement: "How is improvement to be done?" and "How is what is to be done to be measured and evaluated?"

In every school, the first question asks the leadership and teachers to think through and then write down their approach to each process step.

With this question, we seek to unravel the complex processes used for meeting or improving each standard of the winning prescription. With this method, we ask the school to start from scratch, to evaluate all of their methods, their tools, and their different techniques. The second question triggers the feedback of results and the corrective action. Both steps are essential to improve the school's quality control.

Deming is the quality expert who helped reshape the economy of postwar Japan. He gives us the following well-respected standard of continuous improvement. "Constantly improve design of product and service," he advised. "This obligation never ceases . . . everyone, every-day must ask himself what he has done to advance his learning and skill on the job" (Deming 1986, 102).

Achieving quality is a step-by-step process. The quality school avoids reinventing the wheel each time a problem or opportunity crops up. The quality school strives to keep that proverbial wheel turning constantly. In this way, continuous improvement is built into that school's daily practices. Quality activities are not simply grafted onto the school day. The quality school constantly uses two rules of quality thinking — (1) look for feedback from quality actions that can be measured, followed by (2) developing a plan for and the use of corrective actions.

PROCESSES LEAD THE WAY

The winning prescription requires the school to wrestle with the importance of continuous processes. At the outset, the major stumbling block at school may be the difficulty in grasping the crucial consequences of processes. However, only in this way can the school expect to achieve dependable teaching time in every classroom, and that is precisely what we are looking for.

Most people are in the habit of thinking solely in terms of things. We ordinarily think of products and specific elements. Most folks do not think much about the processes or underlying ways in which things — and services — are created and developed.

A process is merely a repeated activity that changes something. Most homemakers know that the process of stirring cream will first produce whipped cream. If the stirring process continues, it eventually changes the cream to butter. Obviously, the processes used in schools are more complex.

Grasping and improving the processes that underpin the winning prescription's six elements is central to school success. Putting it another way, the first step toward success with the winning prescription is the acceptance of what Baldrige and ISO 9000 are trying to get the school to do. It will pay off in reliable classroom teaching. Evaluating and improving all school processes is the challenge for approaching, organizing, and continually improving the reliability of classroom teaching time.

One of the processes badly in need of continuous improvement is determining the readiness of the class when students start a new class. Teachers need to be notified of previous student performance in order to build this vital link into instruction.

Resolving parent complaints is just as much a process as is recruiting, orientating, training, and staff development. Every repeatable school activity throughout the school district needs to be viewed as a process of events. In schools, the processes *are* the system.

The next time one of your neighbors declares that the #@$% school system has a problem, you can correct that angry statement. The problem needing attention is located in one of the *processes* that comprise the system.

A common mistake made by teachers and staff is to think that problems are the possessions of an individual or some special event. Today, we know that most problems are not isolated situations or special causes. They are not disconnected events; they are built into the system. They are chronic problems that persist over time and they are the consequence of some cause and effect that is buried deep in the unstudied processes of the system. These flaws, if allowed to persist within the system, eventually reveal themselves in unexpected ways, and block the school's desired end result.

Again, Deming gives us guidance. His lifetime of experience on the character of the processes that are entrenched in the system results in a startling statistic. Deming is often quoted as saying that fully "94 percent of the troubles an organization has can be attributed to system. Only 6 percent are due to" what Deming terms "special causes" (Deming 1986, 315). Special causes are the occasional glitches that follow Murphy's Law. This bottom line provides guidance to quality experts, parents, and educators with a simple and direct fix. Concentrate on the processes, and the end result you want will take care of itself.

The winning prescription gets us to pay constant attention to the "what" and "how" of processes. It asks school leaders and teachers to describe the sequential activities they use—sometimes unconsciously—and to commit to writing the tools, techniques, and methods used during those schooling processes. Education leaders are urged to think of the Baldrige and ISO directives as a "census of processes" for motivating staff, planning for needs, and assuring reliable quality.

The attention to processes leads us to the desired continuous improvement. We know that by their very nature, school processes can never be permanently solved. School processes either become (1) habit forming and eventually deteriorate, or (2) part of our consciousness and become steadily improved. Once fully immersed in Baldrige and ISO 9000, school staff backs away from solely playing the role of inspectors. In its place, they begin to think like an architect, engineer, and designer. They seek to identify system improvements that create and sustain the results that other staff members, parents, and future employers—the internal and external customers—demand.

The heart and soul of improving system processes is the road to prevention of student failure and the reduced need for student remediation. The target is not to discover defects. Rather, the goal is finding the knowledge and insights needed to improve the processes that lead to defects. We want to eliminate problems before they lead to undesirable consequences. Putting it another way, we are talking about more attention to fire prevention so as to lessen the need for fire fighting.

HELPING PARENTS HELP THEIR STUDENTS MEET STANDARDS

If a student is having trouble meeting the standards, help should always be available. In a reliable quality school district, the entire school community will be at your call. Their responses are aligned to work in support of each student's achievement of the standards. The school administrators and teachers have no greater priority than to assist the student. It remains their top priority! School districts are responsible for providing the resources and support to each student needing extra help to meet the standards. In addition, the quality school is charged with developing an intervention-improvement plan for those students not yet meeting the standards.

As a help to readers who are not professional educators, the following samples of learning standards will give the reader an idea of the basis against which you can evaluate a student's progress. His or her teacher should be always available to help you better understand these standards.

By the End of the Fourth Grade, Your Student Can:

In reading, use a variety of strategies and word recognition skills, including reading, finding context clues, applying their knowledge of letter/sound relationships, and analyzing word structures. Also:

- They can infer the meaning of unfamiliar words in the context of a passage by examining known words, phrases, and structures.
- The fourth-grader can also demonstrate awareness of phonetics, including letter/sound relationships as aides to pronouncing known words, phrases, and structures.
- They can read aloud with age-appropriate fluency, accuracy, and expression.

In mathematics, the fourth-grader can use reasoning abilities to perceive patterns, identify relationships, prescribe questions for further exploration, justify strategies, and test reasonableness of results. Also:

- The fourth-grader can communicate mathematical ideas in a variety of ways, including words, number symbols, pictures charts, graphs, tables, diagrams, and models.
- They can use appropriate mathematical vocabulary, symbols, and notation with understanding based on prior conceptual work.

By the End of the Eighth Grade, Your Student Can:

In reading, use knowledge of sentence and word structure, word origins, visual images, and context clues to understand unfamiliar words and clarify passages of text. Also:

- By the end of the eighth grade, the student can use knowledge of the visual features of texts, such as chronology and cause-and-effect, as aides to comprehension.

- They can also select, summarize, paraphrase, analyze, and evaluate, orally and in writing, passages of texts chosen for specific purposes.
- The student can analyze the effect of characters, plot setting, language, topic, style, purpose, and point of view on the overall impact of literature.

In mathematics, the eighth-grader can use reasoning abilities to evaluate information, perceive patterns, identify relationships, and formulate questions for further explorations. Also:

- They can evaluate strategies, justify statements, test reasonableness of results, and defend work. They can communicate verbal arguments clearly to show why a result makes sense.
- The student can analyze nonroutine problems by modeling, illustrating, guessing, simplifying, generalizing, shifting to another point of view, etc.

By the End of the Twelfth Grade, Your Student Can:

In reading, apply sophisticated word meaning and word-analysis strategies, such as knowledge of roots, cognates, suffixes, and prefixes to understand unfamiliar words. Also:

- The student is able to gather information to help achieve understanding when the meaning of a text is unclear. Identify propaganda techniques and faulty reasoning in texts.
- The twelfth-grader can explain and evaluate the influence of format on the readability and meaning of a text.
- They can distinguish between fact and opinion in nonfiction texts.

In mathematics, they can use reason and logic to evaluate information, perceive patterns, identify relationships, formulate questions, pose problems, make and test conjectures, and pursue ideas that lead to further understanding and deeper insight. Also:

- The twelfth-grade student can analyze nonroutine problems and arrive at solutions by various means, including models and simulations, often starting with provisional conjectures and progressing, directly or indirectly, to a solution, justification, or counterexample.

THE QUALITY DIMENSION IN THE SCHOOL

Baldrige and ISO 9000 always bring us back to quality control. Quality is the cornerstone of the continuous-improvement processes. Customer satisfaction—the enthusiastic acceptance of parents, teachers, and future employers—is its Holy Grail.

As described in greater detail in the previous chapter, quality control and the mystery of its language are easily demonstrated through a common household thermostat. We reliably control room temperature

- by setting the temperature we want. (This is the performance standard of the system.)
- reading the built-in sensor to give us the actual temperature. (The feedback is the assessment of the performance standard.)
- evaluating any difference between the thermostat setting and the room temperature, and offset it by either warmer air or cooler air. (This is the corrective action.)

Quality Control (QC) is the reliable quality-system function that includes the reality of a situation against a desired standard. It does so on an ongoing basis, just as the sensor compares the actual and desired temperatures. If there is a gap, QC takes continuous action to achieve what is desired. You can hear and feel the hot or cold air cut on and off as needed.

QC activates the continuous improvement link between performance standards and their assessment. When the teacher, administrator, and school board systematically apply QC, it results in noticeable changes in the usual staff attitudes toward the results of teaching. This is the attitude of disciplined caring.

If the teaching does not achieve the intended performance standards, the teaching methods and management support are worked on until the student gets it right. In other words, if the student is not successfully prepared, neither the customer (the student and parents) nor the providers (faculty and staff) are blamed. Simply stated, it is the job of the teaching system to teach successfully. If it does not, the reasons for what isn't working are thoroughly investigated. Then, corrective action is put into place.

Understanding Systems

A system is a group of elements that are interconnected to accomplish a purpose. Two main ideas give the idea of a system its powerful and practical power. First, there is the defined purpose of the system. Second, there are the working relationships between components of the system. All systems have purposes, and the various parts of the system must be carefully related or the purposes cannot be achieved. It is easy, for instance, to see the interconnected structure for delivering quality sound with low distortion in the home stereo system.

Each school system is made up of many system components. There is a transportation system for delivering children to and from school, a cafeteria system for feeding them, and a safety system for protecting them. There is a governance system, a management system, a public information system, and an employer/employee system, to name some others. These distinctions are subtle but essential to understand. The leadership of the overall school system needs to understand and be able to track the cause and effect of the interaction of these systems. We need to keep in mind that 94 percent of all problems result from this interconnectedness, but the solutions are seldom apparent. They are often buried deep within the structure of the overall school system.

At the heart of each school system is the teaching/learning system, often called the *instructional system*. It is further composed of subsystems—classroom spaces, students and their parents, teaching materials, and technology. There is the teaching faculty, expertly performing the functions required. The proper functions to successfully guide students toward achieving standards are well known through research and field testing. The administrative staff is there to expertly support the teaching function.

Each classroom is also its own instructional system. When operating successfully, the internal customers, comprised of other teachers and staff, and the external customers, made up of parents and future employers, can readily see:

1. that mandated standards are the goals to be achieved,
2. that criterion achievement tests measure how well standards are being met,
3. that course content and media used by teachers help students reach standards
4. that the teacher uses suitable methods in teaching and classroom management
5. that QC methods are used for corrective action if students do not master standards

We can now see that to accomplish the learning-achievement purposes of a school, it is necessary to keep all school subsystems dependably working together and in sync with one another. They must quickly resolve clashes with each other. Operating at its best, the quality-control function is a primary force for managing the successful coordination of the separate subsystems.

Many states now mandate school standards for student learning in such areas as language arts, mathematics, science, and social studies. The standards clearly describe what the student is to know and be able to do in a given subject area. It goes on to define the kind of student work that demonstrates mastery. Today, these standards represent the learning-achievement mission of the local school.

WHY SYSTEM THINKING?

Sometimes, in order to understand the system, we need to understand the big picture as well as its individual parts. The story of the blind man and the elephant is often used to illustrate this. A blind man is asked to describe what he thinks an elephant looks like. Taking hold of the animal's tail he quickly assumes the elephant looks like a snake. Next, he feels the elephant's trunk and now says he must look like a fire hose. Asked to wrap his arms around one of the elephant's legs the blind man exclaims this must look like a giant tree. Then, after being led over to the animal's ear he finally says in exasperation this animal must look like a big leaf. "It must look like a very strange animal indeed," he finally concludes.

One of the most powerful tools for achieving a reliable quality school is system thinking. It also gives us the means for better understanding how technology relates to the professional practice of education. In simple language, the systems thinker says: "It's better to see the whole problem than just a part of it." System thinking aids us in more clearly thinking about making "good practice" the prevailing classroom teaching practice.

We know a system is a group of essentials, integrated to accomplish a purpose. An automobile is a system of parts and components that work together to provide us transportation. An autopilot and an airplane form a controlling system for flying at a specified altitude. A warehouse and loading platform is a delivery system for helping move goods into a truck. An elephant is a system for moving large loads in India. A school is a system to produce an educated citizen.

A system may include people as well as physical parts. The stock clerk and office worker are part of the warehouse system. Management is a system of people for allocating resources and regulating the activity of the enterprise. A family is a system for living and raising children.

The notion of a system is very far reaching. This gives it great practical power, but if systems are so pervasive, why do the concepts and principles of systems not appear more clearly in educational practice and literature? The answer seems to lie in the evolution of three facts: (1) up until now, there has been little need to understand the nature of systems, (2) until recently, there has been no general theory of systems, and (3) the principles of systems have been somewhat obscure.

In a primitive society, the existing systems were comprised of elements that arose only in nature. Their characteristics were believed to be divinely given and beyond man's ability to understand or control. Man simply adjusted himself to the natural systems around him and to the family and tribal customs. Man adapted to natural systems without feeling compelled to understand them.

As industrial societies came about, systems began to dominate life as they exhibited themselves in economic cycles, political turmoil, recurring financial panics, fluctuating employment, and unstable prices. Social systems became complex and their behavior grew to be confusing. A search for orderly structure, for cause-and-effect relationships, and for a theory to explain system behavior easily gave way at times to a belief in random, irrational causes.

To nail this point to the wall: the fabric of the systems concept is comprised of the system's intended purpose and the coordination of its subsystems to achieve some goal. Schools have many purposes. There are elements and functions that form the school system. These various elements must be well managed to see that all of the principle purposes of the school are realized.

The principal task of the school administration is to keep each subsystem functioning as smoothly as possible in order to avoid conflict. These subsystems should support one another on behalf of the overall purpose of the school. The school bus must get the students to school on time. The food service must accommodate the students' needs within a designated cost and time period. While these subsystems operate independently, it is easy to see that their effectiveness is greatly improved when these subsystems reinforce one another.

The heart of the educational system is the instructional subsystem. One definition of this classroom subsystem could be this: an integrated set of technology (media, methods, materials) and persons (teachers, students, parents, staff) to efficiently and effectively performing the required functions needed to accomplish the learning standards (goals).

By its very nature, systems thinking can cause a remarkable change in teacher and administrator attitudes toward the process of instruction. It is an attitude that is in direct opposition to a tyranny of chance. It is a mindset of professional responsibility for defining and applying what works.

To reemphasize this point: It is difficult to understate the spirit represented by this attitude. It may be the most important single change to try to get into schooling. It has the most direct bearing on school system effectiveness. Applying the winning prescription creates a shared attitude among all the partners in schooling, and this attitude translates into actions. If the instructional subsystem (the teachers, the materials, the equipment, the methods, the time, or any other components that make it up) is not effective and the student does not learn what is expected or required, the subsystem is redesigned until it does. The parents, the teachers, or the students are *not* blamed.

The general functions that make up an effective instructional system have repeatedly been identified in research. A minimum of the following five functions must be present and taught well.

The Specification of Desired Learning Results

Learning is a concept that can only be inferred. We can't really see or touch any learning directly. What we see is a change in condition. The student can now do something that he or she could not do before the learning experience. That something is the purpose of the classroom learning experience.

It has been a long and ongoing struggle to persuade educators to state the learning targets in such ways that they can be measured objectively. There continues to be the common school practice of stating desired targets in highly abstract terms that lack measurement possibility. We often hear of such learning targets as the development of "understandings." Beliefs and knowledge are stated without spelling out how we can possibly arrive at a reasonable estimate of results. We need to know the extent to which the learner understands, appreciates, knows, accepts, or believes what the classroom learning experience was intended to provide. We are talking about the measurable results of goals.

There currently exist tools for describing the learning targets of both education and training. The goals of the learning experience need to be spelled out in such ways that can be convincingly verified by both the providers and the customers. In this way, we can harness the power of system thinking and apply it to reliable classroom teaching.

The Presentation of Knowledge and Performance

Teachers can now employ a variety of teaching technologies such as reading, lectures, graphic aids, television, films, tape recorders, computers, videotapes, and CD-ROMs to serve students.

In the past, presentations were usually one way. They flowed from the teacher to the student. Today, we have readily available and effective two-way or interactive modes. We can look to the work of the learning subsystem—the presentation of knowledge and performance—to improve the classroom learning experience for increased effectiveness and greater efficiency.

The Practice of Knowledge and Performance

The targets of teaching consist of learning the skills and knowledge that are essential for mastering what has been taught. A classroom objective is a meaningful unit of work. A completed task is an example of such an objective.

Here is a case in point. Baking a cake and testing for smog control on a car are two objectives. In the classroom, it is crucial for the teacher to define in advance the knowledge and skills that meet the class objective. For baking a cake, it may be knowing the right ingredients and measurements; for smog-checking a car, it may be the skill of placing the instruments in the correct places. Educators call this transfer of knowledge and skill enabling classroom objectives, because without them the student cannot master the desired learning objective.

To be effective in meeting the objective, the student must practice the task as well as the skills and knowledge components that make it possible. To master any task, the student needs to be provided with adequate practice. Also, it is more cost-effective and less tedious for the student if the teacher provides students with practice of the enabling skills and knowledge at the same time. This can reduce the amount of time required for students to master the full performance.

The Management of the Learning Experience

Managing the classroom learning experience refers to those activities needed to keep students actively engaged in the entire learning experience. Among several recent developments are cooperative learning, newer forms of individualized instruction, and providing incentives tied directly to progress.

Quality Control (QC)

Measuring the student's actual performance serves as the cornerstone of QC. This information forms the feedback that leads the student and his or her teacher to the needed corrective action. Therefore, the performance data on the student must be as valid, reliable, objective, and detailed as is possible in each classroom learning situation.

QC measures how well the class target has been achieved. It helps to identify and initiate the proper corrective action. It includes feedback plus corrective action. This is a basic advance over common classroom evaluations that merely identify a gap between what was intended and what was achieved and assign a grade of A to F on what has happened.

QC produces that remarkable change in attitude among those providing education. It fosters an attitude of mutual accountability for results.

If the learning experience provided to the student does not achieve what was intended (that is, if the student did not succeed), the learning experience is redesigned. Thus, the student is provided with additional opportunities to be successful. Most importantly, nobody is blamed. It is the system's job to deliver the achievement of standards.

THE BALDRIGE AWARD, ISO 9000, AND SYSTEMS THINKING

Peter Senge, in his influential book *The Fifth Discipline* (1990), defines systems thinking as "a discipline for seeing wholes. It is a framework for seeing interrelationships rather than things, for seeing patterns of change rather than static snapshots."

The Baldrige and ISO 9000 provide all those involved with the school system with a discipline for caring. From the outset, the focus is on the success of the entire school organization, including all of the subsystems and how they interact. It helps everyone in the school focus on the interrelationships among people and processes at work within the system. The improvement process begins here. It helps determine the success of the school as well as which patterns of change demand greater vigilance to help the student.

Clearly, the public school operates within more diverse population and complex environment. It is increasingly obvious that the public school cannot hope to improve—or even survive—in a system that relies on the tyranny of chance. The public school remains subject to that tyranny if those in charge do not follow the ground rules for reliable quality.

- Know what their customers (the students, parents, and future employers) require, following the standards set forth by their state department of education.
- Have well-defined processes for translating those requirements into steadily improving internal actions.
- Align all the tasks and processes of the subsystems along common goals and objectives that relate to the optimal achievement of the standards.
- Use key measures to manage by fact, such as honoring measurable quality.

- Involve everyone in the process of continuous improvement.
- Understand and improve all of the crucial processes, which are the ones that relate most directly to closing the gaps exposed by quality control.
- Fully satisfy their customer population, including students, parents, and the taxpayers who support the school district.

The Baldrige National Quality Award itself may or may not be pursued by the school. The school or district may not fully achieve ISO 9000 certification, but using the Baldrige and ISO 9000 criteria for quality control is what really counts. These criteria focus all persons charged with educating students on attaining performance excellence in their schools.

Baldrige and ISO standards outline the yardsticks of the quality-control function that must be included. They do not control any school on how to achieve these standards—that is left completely to the individual school. The Baldrige and ISO 9000 are a bottoms-up, self-directed, provider-driven effort. It provides school leadership with a vision for what must be studied to achieve the quality control for continuous improvement.

According to a study of worker attitudes and behavior headed by psychologist G. Clotaire Rapaille, Americans are most threatened by change when it is imposed (Zuckerman and Halata 1992). They generally feel positive about change when they feel they can control it. The Baldrige and ISO 9000 are completely under the control of the providers, including peer review. If school leadership so chooses, it can agree to be assessed by outside teams for the quality award or certification.

The Impact of the Baldrige Criteria since Its Inception

The Baldrige criteria provide the best initial guide to better understand, assess, control, and improve schools. No other model has the potential for such widespread acceptance.

- Since the Baldrige Award program for business and industry was introduced in 1988, National Institute for Standards and Technology (NIST) has distributed an estimated two million copies of the criteria.

- At least forty-four states in the United States now have their own state quality-award programs based on the Baldrige criteria.
- Several countries, including Argentina, Australia, Brazil, Canada, and India, now base their quality-improvement programs on the Baldrige criteria.
- The criteria for the European Quality Award, first presented in 1992, are patterned after the Baldrige criteria.
- A "who's who" of recognized top-notch American companies, such as IBM, Kodak, and AT&T, have adopted the Baldrige criteria as their internal assessment tool and criteria for their corporate quality awards. Many of their divisions are also ISO compliant.
- Many companies now ask their suppliers and subcontractors to assess their organizations by the Baldrige criteria.

In the book *The Baldrige: What It Is, How It's Won, How to Use It to Improve Quality in Your Company* (Hart and Bogan 1992), the authors explain how these criteria evolved and how companies of all types and sizes use them to continually improve. The book shows clearly how the Baldrige application—when it is completed—is so productive. "It's really a genius document," said Don Clark, president of the National Association for Industry–Education Cooperation,

> because it allows you to go back to the basics and see the common thread that exists in everything you do. Things get down to some very basic fundamentals that you know are at work. If you can put your finger on them, you look at life with a clearer vision of what it's about and why things are happening. (Clark 1999)

The consensus of a host of leaders who have made the Baldrige criteria their management yardsticks is that it helps establish a system that:

- focuses on the customer,
- aligns internal processes with customer satisfaction,
- puts everybody in the group to work on shared goals,
- facilitates a long-term approach to continuous improvement,
- demands measurable quality, that is, management by fact, not assumption,
- promotes prevention rather than remediation,

- values results,
- looks outside for chances to partner and collaborate, and to benchmark; and
- fulfills responsibilities as a corporate citizen.

A Word of Caution

As a former school board member and lifelong corporate planner, it seems to Allen that schools face some special obstacles. When setting out to tackle Baldrige and ISO 9000 for their school system, administrators and teachers need to replace the habit of the culture, which says "that's the way we always did things around here." By this, he means that educators have always seen themselves as "different" from business or, for that matter, from much of the rest of the accountable universe. They have often viewed their mission as "above the fray" or surprisingly "momentary" when related to real-world considerations. Educators need to constantly be aware of the long-term implications of even their most harmless actions. School is a very impressionable time for students.

Throughout this book, we try to make plain that the school and its educators are as subject to sound quality principles as are your doctor, your lawyer, and the engineer who may have helped you overcome an illness, prepare your will, or build the road in front of your house. In fairness, there are some barriers to success that may be unique to educators, but this should entitle administrators, teachers, and staff, as well as parents, to go into Baldrige and ISO 9000 with their eyes open and with a positive can-do mind-set.

Educators may also look upon the school system as too fragmented. They may find it difficult to define system and subsystem boundaries. This definition takes a real labor of thinking, but then, what organization has a better-educated working management and staff to tackle these concepts than the school?

Schools have a very complex leadership structure. This appears as a weakness that can be harnessed into a strong operating system. Every business organization and some schools who have traveled the Baldrige/ISO pathway have successfully crossed this same bridge, and they have survived to praise the virtues of Baldrige/ISO 9000.

In schools, the work processes are often poorly defined or not defined at all. Chance, combined with content knowledge and expediency, has too often been observed. Classrooms seem highly susceptible to the mood swings of the teacher and the students rather than being mission focused. This is a task that can only be overcome with enlightened persistence.

The customer–supplier relationship is also complex. We have and shall continue to repeatedly point out and try to sharpen the reader's understanding of who the customers of the school are. There is not one single customer, but for starters, focus first on the student, then the parents, and then next year's teacher.

For a profession that is in the business of learning, trying to put training resources to work in schools should not be more difficult. Training in education remains unfocused. The many opportunities for improving individual teacher and staff performance are too often blocked by noneducational considerations.

It would be unfair not to acknowledge that schools and educators function under severe time constraints, but so does every enterprise. It all comes down to a matter of priorities. The school's nineteenth-century industrial model is out of date. The fifty-minute class, 180-day semesters, the shortened school year, and the production-line model of twelve grades place an artificial constraint on educators rethinking the quality of the learning process.

Similar to many businesses, school leaders and teachers heavily lean toward concentrating on the short term. Finding time during the school day for quality improvement runs smack into work-related contracts. Businesses have overcome more difficult barriers and implemented quality training. Some school districts have even invited those teachers and staff who are really interested in their own future development to provide the time to become involved in the quality movement. Is there an educator who would now admit that a businessperson is smarter and therefore can be trusted to be more amenable to change than a teacher?

In education, there remains the temptation, much as there is in business, to make the Baldrige/ISO criteria an end itself. It is often tempting for staff to just go through the motions and merely "fill in the quality blanks" so that they can get back to "business as usual." Educators are not alone in this thinking, but this is where educational leaders can really earn their pay.

THE GHOST OF DR. SEMMELWEISS

The image of Ignaz Semmelweiss haunts America's schools and class-rooms. At the turn of the century, Dr. Semmelweiss was an important and well-respected medical doctor in Vienna. As a solid science professional of his day, he studied the reported birth and death statistics. He took special note of the higher incidence of death among women in childbirth who were attended by physicians than among those women attended only by a midwife.

Intrigued, astonished, and curious, the doctor decided to study the reasons why this might be happening. He found that the physicians did not use as common practice the thorough washing of their hands or the washing of their equipment when they treated more than one woman.

When the data he collected became sufficiently large to allow him to make valid predictions, he went to his medical society to share his findings. He alerted his fellow doctors to the dangers of their lack of hand-washing practices.

Understandably, his fellow physicians and former friends were, at first, very skeptical. When he continued to insist that they adopt as standard practice rigorous hand washing, they voted almost unanimously to remove him from the medical society. Further, they discredited him publicly and ruined his reputation as a physician. He died a pauper in disgrace.

Today, a statue stands in his honor in the Vienna Medical Society headquarters. Medical doctors in Vienna, as well as all other doctors, now routinely use as standard operating procedure the good practice of washing their hands and instruments thoroughly before working with a patient.

A patient going to a doctor in Vienna or Toledo, Ohio, does not need to wonder or even be concerned about the reliability of his or her doctor using as standard operating practice in the office or hospital what the profession now accepts as good practice. Practitioners teach proper hand washing during orientation to all new health care employees and daily whenever the need arises. Hand washing is considered serious business and proper practice is enforced. We now know hand washing is important in the home, in schools, and in the workplace, as well as in hospitals. It is the number one prevention against the spread of infection.

With respect to accepting the best that research has to offer, school teaching is a carbon copy of the doctor's mind-set in the Vienna Medical Society when Dr. Semmelweiss made his presentations. Tested, scientifically based teaching practices compete regularly in schools with untested, unscientifically based teaching practices. Worse yet, even when the teaching practices in use are proven to be useless or even harmful for learning, they continue to be used. Customers—the students and the parents, as well as other stakeholders—cannot assume that any particular teacher or school knows about or uses good practice in teaching and learning as their standard operating practice.

Currently, school teaching is an unreliable profession. No parent sending their child to any school in any state can honestly be assured by school administrators that his or her child's teacher will: (1) know her subject, (2) know how best to teach it, and (3) know how best to lead and manage the classroom so all children get maximum benefit.

It is the ghost of Dr. Ignaz Semmelweiss who haunts America's schools and classrooms today. When it comes to receiving reliable quality in classroom teaching, parents, students, and those who care deeply about the quality of schools live under the control of a tyranny of chance. Someday, we need to put the ghost of Dr. Semmelweiss to rest in his job of haunting American education. Given what we now know about how to insure and assure reliability in classroom teaching, continuing to accept unreliability is a disgrace.

CHAPTER 5

Using Quality to Improve the Health and Fitness of Schools

In 1998, after ten years of application to American business, the Malcolm Baldrige National Quality Award was expanded to include quality improvement in health care and education.

Measuring the quality of medical care predominately by heartbeats and body heat is one of the reasons modern medicine got into its current difficulties. It focused more on diseased organs and technology than on the goals of the sick person. Patients do not simply want to survive; they want to survive in order to live a life in which they can recognize themselves and their values are preserved.

The public school is not the only American institution to have suffered from its current form of illness. In the mid-1980s, American business was suffering from the very same chronic malady. It took business about four decades, starting from the end of World War II, to recognize the extent and seriousness of its illness. By looking at the fitness programs taken on by American business, the public school can see the emphasis and direction their return to health must take.

American education is about where American business was in the early 1970s facing competition, accountability demands, customer backlash from poor products and rising costs. They needed to restructure. American business did many things to get more competitive. However, one prominent source of the change was, and still is, the use of quality as a framework for systemic change.

It's one thing to suggest that educators look to the world of business for lessons in quality improvement. It is totally another matter for the educator to grasp the picture of *why* quality improvement has become so crucial to business survival the world over, and, moreover, why this experience—if properly transferred to the school—can yield excellent results.

Another school board experience comes to mind. One evening, Allen's board and staff were meeting to go over the annual budget for the 10,000 students, the vast majority of whom were minority children.

By this time, school busing had overcompensated with 93 percent to 97 percent racial imbalance, having driven 20 percent of school-eligible youngsters into private and parochial schools.

There was a growing need to improve the performance of kids counting on the public schools to provide them with a promise for their future. Minority parents want their children held to a high-performance standard, just as other parents do. These parents came before the board to plead and pressure the schools to get tougher with the students. They insisted that the school district weed out the poor teachers and raise the learning expectations for their youngsters. This was 1973.

During the budget review process, there remained an obvious mismatch between the proposed programs and the way dollars were to be allocated. The more the board probed cause and effect, the wider the discrepancies grew in explanations by the superintendent and staff. The board wanted accurate answers. They wanted to know the benefits associated with each of the major cost categories. How would staff measure results and how would accountability be assigned?

Allen can still see this scene today in his mind's eye, as though it had just happened. In a moment of utter frustration, following an ongoing series of dull-witted responses to probing questions, he blurted out to the superintendent, "This is certainly not the way we would conduct this budgeting process at ITT." At the time, Allen was an operations executive with this multinational corporation. Without hesitation, the superintendent responded, "This isn't ITT." Then, the entire board received a sharp rebuke followed by a lecture from the superintendent on the profound differences between a school system and a business system.

Guess who lost out in the heat of the moment? You guessed it. The needs of the customer were missing. The pleadings of parents of minority students and the struggles of underprepared students were at the bottom of the stated staff concerns. But that was then and this is now. Today, there is growing awareness that well-proven quality business practices can indeed make major contributions to help improve school performance. We will show how.

A QUICK INTRODUCTORY LESSON FROM BUSINESS

Winners of the Malcolm Baldrige National Quality Award (MBNQA) and recipients of ISO certification have generously shared their quality management strategies with other businesses and nonprofit organizations. They have made enormous contributions to building awareness of the benefits of quality to national competitiveness. This unselfish sharing has encouraged many other organizations in all sectors of the U.S. economy to undertake their own quality-improvement efforts.

Baldrige and ISO 9000 help us look at reliability through the eyes of business. A true customer-focused, goal-seeking organization has a much better idea of how to carry out this kind of change. The Saturn project is a good case study.

Several years ago, General Motors (GM) and the United Auto Workers (UAW) agreed to work together on a project that involved rethinking all their preconceived ideas about making and marketing a car. This rethinking included the assembly-line process, the traditional labor–management structure, and building customer satisfaction. After six years of work, they had a car that sold well. It helped advance a model of automobile production and sales that has had an impact on other companies. *Consumer Reports Annual Auto Issue 2001* (May 2001) showed Saturn customer dealer satisfaction continues to rank at an average of 82 percent, putting it at the top of twenty-nine auto manufacturer brands.

What we usually hear about in connection with Saturn is the change in the distribution of power. Labor and management share the responsibility for all decisions, as they have from the outset, but altering who makes the decisions is only part of the story. There's nothing that says a labor–management committee could not build another Edsel, a 1950s Ford-made car famous by the fact that customers rejected it.

The significance of the Saturn experiment to our theories about business and reliable quality lies in the changes made in the production process. At the heart of these changes are Saturn's self-managed teams. In the old production line model, every worker—like teachers—had a single, carefully specified job to perform. The Saturn line is made up of work stations, each with a multistep operation to perform, and staffed by a team responsible for deciding how to set up and work its station most efficiently. This means scheduling, budgeting, and monitoring performance.

One person checks scrap and receives weekly reports on the amount of waste. If the line of the chart is rising, the work team needs to be more careful. Since team members know the cost of each part, they know how much money their scrap costs the company. Once a year, the team forecasts the amount of company resources it plans to use in the coming year. Each month team members get a report on what they budgeted and how much they spent. The teams even get a monthly breakdown on their telephone bills.

But the production teams do more than keep the assembly line running. If they suspect that there might be a better way to install a door, for instance, it's their job to figure out how to change the existing process. They have at their disposal the help of a department that has a simulated assembly line and a staff of engineers. So the production process is constantly being monitored and improved.

How did Saturn find these smart, flexible, and disciplined workers? It didn't find them. It used an impressive training program to give workers from 136 other GM plants the information, skills, and ongoing help they needed to participate in this new way of running an automobile plant.

The original team members received more than 400 hours of training within their first few months at Saturn, and it is still ongoing. New employees take part in a kind of internship. During the first two or three months, they split their time between class and on-the-job training.

Every Saturn employee is expected to spend at least ninety-two hours a year in training. This represents about 5 percent of their total work hours, and 5 percent of their salary depends on their doing so. A central training group offers nearly 600 different courses. As procedures are changed or new ones developed, new courses are also designed to assist employees in learning them.

Imagine what a training program like this could do for people trying to restructure their schools. Or, putting it another way, imagine trying to change things as basic as school culture and the way people teach with a couple of days of in-service training a year and some hours stolen from class-preparation periods. Realistically, that is about all the time most school teams now have in trying to restructure their schools.

It strikes us as ironic that a bunch of people whose business is building cars understands so well the importance of educating their employees. In contrast, people in education seem to assume that teachers and other school staff will be able to step right into a new way of doing things with little or no help. If it takes 600 courses and ninety-two hours a year per employee to make a better automobile, it will take at least that and more to make better schools. If we're not willing to commit ourselves to this kind of effort, we are not going to get what we want.

WHAT'S REALLY AT STAKE?

Why not just keep rocking along with about one-third of our students dropping out and another third being handed a high school diploma that they can barely read? Let's take a serious look around the world we are living in, from an economic perspective.

Global economic trade has been developing for a long, long time, ever since sailing ships could cross the seas. Prior to World War I, British trading companies provided tea and silk from China, opium from India, textiles from Britain, and spices from the Caribbean. British banks funded the building of U.S. and Australian railroads. At the time, technology existed to send information about prices from one edge of the developed world to another, forging a global commodities market. Shipping lines circled the globe carrying commerce.

The nature of a global economy has changed everything. Today, we exchange ideas and freely do business over the Internet and by e-mail. At one time, these contacts demanded a face-to-face meeting or a letter moving first by ship and later by air. Today, it is as easy to communicate around the world as it is to order a cup of coffee. International trade and services have surged. Now, when we say "small world," we really mean it.

More than ever, we all live in a state of global interconnectedness. In the past, global trade was limited to a narrow, elite, and prosperous slice of the population. Today, a banker can move billions of dollars electronically to the other side of the globe in seconds. A software company can take orders for delivery in France with the product being designed in India and manufactured in Ireland, which is second only to the United States in software output. You and I may drive to the shopping mall in an American-brand car, but there is a good chance it may have been assembled in Canada and comprised of parts that come from Asia. At the mall, we browse through goods that come from a collection of nations. The different labels speak to us as a United Nations of producers.

Once upon a time, as the story goes, we went to school, grew up, raised a family, and were buried all in the same town. Other than perhaps dreaming of going to the "big city," we never imagined that we would have to compete for our livelihood with persons schooled or working thousands of miles away.

The winning Baldrige/ISO prescription causes us to focus on searching for dependable and durable breakthroughs in quality and control of results. In this new economy, there are lots of problems to be solved, new knowledge to be applied, many skills to be learned, new resources to be invested, and considerable profits to be made. It is this competitive process which yields a higher standard of living to workers of the most competitive and successful nations. In the new global economy, firms and individuals cooperate when there is a mutual need. They also share risks out of mutual commitment to common objectives.

In this fast-moving economy that circles the globe, individuals, enterprises, communities, and nations have but two choices: (1) they can compete by reducing costs, mostly in the form of lowering wages to workers, or (2) they can improve their overall productivity, which includes greater efficiency, improved quality, and benefits to workers.

That's it. These are literally the *only* variables for choice. On this, there is general agreement. If Americans choose to reduce labor costs to better compete, then direct competition will come mostly from third world nations, and the direction of American wages is predictable—it will slope downward.

The advice from U.S. economists is unanimous. If we do not want to get poor, we must compete by thinking and working smarter. Our workers and managers must learn to compete on the basis of effectiveness, quality, and efficiency. That is the full meaning of productivity.

To continue fostering the economic benefits of the American Dream, there is really only one choice. We must achieve both improved quality and greater productivity at the same time. In economic terms, it can be seen as a supply-and-demand decision. The questions are simply these: Do Americans want the new jobs? And what do Americans need to do to keep getting the higher-paying jobs?

If the quality and productivity route is chosen, and there doesn't seem like much incentive to take any other path, several key concerns must be squarely faced. First, there is an increasing need for worker knowledge and skill. This means that all workers will need higher-order thinking skills in the workplace. Mind-power is the energy that fuels the quality/productivity choice. While mind-power was always an important factor before, it now becomes the primary source of economic power.

High-performance organizations are the engines that increase productivity. The quality of human resources—its people—determines how well an enterprise can be organized for high performance. These are the criteria that the schools need to prepare students to successfully handle.

Gross Domestic Product (GDP) is the total of all goods and services produced in the United States. The payoff for making improvements in human capital (better knowledge and skills) is greater than that in any other form. Take this example: Labor (total worker earnings) represents roughly 70 percent of America's GDP; capital (total money invested) is roughly 30 percent. Therefore,

- A 5 percent increase in capital (the money invested per worker) increases productivity by 1.5 percent ($.05 \times 30 = 1.5\%$).
- The same increase in labor skills and knowledge—the human capital—boosts productivity by 3.5 percent ($.05 \times 70 = 3.5\%$).

The improvement in knowledge and skills shows a more than a twofold advantage spread over more than twice the amount of GDP. In other words, more people benefit financially from increased productivity. This makes it clear that the combination of productivity and quality is the preferred choice. It offers the greater potential payoff for each worker.

Doing so successfully means all U.S. workers must gain both the knowledge and higher-order thinking skills that are required. It is no longer realistic or do-able for business and workers to depend solely on the 25 percent who went to college. These persons previously made up the backbone of our professional, technical, and managerial work force. Today, all workers need to continue learning and to improve their knowledge and skill base.

Looking back for a moment, to the America of the 1950s, 60 percent of all jobs required few skills beyond the willingness to work hard and show up on time. Many of the jobs, especially in the nation's booming post–World War II mass-production economy, were well-paying jobs. For the most part, this offered a secure financial future for high school graduates and dropouts alike. In 1950, 73 percent of manufacturing jobs were unskilled. By the 1990s, only 35 percent of jobs in America were unskilled. The figure is expected to drop to as low as 15 percent early in this new century.

The twenty-first-century information economy demands a different set of work skills than those traditionally achieved and held by the vast majority of the American workforce. The consensus about the required skills for a world-class American worker is the ability:

1. to learn,
2. to think for oneself,
3. to make independent judgments,
4. to read and think analytically,
5. to communicate effectively,
6. to work well with others, and
7. to take responsibility for oneself.

Let's look at the ongoing battle raging among computer software leaders, phone companies, and other communications giants. Microsoft, AOL, AT&T now with its own cable companies, "Baby Bells" in the long-distance markets, wireless companies, and Internet Service Providers (ISP) are all devoid of labor in the traditional sense. The innovative genius of product managers, software developers, marketers, and technical service specialists gives them their competitive edge.

Contrast, if you will, today's complexity of services with the simplicity of services just a few years back. Today, picking a phone company means choosing among a myriad of offers and services. The neighborhood TV and hardware store sells and installs an 18-inch dish that you can mount outside your residence. You can now receive several hundred cableless channels from satellites circling in the heavens.

For the foreseeable future, in the twenty-first century, what will count for maximum competitiveness is the ability to attract, hold, and continually improve the capabilities of knowledge workers. This requires providing a management environment that breeds ingenuity and productive change. In such a world, an organization, whether global or neighborhood-sized, can be competitive only so long as its workers can learn faster than either its present or emerging competitors. Since almost any product can be copied in this race for new markets, only lifelong worker and organizational learning can provide a real competitive edge.

Beretta Firearms—A Case Study of Organizational Learning

It is helpful to examine the unique history of the Italian gun maker Fabbrice D'Armu Beretta (Beretta). Seldom are we able to track the

500-year history of a single firm. Beretta provides us with a singularly unique perspective. We can look at the impact of technology on its workforce development, management fads, and eventually market changes over an exceptionally long period of time. The important changes in Beretta's long history were triggered by technological episodes that took place *outside* the firm.

It is also valuable to look at the effect of these changes on Beretta's production workers. This includes the changing demands for higher-order thinking and work skills. Hopefully, these lessons are not lost on U.S. educators.

Reviewing such experience from an unusually long view helps us see five important lessons:

1. The evolution of management thinking;
2. How technology affected management behavior;
3. How today's technology hastened the return to a modern form of product customization not seen or experienced since the guild craft era;
4. The impact of advanced manufacturing processes; and,
5. *Why* the evolution and subsequent demand for a new type of knowledge worker exists.

Given the central role played by war and guns, it is safe to say that Beretta has been a factor in global trade since the earth was last viewed as flat. At about the same time that Christopher Columbus "stumbled" upon the New World, the family firm Beretta was founded. It was 1492, during what historians called the *guild system era*.

At first, all Beretta guns were handmade by master gun makers. The master used calipers, jigs, clamps, and files, and an apprentice watched to learn the craft. All activities centered on fit. Parts were hand-modified to fit tightly with other parts. As a result, every gun was a one-of-a-kind. In those days, parts were *not* interchangeable. Highly skilled and trained workers, much the same as cabinet and clock case makers of the day, crafted these early instruments of war.

In 1800, the Industrial Revolution established the English system of then-modern production. The Industrial Age brought with it, for the first time, the development of new and uniform tools and universal fabrication, for example, metal lathes. The new industrial system separated the production function from the processes used to make Beretta firearms.

In the nineteenth century, apprentices were taught proficiency on a particular tool, rather than on a particular gun product. An era of worker specialization was evolving which enabled process improvements to be made independently of which gun products were to be manufactured.

Beretta introduced early mass production. Their workers were expected to have fewer universal skills, but the worker needed to be trained to be more specific and tool-centered. This uniformity led to fully interchangeable parts, but also to de-skilled workers. Such production systems became popular and widespread throughout industrial Europe and then on to America.

The American system of production, developed in the 1850s, moved into a new phase. High-volume production of products with interchangeable parts became the order of the day. Driven by mechanization, the workers became interchangeable, but still viewed as only a by-product of production. In the American system, the Beretta product line was pared down to three models. Rigid production processes and worker efficiencies became the rationale for avoiding product customization.

Next, along came Frederick W. Taylor seeking to refine the early Industrial Age production methods. In his book *The Principles of Scientific Management* (1911), Taylor discussed his methods. The *Taylor Scientific Method*, as it became known, sought to make labor as efficient as machine tools; both became specialized. Following Taylor's methods, work was redesigned through time and motion studies. It used man–machine process interaction to determine the most time- and cost-efficient organization.

With these efficiencies and product shifts, Beretta was able to increase its product catalog from three weapons to ten. Job responsibilities were broken down to specialty-trained workers. Work discretion was replaced with Taylor's "one best way to perform the task." Beretta management controlled all aspects of work, comparing product and worker performance to preset standards. Taylor's industrial methods have been overtaken by time and modern events, but one piece of his counsel still gives a ring of good advice for teachers and managers.

> This change can be brought about only gradually and through the presentation of many object-lessons to the workman, which together with the

teaching which he receives, thoroughly convince him of the superiority of
the new over the old way of doing the work. This change in the mental attitude of the workman imperatively demands time. (Taylor 1911)

By the end of World War II (1945), statistical process control had
come into wider use. The North Atlantic Treaty Organization (NATO)
required M-1 rifle parts with tolerances calling for perfectly interchangeable parts. Beretta responded to customers' needs by building
new manufacturing equipment for the task. Beretta used regular sam-
pling for quality control, but only defects were inspected at this time.
No best way to operate had yet been found. Quality engineering occurred at the end of the production line, while problem-solving teams
watched over machine performance. There still remained potential
quality gaps in the production process. At the time, the manufacturing
process was not yet recognized as needing to be seamless.

By 1976, Beretta began applying Deming's "Methods of Numerical
Control," then successfully proven as having brought about the postwar
"economic miracle" of Japan. Deming's genius was in recognizing that
what the Japanese call *Kaizen* is deeply ingrained in the culture of a
people dedicated to continuous improvement in all facets of their
lives—product, production, and personal. To this day, the brilliance of
Deming's methods resides in the fact that it is both a motivator as well
as a natural extension of the way the Japanese see life. We look at the
subject of *Kaizen* more in chapter 7.

Information processing could now be used to automatically and nu-
merically control Beretta machines. It could perform in sequence all of
those tasks that had previously taken multiple pieces of equipment. At
the time, line workers represented just half the Beretta total company
employment. With new forms of statistical control, it was now possible
to increase the management span of control to five times greater while
covering several machines at once. The new standardized product demanded a much better trained Beretta worker than at any time since the
eighteenth century.

Another new era began at Beretta. New production equipment and
new management methods allowed the company to bid a price one-half
of that of their U.S. competitors. The transportability of numerical control programs enabled Beretta to meet the U.S. Army's (the customer)
stipulation of delivering guns from full U.S.-based production.

In the early 1980s, Americans were shocked to learn that the Beretta 9-mm Parabellum won the U.S. Army contract, replacing the historic Colt-45 sidearm. What had been the mainstay of the U.S. military for over 150 years had now fallen to a global competitor—a story often repeated throughout other sectors of the U.S. economy.

With numerical control, Beretta now evolved from a user of information to an information-based company. Data needed to manufacture products were stored digitally on computers rather than on blueprints, dies, and molds. In 1987, computer-integrated manufacturing (CIM) became the norm at Beretta, linking together the entire company with computer networks to perform computer-aided design (CAD), engineering, and flexible manufacturing systems right on the factory floor. This process used:

- A computer-controlled team of semi-independent workstations connected by automated material handling systems. The looped conveyors carried pallets bearing individual work pieces.
- Supervisory computers carried information about these work pieces. It directed the movements of material and components through the manufacturing process and assigned priorities and queue.
- Information-driven machines react to changing situations by loading the correct numerical programs in the proper machines and continually monitoring results.

At Beretta, the effect of computer-integrated manufacturing (CIM) proved startling. First, there was a three-to-one jump in productivity. The Beretta factory floor was now down to thirty machines (which was the lowest in 150 years). Thirty people was the minimum staffing, fewer people than Beretta employed at the end of the seventeenth century. Rework had fallen to zero. Staff positions comprised of knowledge-workers now represented two-thirds of the Beretta workforce.

Beretta evolved to a service company. Customized products are made available to special market segments—police, military, and gun collectors around the world. In turn, this technology-driven change has raised the demands for highly skilled, knowledge-based workers at every level of the company.

For the first time since the guild days, over 300 years ago, Beretta is theoretically capable of creating numerous custom products. Customization is almost an unlimited capability today. Guild-Era crafts-manship has returned in a twenty-first-century model. Beretta has brought us full circle.

LEVELING THE GLOBAL PLAYING FIELD

Coopetition (COOPEration + compeTITION): The phenomenon of companies, located anywhere in the world, joining their competitors on a project-by-project basis. The products have sometimes been called "Alliance Ware."

When implementing the winning prescription for reliable classroom teaching, schools and school districts can find willing partners in this effort within the business community. At times, schools have seen themselves as being in competition with private enterprise, but in real-ity, school leaders and business leaders have much to offer one another. The Baldrige and ISO 9000 criteria are increasingly applied in business. These firms already have experts on staff in each subject area who can be allied with their local school district to help schools navigate these quality criteria.

The standard economic textbook could have difficulty with *coopeti-tion* (cooperation and competition with the same party). In 1994, the authors first studied this phenomenon. Through workshop papers, they developed a simple twelve-point checklist to help smooth the long-established mind-set in shifting from the traditional either-or to the both-and approach to building effective alliances. These steps are:

1. to build commitment from the outset; people make collaborations work.
2. to devote time to the effort, otherwise stop; all ventures require coaching.
3. to get issues on the table early; to trust is an underpinning.
4. to think win–win, since you have to give up something to get something.
5. to file legal contracts and build understanding during the contrac-tual process.
6. to recognize your partner's problems because situations change; to be flexible.

7. to define expectations and time frames; to encourage partners similarly.
8. to develop personal relationships, because friendship helps overcome adversity.
9. to prize different cultures; to work toward understanding them.
10. to remember partner-independence; to think different interests and win–win.
11. to put facts and risks on the table early so there are no surprises.
12. to share the fruits of victory; to celebrate success as would a family.

Does coopetition work? Sometimes yes, sometimes no. Coopetition is first a mind-set driven by the overriding objective that mutual success is the superior and most desirable result, and the necessary working agreements follow. A typical regional shopping mall is a living example of these principles in action. Both J.C. Penney and Sears anchor many of the same malls.

Ford Motor Corporation (U.S.) and Mazda Motors Corp. (Japan) have enjoyed a profitable international venture since 1979. For Ford, the payoff has come partly in new car design and expanded Mazda-labeled sales. In 1992, the auto industry mobilized the White House to join their team in an effort to break down Japan's closed doors to U.S. car and auto parts sales. At that time, Ford already was the top-selling foreign nameplate in Japan for several years. Ford cars were sold through a jointly owned dealer network with Mazda.

In 1985, Ford built a new plant in Mexico using the successful Mazda Japan factory as a model. An improved line of Ford cars and trucks was also influenced by Mazda and brought to market through joint styling and engineering. Ford-partnered Mazda cars and trucks were also introduced. Ford used the Mazda coopetition model to introduce a joint Nissan-designed minivan.

Since that time, the annual Ford and Mazda product changes reflect a unique blend of new thinking and cooperation. Ford has purchased a larger stake in Mazda and the relationship continues to evolve, as would any marriage in its stage of growing together. Ford and Mazda dealerships stand nearby one another on most automobile merchandising rows, where they battle it out for the customer's dollars.

On the other hand, General Motors (GM) has had its ups and downs. It sold its interests in Daewoo (South Korea), which finally went on the auction block. GM continues a somewhat rocky relationship with Isuzu (Japan). Isuzu expanded its truck production for the Honda and Acura U.S. sport utility vehicles. Soon, GM jumped back in with active working deals with European and Korean carmakers. They now market several German-made cars under their U.S. labels.

Ford's international success story resulted in their buying such long-standing car nameplates as Volvo Autos (Sweden), Jaguar (Great Britain), and Rover (Great Britain). Daimler-Benz (Germany) bought Chrysler (United States) and extended its global reach, buying a 33 percent share of Mitsubishi (Japan). Renault (France) purchased part of Nissan (Japan).

Driven by technology and the demands from their customers, the world's three largest auto manufacturers agreed to cease development of their separate e-commerce exchanges and formed an independent company that will provide a single e-business marketplace for the auto industry. Established in early 2000, the business-to-business (B-2-B) exchange will provide capabilities for e-procurement, forecasting and online development collaboration, financial services, payment, and logistics. This is intended to put an end to confusion among auto parts and materials suppliers using different technologies for each company. This move, using the coopetition model, will establish a uniform standard among the Big Three by easing pressures on suppliers to operate different exchanges.

Such unprecedented agreements allow companies with competing interests to work together with suppliers who are strategically positioned among customers interested in aggressively pursuing lower cost development. This is a win–win situation for suppliers and, most importantly, for customers. Working together can resolve the manufacturing and integration challenges unique to the new technologies. This will greatly reduce customers' costs and development time, while also helping them to quickly tap the potential for the new technology.

WHO WILL YOUR STUDENT WORK FOR SOMEDAY?

Long considered to be the mainstay of the local community, U.S. public utility companies have become increasingly attractive to foreign owners. In early 2000, National Grid Group of London completed a $3.2 billion deal for Massachusetts-based New England Electric System. PowerGen, also from London, is seeking to complete the purchase of LG&E Energy of Kentucky. In 1999, Scottish Power bought Pacific Corp of Portland, Oregon. Iberdrola of Madrid, Spain, after having assembled utility companies in Guatemala, Brazil, and many companies have held on-again/off-again talks with Florida Power & Light Company, which serves almost four million customers.

In the information age, coopetition takes on multiple dimensions. "It's increasingly important to be able to compete and cooperate at the same time, but that calls for a lot of maturity," writes Microsoft former chairman Bill Gates in his book *The Road Ahead* (1995). The almost head-spinning growth of Internet usage has already brought forth many innovative agreements. The America Online (AOL) subscriber base grew to over twenty million at the turn of the century, up from six million only four years earlier. AOL then acquired one of the world's strongest old-line media companies, Time–Warner, owners of CNN.

Another business success model, the Oracle Business Alliance, fosters expanding relationships with leading information technology companies around the world. Their stated objective is to provide mutual customers with a broad range of products and services. Oracle has crafted alliances of different characteristics, depending on the partner's capabilities. Among the programs are Oracle Alliances with independent software vendors and hardware and operating system providers, professional services and systems integration providers, value-added distributors, and education and training services providers.

Oracle's Business Alliance support programs are equally impressive, including a full array of services for members such as technical support, benchmarking services, user and developer conferences, technical training, global sales support, joint market development, catalogues, worldwide web services, publications, Business Alliance conferences, consistent worldwide business practices, flexible financing, and contracts.

The Business Alliance promotes global sales opportunities for competing companies that provide Oracle-based products and services. Oracle, a global market leader, offers advanced technology and products. They bring value-added propellant to an alliance engine to help partners increase market share, and improve their bottom line.

All too often, partners may duplicate resources rather than making them mesh. Avoiding duplication and redundancy, both hallmarks of a management bureaucracy, usually signals management's real commitment to working together.

These unprecedented agreements allow companies with competing interests to work together with suppliers who are strategically positioned among customers interested in aggressively pursuing lower-cost development. This is the win–win situation we repeatedly speak of for suppliers and, most importantly, for customers. Working together can resolve the production process and integration challenges unique to the new technologies. In turn, this will greatly reduce customers' costs and development time, while also enabling them to quickly tap the potential for the new technology.

INFORMATION: NEW TECHNOLOGY FOR NEW TIMES

Changes in technology normally have taken place over time. Some have been the drivers of dramatic transformations in our work and personal lives. The shift to the Industrial Age was clearly one of these transformations, such as experienced at Beretta. More than five hundred years ago, the invention of the printing press combined with the invention of paper was another. Suddenly, the ability to easily share information and ideas was vastly expanded. Books of Greek philosophy were printed in one country and distributed throughout Europe. The ideas of the Reformation were quickly and widely spread through pamphlets.

Today, we are in the middle of another major transformation as our lives and workplaces are speedily transformed from an eighteenth- and nineteenth-century Industrial Age to a fast-moving, twenty-first-century information age. The technical evidence of this change is wrapped up in the Internet and World Wide Web. This combination will undoubtedly have as great or greater impact on our students' lives as did the printing press and paper. This dynamic duo allows us to share ideas and information all over the globe as never before imagined possible. NBC's Tom Brokaw told journalists that they will have more power than Citizen Kane ever dreamed of having.

This, too, is what is forcing a more level playing field, with global market opportunities and a virtual workforce. It allows persons to live and work in any lifestyle they prefer. This is the kind of shift that will have social, economic, and political implications more powerful than the shift from the Agricultural to the Industrial Age or from one president of the United States to the next. It is already happening quickly.

With all this rapid change, many crucially important rules are giving way to new rules. Intellectual property rights, copyrights, biotechnology, and the availability of information from computers to DNA are but a few examples. This information revolution is widely recognized. There is no shortage of those commenting upon these events, including a variety of leading thinkers, economists, futurists, academicians, and technologists.

Interenterprise collaboration is becoming the norm. Once hard and fast distinctions between competitors, customers, and suppliers have given way to totally new circumstances and more fluid situations. The spawning of coopetition is part cooperator/collaborator while remaining part competitor. With unprecedented economic shifts, the competitive boundaries are continuously moving. Witness, for a moment, the birth of the "infotainment" industry, which produces a steady stream if infomercials and entertainment news shows. This raises some vexing questions for business:

- What types of interenterprise relationships need to be forged in response to escalating market changes?
- How will an old-line company need to manage new alliances?
- What role will outsourcing play?
- How will a company determine with whom to team in the information-rich global marketplace?

Implementing the winning prescription for schools asks the educator to similarly answer tough questions. How will staff and teachers prepare their students to perform, persist, and prosper for themselves? Soon their future employer, or more likely employers, will impose increasing and conflicting demands in a rapidly changing economic climate.

Case Study in Coopetition: Scotland's Silicon Glen

Most of the business press concentrates their "babble" on the competitive economic activities in Southeast Asia, particularly from Japan.

Quietly, halfway around the world, the principles of coopetition are played out every day in an out-of-the-way place. It offers the educator and parent yet another compelling lesson in the magic of learning and earning.

Silicon Glen, Scotland, is where more computers are made per head of population than any other country in the world. Silicon Glen hosts a large number of Scottish companies ranging from startups to established mature companies. These include Sun Micro Systems, Motorola, Agilent (formerly HP), IBM, Microsoft, Oracle, Cap Gemini, Wind River, Compaq, Cadence, 3Com, and Adobe. There are also a large number of universities in the area, including the universities of Glasgow, Edinburgh, Stirling, and Dundee. These universities produce a constant supply of world-class graduates for Silicon Glen companies. At last count, the Scots hold 10 percent of the world's PC market and 40 percent of Europe's PC market.

Why? Scotland has a highly skilled technical workforce. It has an abundance of engineers. The Scots have a solid work ethic. The country has great sporting and recreational facilities, fantastic scenery and wide-open spaces, low-cost housing, and few traffic problems. It has much to offer culturally as well.

National Semiconductor (NSI) located its largest plant outside the United States in Scotland. NSI builds all of their analog chips there; Intel is their largest customer. Analog chips are widely used in audio equipment, in air conditioning, in fuel injection, in ABS braking systems, and in the computer hard drive and mouse. In fact, there are more analog chips in the modern PC and MAC than digital chips.

In Scotland, there is also a different work ethic, even among competitors who share facilities in the event of emergencies. It is not uncommon for one manufacturer to offer the use of their production lines to a competitor in times of emergency need.

NSI also picked Scotland for its worldwide training center. Here, workers are taught and learn the entire process—both strengths and weaknesses. NSI demonstrates the belief that those who learn faster remain ahead of their competitors.

IBM came to Silicon Glen to build its new worldwide headquarters for video displays, monitor design, and manufacturing. All monitors must be adjusted for their physical location in relation to the earth's magnetic fields. In Silicon Glen, IBM has created a virtual world in order to properly calibrate monitors to work at the ship-to locations anywhere on the face of the globe.

More than three dozen firms got together and established Glen Net, an ISDN (high-speed) network that ties together all of the firms. This coopetition includes the friends or foes, suppliers or competitors, that are located in the Glen. Cooperation is high among engineers in competing and supplying companies. One engineering manager was quoted as saying that design problems that used to take weeks or even months to resolve through meetings, fax, and missed phone calls are now cleared up in five minutes.

AT&T also chose Scotland as the place to develop its next generation of automatic teller machines (ATM). The new ATM is intended to be the last stop for paper in a paperless banking system. The ATM is intended to actually endorse checks, do the necessary accounting, and complete all transactional events. For bank customers, it can cut waiting time; for the bank, it lowers costs.

COOPETITION BRINGS A NEW VIEW OF CONTROL

As America's business managers cautiously proceed toward the inevitable growth in the number of coopetition agreements in the global marketplace, it needs to overcome the delusion that total control ensures the chance of success. Control does not necessarily lead to a better-managed enterprise. You cannot manage a global enterprise or even a small business through muscle. In fact, this form of control is a last resort. It's what you fall back on when all else fails and when you are willing to risk demoralizing workers and other managers.

The need for control is deeply rooted. Traditions of American enterprise, driven by legal and accounting rules, have taught generations of business managers the following incorrect arithmetic; that 51 percent control equals one hundred percent and that 49 percent control means zero percent. Fifty-one percent control may buy an organization full legal control, but this is control of rapidly changing markets and globally based customers about which the management may know little. The 2001 U.S. Senate, with a 50–50 split of party membership, entered into an unprecedented power-sharing agreement for committee membership. Valuable partnerships have emerged as one essential in achieving quality change.

This explains how coopetition has come about as the only reasonable approach to holding your own in the brutally competitive, yet necessarily collaborative, new economy. Coopetition requires loyalty among competitors; and trust, craftsmanship, and cooperation, as well as power sharing, among employees.

Now, quality reenters the picture. *Webster's New World Dictionary of the American Language* defines quality as "the degree of excellence which a thing possesses." Excellence is "the fact or condition of excelling; superiority; surpassing goodness, merit." Most people support this notion of quality. They link the concept of quality with the idea of being best either as a product or a service. There is a problem with this notion of quality and it is a severe one in this age of transition between economies.

Business has learned that the definition of quality that best meets the demands of the customer is: *fitness for use as judged by the customer or client*. It is the customer who determines what is an acceptable standard of quality, not the producer. There can be little disagreement that you, the owner and driver of your new car, determine whether it is a quality automobile and if it meets your quality standards.

Experts agree that quality improvement requires a marked change in perspective. This also means a shift in the culture itself of an organization or enterprise. Since the customer is finally acknowledged to be always right, the organization needs to mold new partnerships with the employees. First, the employees, be they clerks or teachers, are the direct link with the customer. Second, this view means that the system, not solely the employee, is recognized as the major cause of quality problems. Business has learned that this shift, driven by the new definition of quality, requires two essential actions: (1) create new partnerships with employees, and (2) keep in mind that the system, not the worker, is viewed as the major cause of quality problems.

LEARNING FROM BUSINESS

We do not wish to belabor the point of what local education leaders can learn from business, but the following lessons briefly cap the ISO 9000 and Baldrige experiences of some selected school districts.

Lesson #1–Making Education History

On February 18, 1999, the first U.S. school district at Lancaster, Pennsylvania, received ISO 9001 certification and with it made educational history. Speaking for the city of Lancaster, Mr. Charles Smithgall summed it up this way: "The job readiness of our youth has never been more important. A quality system like ISO 9000 obligates us to provide the best education for our children. They deserve it and our economic future depends on it" (Lancaster School District press release 1999).

"This is a milestone in our collective journey towards excellence," said Superintendent Vicki Phillips. "The excitement about this incredible accomplishment is soaring through the community, from parents, students and teachers, to business and community leaders and state and local legislators" (Lancaster School District press release 1999).

Board member Art Mann, self-employed president of DONSCO, Inc., already an ISO-certified company, first proposed the Lancaster ISO project to the Lancaster District school board. In 1997, Leon went to Lancaster to confer with Dr. Bill Kiefer, who went on to successfully spearhead this history-making effort. Allen spent several hours in phone talks with Dr. Kiefer. During their subsequent three years of intensive teamwork, the Lancaster staff created a district-wide quality manual covering all ISO standards. Hours of hard work, including overtime, paid off for this district of 11,500 students. Bill Kiefer's experiences are chronicled in the afterword to this book.

Lesson #2–Raising Our Sights

On October 14, 1999, the Jefferson County Public Schools in central Colorado became the largest school district to date to achieve ISO 9001 certification and only the third in the nation. The certification covers 144 schools, from elementary through high school. The district employs approximately 11,000 personnel, responsible for the quality education of 89,000 students.

"For us this is just common sense thinking to take the principles used in successful businesses worldwide and apply them to education," said Jane Hammond, superintendent of Jefferson County Public Schools. Standardized curriculum, clear operating and instructional procedures, identifiable cost savings, and increased efficiency and accountability are expected benefits (Jefferson County School District press release 1999).

Lesson #3–Seven State School Systems Use Baldrige

The National Alliance For Business (NAB) launched a nationwide campaign to speed up state and local reform efforts to improve student and system performance through the use of the National Baldrige Quality Award for performance excellence. As of December 1998, school districts representing 65 percent of all North Carolina K–12 students participated in this effort.

A total of six states have chosen to participate in the NAB initiative using the Baldrige criteria in their public schools. The states are Maryland, Indiana, Illinois, New Mexico, Texas, and Ohio. In 1998, Leon and Allen spent a week in New Mexico studying their statewide quality program.

In New Jersey, the state legislature went a step further. New Jersey enacted into statute that; school district meeting the Baldrige criteria is considered to have also met state education performance standards.

Lesson #4–The Press Recognizes the Baldrige/ISO 9000 School Quality Connection

In a July 14, 1999, *Washington Post* article titled "Good Business in the Schools," nationally syndicated columnist David Broder wrote,

Mike Ward, the North Carolina superintendent of education, explained that the Baldrige model, introduced in seven school districts in 1992 and now being used in seven times that number, has helped his state achieve greater gains in standard test scores, along with Texas, while dramatically reducing school violence and boosting teacher standards and salaries. . . . Recently, with support from Congress, the Baldrige process has been applied to another threatened area of American enterprise—the public school system. And, judging from what I saw last week at a briefing arranged by the NAB . . . the benefits may be just as great. (Broder 1999)

Based on our observation of progress in the United Kingdom, the authors feel that Lancaster's ISO initiative will be recognized within the United States as one of the most ambitious attempts yet to take something that works in business and apply it to public education. A few ISO-certified businesses located in the Lancaster area include

R.R. Donnelly & Sons, Armstrong World Industries, Hamilton Precision Metals, Clark Filter, and Manpower International.

Business columnist Jim Barlow, writing in *The Houston Chronicle* (July 23, 1999), said: "Let's look at what happened in Brazosport (Texas), a school district of 13,000 students. . . . It had the kind of student performance you find in a typical district. On standardized math, reading and writing tests, white students—who tend to be from higher socioeconomic groups—scored in the 80th percentile range. Minority students—who generally have poorer parents—scored in the 50s."

Having set the stage with what is a fairly typical school performance picture Barlow goes on. "That changed when the district hired a new superintendent, Gerald Anderson. Several members of the school board, who worked for Dow Chemical Co., which had successfully used a Total Quality Management approach productivity at the company, urged Anderson to use the same methods in the district."

"Quality became not an abstract principle," Barlow sums up, "but something to be used in the classroom . . . the result is apparent. Look at the scores. All went up. Now, on average, all students—white, Hispanic, African-American, economically disadvantaged—are scoring in the 90th percentile in math, reading, and writing."

SUMMING UP

The organizational processes and leadership best suited for the twenty-first-century Information Age is a far cry from those that dominated the twentieth-century Industrial Age. Leadership is no longer the exclusive domain of the CEO or the superintendent. In an educational organization, the teacher now comes to share the leadership role with the principal and superintendent in carrying out the dimensions and intentions of quality.

This partnership will come to promote a new sense of ownership among teachers and staff. It will foster the vital commitments so necessary to a new understanding of quality. Those who gain a sense of ownership in their work will see themselves as responsible for its quality. The leadership who manages the enterprise, be it a business or school district, also creates the system. Only the leadership can alter it. They are responsible for ensuring that the system pursues continuous improvement of its processes and its people.

CHAPTER 6

A Reliable Organization Inspires the Health of Public Schools

Transitions take time. More than anything else, however, they take dedication to an idea. This book describes the beginnings. It doesn't matter how long it takes. It isn't some ultimate goal that counts; it's the path to improvement.

Here's the paradox in medicine: The physician cares, but the medicine itself is uncaring. When young medical students enter school, they are full of enthusiasm for taking care of and helping people. They are deeply interested in the patient's stories of illness and medical care. They are solicitous of patients. By the time they finish three years of medical school plus their internships, they often become cynical.

It is the structure and culture of the health care organization within which they eventually practice that greatly influence their future effectiveness as a doctor. The organization gears itself to meeting the needs of its patients. It tries to treat each patient as though it was the only patient it has. Working in a city-owned hospital treating knife and gunshot wounds in the emergency room on a Saturday night is altogether different than practicing medicine at the Mayo Clinic.[1]

A school cannot, and most likely will not, become a high-reliability organization (HRO) on its own. If history is any lesson, school leaders will need to be shown and prodded along the paths into the necessary process changes. As shown in the previous stories, it's not that easy to modify school culture and to rethink the school mission, but it can be done. It is being done right now.

---

[1]The authors are indebted to Professor Ken Leithwood, head of the Centre for Leadership Development of the Ontario Institute for Studies in Education at the University of Toronto, for sharing the initiatory work of Sam Stringfield on schools as high reliability organizations (Stringfield 1995). Professor Stringfield is at the Center for the Social Organization of Schools, Johns Hopkins University.

HRO, BALDRIGE, AND ISO

Is it possible to write a winning prescription for high reliability in the quality of classroom teaching?

Leon once heard a distinguished physician describe how he went about designing a treatment for a sick patient. First of all, he knew what the healthy condition was. That was his purpose. Secondly, he knew what worked reliably as a treatment process to improve the sick condition and move toward the healthy one. Finally, he knew that his job was to actively pursue whatever was needed to achieve his purpose—the health of the patient.

As a professional, he had a great deal of theory and knowledge of good practice as standard operating practice to help him select the proper components of the treatment. He was not satisfied merely to make a prescription. He arranged to see his patients to see if the treatment was working as intended. If it was not, he did not insist that the treatment was right. He changed it until he directly observed the desired results.

It is exactly in this medical sense that we use the term *prescription* for use in curing school failure. There is a great deal known about high-reliability organizations that achieve quality service consistently. Airport management for getting airplanes to take off and land safely is one example of such an HRO. Developing and using nuclear energy is another. Given the need for mastery of the basics to survive and flourish in our country, it is hardly an exaggeration to claim that schools must also be HROs.

We know the chief characteristics of high-reliability organizations. There are six that are particularly important for schools to be an HRO.

1. A Clear Mission

An HRO school will communicate a clear mission and achievable goals to its staff and stakeholders, and will passionately focus on seeing that they are actually achieved.

One of the primary actions a reliable classroom teacher consistently follows is to clearly state her or his student achievement goals aligned to the standards set by the school. At the classroom level, these goals are called *objectives*.

We are not talking about a single classroom in a school. In an HRO school, all the classrooms teaching a given subject will have the same clear objectives. If classroom reliability is to be accomplished, allowing modifications in student achievement objectives that are tied to standards cannot to be permitted.

2. Clear Objectives

HRO school staffs show a strong sense of mission in helping all students achieve the standards reflected by the objectives.

To be sure, a given teacher might also like to achieve other important objectives than those specified by the standards for that subject. This understandable desire is a trap and a major cause of unreliability. There are lots of "most important" goals that a teacher can pursue. Such goals are probably not aligned to the school's mission if they are not reflected in the standards represented by the classroom objectives.

A prerequisite of all high-reliability classrooms is that they communicate, honor, and vigorously pursue the achievement of the standards set out for them in their subject fields.

3. Good Practice

High reliability in classroom teaching is plainly built on the use of good practice as standard operating practice. The following is an example of a quality standard operating practice for teaching reading in the elementary grades and why it must be used.

Sample standard operating procedures. The lack of attention to standard operating practices (SOPs) in classroom teaching is the hallmark of the tyranny of chance. There is an erroneously held notion that SOPs do not exist for classroom teaching, that teaching is some kind of a uniquely personal act, and that the desirable end of all teaching is creativity. Nothing can be farther from the truth.

The use of standard operating practices in the classroom is the major key to achieving reliable classroom teaching. Following two years of intense study and discussion, the prestigious National Commission on Teaching and America's Future in a 1998 report concluded that the reform of elementary and secondary education depends first and foremost on restructuring its foundation—the teaching profession.

The commission said:

It is now clear that most schools and teachers cannot produce the kind of learning the new reforms demand—not because they do not want to, but because they do not know how, and the systems they work in do not support them in doing so.

When it comes to widespread change, we have behaved as though mandates could, like magic wands, transform schools. But successful programs cannot be replicated in schools where staffs lack the know-how and resources to bring them to life. Wonderful curriculum ideas fall flat in classrooms where they are not understood or supported by the rest of the school. And increased graduation and testing requirements create only greater failure if teachers do not know how to reach students. (National Commission 1998)

The winning prescription emphasizing schools as high-reliability organizations speaks directly to this disturbing finding. An April 2000 report of the work of the National Reading Panel published a study about the most effective methods of teaching reading. It is the largest, most comprehensive, evidence-based review ever conducted of research on how children learn reading.

The panel was established in response to a 1997 congressional directive. Specifically, Congress asked the director of the National Institute of Child Health and Development, in consultation with the U.S. secretary of education, to convene a national panel to review the scientific literature and determine, based on the evidence, the most effective ways to teach children to read. The panel consisted of leading scientists in reading research, representatives of colleges of education, reading teachers, educational administrators, and parents.

They examined approximately 100,000 reading research studies published since 1966 and another 15,000 that had been published before that time.

"For the first time, we now have guidance based on evidence from sound scientific research on how best to teach children to read," said the director (National Reading Panel 2000).

The standard operating practice in reading. Reliable quality reading teachers know that identifying the words on a page is not the ultimate goal of reading. The ultimate goal is for the student to comprehend and apply what they read. But first, the student must be able to decode the words on a page.

Teachers must teach students to break apart and manipulate the sounds in words (phonemic awareness). They must help students understand that the sounds are represented by letters of the alphabet that when blended together form words (phonics). Teachers must have the student practice what they've learned by reading aloud with guidance and feedback (guided oral reading) from the teacher. They must have the student apply reading comprehension strategies to guide and improve their reading comprehension.

The greatest improvements in reading come from systematic phonics instruction. This type of phonics instruction consists of teaching a planned sequence of phonics elements, rather than highlighting elements as they happen to appear in a text, as is done so often in other programs. For students with learning disabilities and children who are low achievers, systematic phonics instruction, combined with synthetic phonics instruction produces the greatest gains.

Synthetic phonics instruction consists of teaching students to explicitly convert letters into phonemes and then blend the phonemes to form words. Moreover, systematic synthetic phonics instruction is significantly more effective in improving the reading skills of students from low socioeconomic levels. Across all grade levels, systematic synthetic phonics instruction improves the ability of good readers to spell.

Teachers must explicitly and systematically teach students to manipulate phonemes to improve both reading and spelling abilities. This required phonics instruction produces significant benefits for students from kindergarten through sixth grade and for students having difficulties learning to read.

First, before reading words, students should learn to manipulate the sounds that make up spoken words; for example, teachers break a word into sounds, then the student puts the sounds together to make a word. Example: "mmm aaa nnn What word?"

Here is a different way students manipulate sounds: Teachers say a word, then the children break the word into sounds. Example: SAT. "Every time I hold up a finger, say a sound from the word SAT. sss aaa t" Manipulating sounds is called *phonemic awareness*. Teaching phonemic awareness is the first component of a balanced reading program.

Second, students learn the most common sound for letters and letter combinations. This is called the *alphabetic principle*. For example, given the letter A, children say "a a a."

Third, students receive systematic, explicit instruction in phonics. Spoken words are made up of sounds. Printed words are made up of letters.

To read words, students must learn that the printed letters they see in words represents the sounds the students hear. With phonics, students say the sound for each letter and letter combination and then say the word. For example, the student points to the letters in the word *ran* and say the sounds "r a a n-ran." Over time, the student learns to read words without sounding them out.

Fourth, students practice their phonics by reading decodable stories made up of words they can sound out and irregular words that the teacher has introduced earlier. During this stage, the student does not read literature that isn't closely tied to their phonics instruction.

Fifth, students develop their comprehension by answering questions about the decodable stories and by listening to and answering questions about literature the teacher reads aloud. This is the key to an effective reading program for kindergarten and first grade—teaching decoding with decodable stories and teaching comprehension by having students listen to literature and answer questions.

Good practice in all classroom teaching. Meeting standards requires schoolteachers and principals to thoroughly understand the importance of skill in standard operating classroom teaching processes.

A process is simply a repeated standard operating activity that reliably achieves goals. Coming to grips with the importance of skill in using reliable classroom teaching processes is a most crucial challenge for succeeding in a standards-based school system.

Standard Operating Practices (SOP)

Standard operating practices should include procedures for meeting the following standards: (1) determining the readiness for teaching when children start a class; (2) informing the teachers of previous student performance to build continuity into instruction; and (3) using what dependable research proves works as classroom teaching practice.

As these guidelines are taken from our sample standard operating procedures, many of these will be repetitious to those who have already read portions of these book. However, we have listed the information again here—sometimes almost word for word—in order to provide a concise set of guidelines for use in local schools and in order to reinforce our belief in the importance of these issues.

Resolving complaints are part of a process, as much as is recruiting, orienting, training, and developing teaching and administrative staff in understanding and using what works reliably in the classroom for student achievement. Virtually every repeatable activity in a school and its school system can be—and should be—viewed as a process of events. Indeed, processes are the system.

Almost instinctively, every parent knows that it is foolish and even dangerous to gamble with his or her youngster's classroom schooling— especially in core subjects like reading, writing, and math. The classroom is not a gambling casino. It is not the place for a game of chance.

We have all spent time in school classrooms. Common sense tells us that school classrooms are workplaces that assign teachers to run them properly. Running an orderly, learning-focused, and academically sound school workplace is a teacher's most important task. There is *always* higher student achievement in an orderly and safe classroom that is run in a knowledgeable and businesslike manner using methods that research and field testing have shown repeatedly to be effective.

The Standard Operating Practices

1. Every reliable teacher will, as standard operating practice, show evidence of good planning in teaching.

2. Every reliable teacher will, as standard operating practice, show evidence of good communication of lesson goals and objectives to children and parents.

3. Every reliable teacher will, as standard operating practice, show evidence of consistency with teachers in the same school in choosing subject matter to be taught.

4. Every reliable teacher will, as standard operating practice, show evidence of correct use of classroom time for subject matter.

5. Every reliable teacher will show, as standard operating practice, evidence of not labeling and using different approaches to groups of students.

6. Every reliable teacher will, as standard operating practice, show evidence of using valid and effective teaching methods.

7. Every reliable teacher will, as standard operating practice, show evidence of good pacing and sequencing of student work, the process of the lesson, and covering the course material.

8. Every reliable teacher will, as standard operating practice, show evidence of good management of student discipline.

9. Every reliable teacher will, as standard operating practice, show evidence of good motivation and evaluation of the students.

10. Every reliable teacher will, as standard operating practice, show evidence of evenness and quality control in classroom instruction.

11. Every reliable teacher will, as standard operating practice, show little evidence of ignorance of or apathy toward what works to reliably achieve excellent student achievement.

4. Continual Quality Improvement

High-reliability organizations obsess over the quality of their workplace processes and insist on taking steps to continuously improve them.

Processes literally make up the heart of the school and the school system. Processes that are put in place because they are known to work and then are subjected to scrutiny over time for corrective action and improvement are the *sine qua non* of HROs.

5. The Nature of Quality Control

There is a climate of fear among school personnel that pervades even trying to look objectively at school processes, which have an aura of being sacred because they have for so long been customary. The fear is that if the processes are found wanting, the messenger will suffer. Sadly, this is often exactly what will happen.

This ubiquitous fear must be recognized and dealt with straight away. It is our hope that this book will show why this is vital and what can be substituted for fear. The key is sharing the knowledge that an examination of processes is always followed by corrective action for improvement. When people understand that this is the nature of quality control, and not designed as faultfinding, they enthusiastically embrace it.

An obsession, therefore, with perfecting the basic workplace processes is completely understandable. The process determines the end result. An informal example is cooking using a recipe. As every cook knows or soon learns, the quality of the cake or the pizza lies both in how good the recipe is to begin with and the diligence with which it is scrupulously followed. If both conditions are met, the product desired will reliably have the quality intended.

Leaders of the HRO do not fear exposing the problems they may find as they follow their calling. For them, the hunt carries a tangible payoff in improvement. They use quality tools suggested by Baldrige and ISO for the hunt.

Because the fundamental mind-set behind every HMO is continuous improvement, a problem found is never an admission of failure; it is an opportunity for inventing and deploying corrective action aimed at making the process work even better. Further, this basic *Kaizen* mind-set, a subject discussed in great length in the next chapter, includes follow through. The corrective action employed is not assumed to work. It is checked on after a period of time to see that it shows the specific improvement. If it does not, another corrective action is taken.

QUALITY CRITERIA LINK TO THE HRO

The principle of the high-reliability organization rests on an underlying philosophy of quality. This leads the HRO:

- to routinely analyze its systems for variance-making decisions based on fact,
- to consciously define the organization's internal and external customers, actively seeking input from both,
- to drive out fear by encouraging its members to risk making mistakes in order to learn more about the system,
- to remove any military-type command-and-control barriers by establishing clear and open lines of communication,
- to educate and retrain teachers and staff, and
- to thrive on fostering teamwork and interrelationships.

The HRO creates a structure favorable to the never-ending, step-by-step quality improvement as advanced by ISO and Baldrige criteria. It fosters cooperative labor-management relations.

In education, the *focus* is the student, the *concern* is classroom effectiveness, and *assessment* is the means by which educators gain feedback about what works and what needs to be improved. With quality improvement, the HRO constantly seeks to improve the quality of what it uses, does, and delivers. The definitive goal is to assure the reliability of classroom teaching in order to improve student learning.

COMMON THREADS TYING QUALITY SYSTEMS TOGETHER

First, each school views its students as customers. This brings a heightened awareness of their needs. Initiatives with the greatest involvement are those where top administrators actively participate in reform. Next, each school customizes its staff and teacher development to meet its specific requirements. Most combine active learning, continuous quality improvement, and teamwork. Third, all include classroom assessment as a key. Each school either realigns current fiscal resources or finds new money to support their moves into Baldrige and ISO. Lastly, and most crucially, people at all the schools seem to understand and accept the fact that change takes time.

There are always concerns among teachers and staff about any new program. This can be especially so with a major process change carrying far-reaching implications, such as part of the quality improvement. Briefly, let's acknowledge these concerns:

Standardization. It is easy to see how technical and professional classes like mathematics or science readily accept setting standards. This may be because measuring student results is more direct than with softer subjects like creative writing and language. In areas like these, who defines quality? Who sets standards that are measurable?

Benchmarking and customer focus. Benchmarking means setting your standards with a successful school. Combined with meeting customer needs, these benchmark standards are cornerstones of quality improvement, but does setting our sights on goals, based on even the most current information, provide enough flexibility to see the future? Will schools committed to becoming an HRO consign themselves to the perpetual role of the want-to-be-follower? If an HRO is an example for others, can it both lead as well as continually gauge its progress in relation to other schools?

Teams. Teams and teamwork take time, training, and energy—they do not just happen. Grouping people and assuming that they will work together can scuttle the best of intentions. We may forget to ask the obvious. Do faculty and students know how to work in teams? If the answer is no, do we have the drive to teach them?

Quality. The HRO continually strives to improve the quality of its processes. In effect, the challenge becomes doing what we already do, only doing it better. Rarely do we question what we do. The future is filled with uncertainty, greater public scrutiny, and more calls for accountability, rapidly exploding knowledge, and more diverse communities. We must ask ourselves, is continuous quality improvement enough?

Experienced meeting-goers can relate to the following observation from the notes of an actual, but typical, quality-improvement meeting observed by Allen.

> The feedback received was that the assistant superintendents don't know where this project is going and they don't see where the great advantage to it lies. In other words, "What's in it for our district?" Part of the problem is that at least half of the participants were not in the kickoff meeting where much of this was explained. The other part is the same reaction I saw in businesses; people have more to do than they can do. This sounds like one of those "nice things to do" but not as important as whatever is on their desk today.

In 1997, *A Cultural Study of ISO Certification* by Mallak, Bringelson, and Lyth identified organizational cultural values that contribute to the success of those organizations successfully achieving ISO 9000 certification. As mentioned earlier, the ISO program seeks to achieve and maintain product/service quality, ensure management that quality standards are being achieved, and provide consistent products/services to consumers. Their findings strongly suggest that achieving ISO 9000 certification requires such values as decisiveness, team orientation, risk aversion, cooperation, and attention to detail.

The authors' findings support these conclusions, as well for the development of the HRO and putting Baldrige criteria to work. The fact that organizational culture influences the success or failure of implementing quality-improvement programs is a given. Most organizations that pursue the link between the HRO, Baldrige, and ISO 9000 enhance their long-term ability to perform effectively. To fly the ISO banner from the school flagpole or be acknowledged as a Baldrige quality leader is quite an honor. The recognition of customers and constituencies help spur HRO leadership, staff, and teachers to ever more innovative quality improvements.

MAKING HRO WORK WITH BALDRIGE AND ISO

One of the basic processes followed by HROs is designed for use in motivating, training, supervising, and evaluating employees. It is based on meeting date-specific timelines with due care, diligence, and regard, all of which are discussed in greater detail in the next chapter. Summarized below are the essential linkages between the criteria that Baldrige and ISO ask the school leaders to follow, and the steps to creating the HRO in the public school.

Define What's Coming

The first step is to prepare school staff to what's coming. Outline the essential elements of Baldrige or ISO that you intend to follow. Every teacher, administrator, and member of the support staff needs to know what is expected of him or her. This puts the staff members at ease and helps remove the natural anxieties brought about by changes in processes and procedures.

It is essential at this stage to clearly outline what the job is. It is also crucial to learn what each staff member thinks they already know about what's coming. In this way, leadership can help get staff members more interested in the task that lies ahead. It will help cushion the cultural changes that are intended to come about through the deeper examination of and subsequent changes in school operating processes. These early steps can help put staff members in the correct position for easier acceptance of change, a hallmark of the HRO.

Provide Assistance

The second step is to assist school staff by clearly presenting the newly proposed operation. The leader tells, shows, and illustrates one important step at a time. One of the common vulnerabilities of a highly educated workforce, such as the teamwork called for among administrators and teachers, is to erroneously assume that other team members can properly interpolate the details between the lines. Nothing could be further from the truth.

The leader needs to stress each key point to be followed in the quality system. Change means difference, and the change elements are indeed comprehensive. The leader needs to instruct and guide clearly. All essential elements must be included in the explanations so that the transfer of school quality improvement steps is complete. The leader needs to be calm and patient when teaching. He or she must try to avoid transmitting no more than the staff member can master at a given time.

Test Important Changes

The third step is to try out some of these new ideas. In this way, the leader gains a fairly quick grasp on how things are working. Knowing the results of actions early on helps both the leader and staff member. Having staff members proceed with certain aspects of the quality-improvement program best accomplishes this. Baldrige and ISO repeatedly provide opportunities to put new ideas into action. In this way, the leader can correct errors before they go too far.

Encourage staff members to explain each key point in the quality system stage that is being pursued directly back to the leader. As the staff member proceeds with that aspect of the quality assignment again, he or she gains greater confidence and "buys in" to the entire process. This also gives the leader the chance to make certain each staff member understands the nature and meaning of all steps in the quality process. The leader needs to repeat this process until he or she knows the staff member has understood it.

Use Follow-Through

The fourth step is to follow up. During this stage, the staff member learns which of the corrective actions are most crucial to the quality-of-results mind-set. The staff member needs many chances to get it right. The cultural changes that the organization is embarking upon are too important to be short-circuited by sloppy or inadequate follow-through.

By putting the staff member on his or her own, the staff is given the model for expanding their creative thinking. Each staff member also needs to know who is designated as his or her mentor during the quality-building stage. The leader needs to check frequently and to encourage questions. As the leader observes the expected progress, the leader can taper off extra coaching and close follow-up. In this way, the HRO becomes fully rooted within the school's cultural and operational processes.

SUMMARY: THE MALCOLM BALDRIGE QUALITY STANDARDS IN EDUCATION

We have stressed that the world of work has changed, but schools seem to continually break down around the issue of reform. While global business competition abounds and customers demand more for less, workers demand more say in what they do while government agencies add more restrictions. These are sharply contrasting events.

This new workplace is where students will need to perform, thrive, and survive after their school years. They will experience technologies that shake up their employers. They will see once-profitable companies and markets vanish overnight. Every time they learn the "rules," the rules will soon change.

Schools are just now coming to grips with a new truth. Delivering world-class results flows directly from a school that is an HRO. The HRO school uses measurable quality to achieve continuous improvement.

The Baldrige criteria for evaluating a school involve the following key points:

- Leadership
- Strategic planning
- Student and stakeholder focus
- Information and analysis
- Faculty and staff focus
- Educational and support process management
- School performance results

In 1997, one state legislature recognized these trends and took action to meet the need. "It is the goal of the State of New Jersey to prepare its students to be internationally competitive and to meet world class standards through our system of education." The New Jersey Legislature further declared the need for local communities to work collaboratively to promote quality and accountability in the delivery of educational services. To meet this end, the New Jersey Legislature provided that:

> A school district at Level 1 may apply to participate in an alternative program of monitoring and evaluation for the purposes of certification . . . the criteria shall include but not be limited to, the criteria used in the education eligibility category of the Malcolm Baldrige National Quality Award.

ISO STANDARDS FOR EDUCATION

ISO education guidelines were thoroughly reviewed by leading educators around the world. Committee members representing the American Association of School Administrators, American Society for Training and Development, National Society for Performance and Instruction, National Education Association, American Federation of Teachers, and all members of ANSI Z-I and the U.S. Technical Advisory Group to ISO TC 176 reviewed the education guidelines. Validation of the guidelines consisted of a development and review process. Authorities in instructional design and application conducted these reviews. It also included the educational and training design principles for institutions, which involved experienced quality professionals.

The ISO 9000 standards for education, like all other standards, are simply a set of tools to be used to achieve a set of objectives. The guidelines combine two systems, begun in the early decades of the twentieth century, and have undergone further development since World War II. The first, the instructional system, has been used to design, develop, deliver, and assess instruction in military, industrial, service, education, and training institutions. The second, the quality system, has been used to ensure quality in many of these same institutions.

Those experienced in systems approaches will find the language and logic of ISO familiar. Experienced quality professionals will find the rigor of quality practice intact. Experienced educators and trainers will find suggestions on implementing quality systems directly related to their current practice. ISO education and training guidelines are written to be user friendly.

The ISO 9000 standards represent an international consensus on good management practices with the aim of ensuring that the organization can, time and time again, deliver the products or services that meet the client's quality requirements. These good practices have been distilled into a set of standardized requirements for a quality management system, regardless of your organization, its size, or whether it's in the private or public sector.

As repeatedly stressed throughout this book, the existence of an organization without customers, or with dissatisfied customers, is in danger. To keep customers—and to keep them satisfied—a school's service needs to meet their requirements. ISO 9000 provides a tried-and-tested framework for taking a systematic approach to managing operational processes (the school's activities) so that it consistently turns out products and services conforming to the customer's expectations. That means consistently happy customers.

The requirements for an educational quality system have been standardized, but most of us like to think our school is unique. So how does ISO 9000 allow for the diversity of say, on the one hand, an urban school district, and on the other hand, a suburban school district?

The answer is that ISO 9000 lays down *what* requirements the quality system must meet, but it does not dictate *how* they should be met in the school—which leaves great scope and flexibility for implementation in different school environments and differing school cultures, as well as different national cultures. ISO is being used in schools in China, Singapore, Israel, Saudi Arabia, Great Britain, and France, as well as (more recently) in the United States.

ISO includes a standard on terminology and other standards, which can be described as "supporting tools," which give guidance on specific aspects, such as internal and external auditing of quality systems.

The school organization carries out auditing of its ISO 9000-based quality system itself to verify that it is managing its processes effectively—or, to put it another way, to check that it is in full control of its activities. In addition, the school organization may invite its clients to audit the quality system. This gives external stakeholders the confidence that the school organization is capable of delivering students and services that will meet their requirements.

Last, the school organization may engage the services of an independent quality system certification body to obtain an ISO 9000 certificate of conformity. This step has proven to be extremely popular in the marketplace because of the increased credibility brought about by an independent assessment. The school may avoid multiple audits by the school's clients and reduce the frequency or duration of client audits. The ISO certificate also serves as a reference between the school and its potential customers, especially when school and customer are new to each other.

In 2000, ISO revised ISO 9001 and ISO 9004 standards as a "consistent pair" of standards. Previously, ISO 9001 clearly addressed the quality-management system requirements for an organization to demonstrate its capability to meet customer needs. The revised ISO 9004 is intended to lead beyond ISO 9001 toward the development of a comprehensive quality-management system, designed to address the needs of all interested parties. This now reaches out to constituents and all school stakeholders.

The revised ISO 9001 and 9004 are based on eight quality-management principles that reflect best management practices and have been prepared by international quality experts. These eight principles are:

- Customer-focused organization
- Leadership
- Involvement of people-focused organization
- Process approach
- System approach to management
- Continual improvement
- Factual approach to decision making
- Mutually beneficial supplier relationship

The new revisions will have a single quality-management requirements standard. ISO 9001 applies to all organizations, products, and services. This will replace the current three standards (ISO 9001, 9002 and 9003) in the 1994 version.

- ISO 9001 will be used for the certification of quality-management Systems.
- ISO 9004 will be the quality-management system standard, designed to go beyond quality-management requirements, to a holistic

approach to quality management in pursuit of improvement of organizational performance, and benefits to all interested parties through sustained customer satisfaction.

The new consistent pair of standards are structured and sequenced to facilitate an easy and useful transition between them. Similarly, Baldrige criteria stand alone. Although each remains as a stand-alone standard, the winning prescription for curing the illness of public schools promotes synergy between Baldrige and the ISO 9001–9004, which aids organizational efficiency and effectiveness. After all, this synergy is the heartbeat of the high-reliability organization.

CHAPTER 7

Continuous Improvement Helps Shape School Performance

Anecdotes are knowledge; they are stories that speak for themselves. Carefully constructed anecdotes that are accurate about events are accurate reporting. When retold at the appropriate time, they are effective knowledge. Telling an anecdote is a crucial clinical skill.

In health care, attentive observers are always observing. It is important to separate the observation from the interpretation. It is crucial to appreciate the relationships between the observation and the world that surrounds the patient. It is not an isolated event that is observed, but an event in an unfolding process. An attentive observer does not leave a field of view prematurely. Observations serve the goals that anchor them to their observations.

Almost every American living today has been touched by the "economic miracle" of postwar Japan. At the middle of the twentieth century, atomic bombs had leveled two of its major cities, its stubborn army had been defeated, and its navy lay at the bottom of the Pacific Ocean. The resilience of the Japanese people demonstrates their unique understanding and appreciation of the power and use of *Kaizen,* continuous improvement. Today, the reliable quality of Japanese goods and services is recognized the world over, but this achievement did not take place overnight. Gradual change is prevalent in the East, but not common in the West. We're an impatient people and when we turn our attention to a problem, we usually want quick results. Investors want their stocks to rise in a matter of days or weeks rather than waiting months or years. We want our streets fixed now, not next month. We look for the breakthrough, the startling, or the innovative. The key difference between the Japanese and American views of how change is achieved lies in this essence of the *Kaizen* concept.

The cultural idea of *Kaizen* is pretty straightforward. *Kaizen* means ongoing improvement involving everyone, including managers and workers, leaders and followers. The *Kaizen* beliefs assume that a way of life—be it your working life, your social life, or your home life—deserves to be constantly improved. This simple but powerful concept is widely known to be a uniquely Japanese management practice.

But can we in America benefit from such a simple idea? Must it remain unique to the Japanese? Could there already be an American counterpart, an American *Kaizen*, which—if made widespread in schools—could improve every child's future way of life?

Our basic argument is that the multicultural United States has a similar push for achieving continuous improvement. That pressure is focused on processes that protect certain fundamental rights that people are guaranteed under our Constitution. It is built, brick by brick, through legal precedent.

Our line of reasoning continues with an illustration of how it currently applies to a protected class of public employees—public school teachers. We conclude with a discussion and demonstration of how it can be applied in a major way to master objectives in today's knowledge and information economy.

Three principles from English common law that are enshrined in tort or contract law in America provide the thought structure for an American version of continuous improvement. The legal principles are *due care, due diligence,* and *due regard.*

Thinking about these principles helps discover how the American equivalent of *Kaizen* gathers together the basics for dealing with pressing change—common sense, common virtues, and common goals.

AN AMERICAN MODEL OF JAPANESE *KAIZEN*

The American legal system operates under the overarching constitutional framework of due process. Here we refer to *substantive* due process as opposed to simply *procedural* due process. With substantive due process, you are concerned with your fundamental rights as opposed to just legal technicalities. There exists a set of universal concepts and practices either unknown, neglected, or misunderstood by educators and the public. When properly applied, these can help solve our present learning achievement problems in our schools.

Taken together, the principles of due care, due diligence, and due regard offer a powerful means to desired results. This is the personal caring for each student that is so sorely needed for reliable quality in classroom teaching.

At present, laws mandate this framework as a protection of the employment rights for public school teachers. Interestingly, the same mandated framework formed the principles for the guided learning experiences that were successfully used to train virtually all American workers to produce the war materials for World War II. Today, if properly working in our schools, this framework would provide a proven process for continuous development of human skill, knowledge, and attitude for every child to be a winner in school.

When widely understood and practiced to improve learning in our schools, this framework can become a tool of American economic advantage. It could give a child a leg up when ready to enter the fiercely competitive yet collaborative global workplace.

Here, we unabashedly call upon the concept of American *Kaizen* as a leading candidate to help any school. What follows is a brief account of the legal framework for the use of a model standard operating procedure for guiding reliable quality into classroom teaching.

Legal Framework for American *Kaizen*

In repeated court opinions, substantive due process, the foundation of due care in common law, is found to consist of five elements:

1. Known *expectations* of what is required to be achieved,
2. Documented *assistance* in meeting the expectations,
3. Timely knowledge of *results*,
4. Feedback from the results to construct necessary *corrective action*, and
5. *Many chances* to be successful through repetition of all the previous elements.

It bears repeating that knowing what's expected, getting assistance, knowing the results, taking corrective action, and having repeated chances are the "stuff" of the guided learning experience. These are the five essentials of due care.

There are two other ideas needed for you to be faithful to the *spirit* of substantive due process. These are due diligence and due regard:

- Due diligence is the obligation for you to be aware of problems and dangers *before* they occur. It mandates a proactive approach to prevent problems.
- Due regard represents the caring spirit of substantive due process. It basically means *respect for every person with no strings, no requirements, no reservations attached, because of gender, race, age, physical or mental handicap, religion, or ethnicity.* It reflects the common law's insistence on *fundamental fairness.* It hardens American *Kaizen* into a discipline of caring.

Through the elements of due care (guided learning experience), due diligence (prevention of problems), and due regard (respect and caring for each person), American *Kaizen* gives us a system of caring in which:

1. You know what is expected and have an opportunity to influence what is expected. The step is symbolized as KOE (Knowledge of Expectations).
2. You are given proactive assistance to successfully meet each expectation, such as meeting standards. This is KOA (Knowledge of Assistance).
3. You are given timely feedback so you know how well you are meeting expectations. Timely knowledge of results is the basic principle for mastery of a skill, attitude, or knowledge. The element is KOR (Knowledge of Results).
4. You are guided to successful learning through the joint development of a corrective action plan matched to expectations not yet satisfactorily met. This element is KOCA (Knowledge of Corrective Action).
5. You are given multiple chances to succeed. A reasonable person, the hallmark of common law, knows that it takes time to master new skills, attitudes, and knowledge. The element is KOMC (Knowledge of Many Chances).

GUIDED LEARNING EXPERIENCE: A WORKER TRAINING CRISIS IN WORLD WAR II

Revisiting the *Training within Industry* program of World War II gives us a dramatic example of the American *Kaizen* process in action. A major phase of this program, *Instructing the Workforce,* was a four-step sequence dubbed "How to Instruct." It was a universal process and fit all training needs, regardless of the product or service being needed for the war effort.

How to Instruct: A Universal Process of Training within Industry

Step 1: Prepare the worker (Knowledge of Expectations).
Put him or her at ease.
State the job and find out what he or she already knows about it.
Get him or her interested in learning the job.
Place him or her in the correct position.

Step 2: Present the operation (Knowledge of Assistance).
Tell, show, and illustrate one important step at a time.
Stress each key point.
Instruct clearly, completely, and patiently; but no more than the student can master.

Step 3: Try out performance (Knowledge of Results).
Have him or her do the job—correct errors.
Have him or her explain each key point to you as the student does the job again.
Be sure he or she understands.
Continue until you know the student has mastered the task.

Step 4: Follow up (Knowledge of Corrective Actions and Many Chances).
Put him on his own. Designate person to whom he goes for help.
Check frequently. Encourage questions.
Taper off extra coaching and close follow up.

Here is its significance: Despite the vast variety of products, processes, operations, people, and time pressures associated with the conduct of World War II (literally millions were needed from all backgrounds and learning levels), these simple four-step rules fit all work situations. They are truly universals on how to instruct for on-the-job training experience. These steps in the universal process led to the expertise (the human capital) needed to create what was called during the war an "arsenal of democracy."

A CURRENT CASE STUDY OF AMERICAN *KAIZEN*

Public school teachers are a protected class of worker by statute and by aspects of the Fourteenth Amendment to the Constitution and by common law, as codified in tort law. Teachers have been ruled to have a property right to their positions. They may not be removed from their employment without due process (both procedural and substantive). To terminate a public schoolteacher's employment, the school district must take on an American model of *Kaizen*. Since the full framework as described earlier is either unknown, neglected, or misunderstood, few teachers are ever removed, even for cause. Worse yet, as will be shown later, the school district's failure to know how to use the American *Kaizen* model needlessly results in the failure of some teachers and some students.

States are required by statute to make it very difficult for any public schoolteacher to lose his or her job. Before a teacher may be discharged, statute-driven steps must be documented by the administration and hearings held by the board of education. The documentation to be provided must be of such a nature that a hearing officer or court will have detailed knowledge of the administration's efforts in carrying out the American *Kaizen* framework. The following shows the process in action in the case of a teacher being considered for employment termination.

Step 1: *Knowledge of Expectations* (KOE). Each teacher must know *what* he or she is expected to do to be successful, and *how* and *when* each expectation will be judged. Further, there must be documentation that the teacher has had an opportunity to influence, but not decide, what is required.

Step 2: *Knowledge of Assistance* (KOA). Each teacher must have been given assistance in successfully meeting the expectations (KOE).

Step 3: *Knowledge of Results* (KOR). Each teacher must be given timely feedback on how well or how poorly he or she is meeting what is expected (KOE). If an expectation has not been met satisfactorily, the principle of corrective action must be employed.

Step 4: *Knowledge of Corrective Action* (KOCA). For each expectation not met satisfactorily as expressed in (KOR), a plan for specific corrective action must be developed with the teacher. The sequence of the first three principles of American *Kaizen* must then be employed.

Step 5: *Knowledge of Many Chances* (KOMC). The teacher must be given many chances to succeed before the final formal notice is served (essentially a repetition of the preceding).

Discipline of Caring

American *Kaizen* is a true example of a discipline of caring. Caring is the central emotion that supports life itself. Such a claim calls for elaboration, but first, what is caring? In what sense can it be said to be a *discipline?*

Caring centers on (1) dealings with people, as well as (2) connections with what is considered important. You can observe the universal process of caring in its ideal form in that most basic of all life-supporting and life-enhancing relationships, your care for your children.

Have you ever been faced with the cynical question, "Why care?" Or wondered how to reply to the person who voices the cliché about something you think important, "Well, I couldn't care less." Through your caring for others, for your community or your school, for a place, for ideas, or even for some things, you give the meaning to your life. Without "cares," your life is empty of meaning. Through your caring and being cared for, you find your place in the world. Caring orders your values and your activities around it.

> "In the sense in which a person can ever be said to belong in the world, he is at home not through dominating, or explaining or even appreciating, but through caring and being cared for."
>
> —Milton Mayeroff, *On Caring*

Most planning for the improvement of people's performance gives the true meaning of caring short shrift. The dictionary defines it as the action of the verb "care," and "care" has a number of definitions. These range from a burdensome sense of responsibility, to painstaking attention, to loving or liking, and to token management or custody as "under a physician's care." Yet, as you have seen by now, caring implies more than unthinking concern. It implies your broader concern for the whole person, rather than just for that person's particular problem.

Example from Medicine

Some of the history of medicine and the processes used by physicians to care for patients help illuminate the power of caring. A family example may provide insights into important aspects of that medical history.

Samuel Lessinger was born in 1886. In 1910, at the age of twenty-four, he became a pharmacist. Eight years later, he began his practice as a physician.

He told vivid stories of his training and medical practice. He showed how he rolled his own pills, the nature of the pharmacopoeia, and the medical practice of the time, which expected the doctor to stay with a woman during the last stages of her pregnancy.

The year he died, 1966, he estimated that he would probably know less than 10 percent of the preparations physicians were then using. He was willing to concede that the young doctors knew more than he did at their age, but he wondered if they still had *compassio medici,* a basic regard for the human condition.

What Samuel Lessinger wondered about were the qualities he had in abundance, and which the great physicians of the prescientific/technological era required in a doctor.

Dr. Francis Peabody observed in his classic dissertation in 1927: "The most common criticism made at present by older practitioners is that young graduates have been taught a great deal about the mechanism of disease, but little about the practice of medicine—or, to put it more bluntly, they are too 'scientific' and do not know how to take care of patients.

"The good physician knows his patients through and through, and his knowledge is bought dearly. Time, sympathy and understanding must be lavishly dispensed, but the reward is to be found in the personal bond, which forms the greatest satisfaction of the practice of medicine. One of the essential qualities of clinician is interest in humanity, *for the secret of the care of the patient is in caring for the patient.*" [emphasis added]

In this country, 1910 marks the transformation of medical practice from what it had been from the dawn of recorded time to what it has now become. The year Lessinger opened his drug store (1910), the famous Flexner Report was published. By the time he began his medical practice, the Flexner "revolution" in medical training was spreading across the land. The revolution placed the major stress in training on knowledge and use of scientific principles to enable the achievement of technical proficiency. When doctors became medical scientists and technicians, they added the potential of competence and confidence to their primary "C" of caring. So how fares the first one, caring, at the end of the century that began the revolution in medicine? And what does caring in medicine really mean today?

"There are numerous examples of physicians who are absolutely superb technicians, with all the latest knowledge and skill, but who approach patients in such a cold manner as to prompt doubt and distress. Members of medical society boards of censors are keenly aware that patients are often so unhappy with that kind of care that they file a formal grievance. In the investigation of such complaints, it becomes clear that, more often than not, the breakdown has been in the 'caring' aspect of the physician–patient relationship—not in the quality of technical care and treatment provided."

—Walter Menninger, the Menninger Foundation
Institute of Medicine of the National Academy of Sciences
Washington, D.C., 1974

Medical scholars have shown that the skills involved in caring for a patient can be acquired. This is why it is sound to think of caring as a discipline. For the physician, caring begins with the dictum *primum non nocere*: above all, do no harm.

There is a universal method for successfully training interns and physicians in the skilled caring for patients. Its five steps are:

1. Establish clearly defined student performance objectives that both the trainer and the learner can recognize when success has been achieved;
2. Teach the parts and the whole in an organized, progressive way;
3. Integrate any particular aspect of training with the student's overall training;
4. Provide the student ongoing clinical experience to allow practice for mastery;
5. Provide ongoing standardized evaluation of student progress with feedback to the student; provide opportunity to improve skills through additional practice.

Observations about the caring of physicians clearly show a broader issue. An identical case for a discipline of caring (that is, the three Cs: *competence*, *confidence*, and *caring*) can be made for teaching and managing. As a human organism, you simply are not designed to survive very well in any environment that treats you like an object. Cairnes (1949), in describing a good doctor, wrote: "He is a person who never spares himself in the interest of his patients; and in addition he is a man who studies the patient not only as a case but also as an individual."

Relationships

Relationships are the primary stuff of life. The degree of success in life becomes in large measure a function of the quality of those relationships.

Caring transforms all relationships, whether they are with people, with living things, with objects, with places, with organizations, or with ideas. It transforms by creating leaders who seek to serve the economic, the psychological, the physical, and the spiritual advantage of the one cared for.

Caring reflects love. It requires knowledge, dedication, faith, and patience. You know when you care. You know because there is congruence between what you ought to do and what you want to do. You know because you are ready to respond to the needs of your "other." You know because you feel remorse if an "other" says, "Where were you when I needed you?"

For the tough-minded, caring has additional value. Skilled caring can directly affect the balance sheet in business. It helps win sports contests. Such caring in an organization, for example, can decrease human failure. This saves costs and prevents harm. The amount saved is roughly the average time spent in dealing with each person who is not working at optimal level. The most crucial, the amount of harm prevented, is harder to measure in dollars, but it can be surmised. It consists of eliminating the friction, the loss of morale, and the injury to the reputation of an organization that occurs from the actions of fearful, apathetic, sullen, or resentful people who can be changed.

Restoring American Common Sense

Revisiting the common law allows us to gain greater insight into its basis in common sense. In America, the common law is a storehouse of practical and legal wisdom. We inherited that storehouse from England and have enriched it through more than two hundred years of the American experience. It provides the principles that govern our relationships as citizens. Common law has given us commonsense (to us) ideas, such as that reasonable people can judge right from wrong behavior. The common law is not a set of statutes developed by legislators. It is the synthesis of standards for human behavior derived from countless court decisions made over centuries.

Some commonsense ideas include, among others, the following:

- You must drive your car reasonably or be accountable for those you injure.
- You are entitled to be judged by a jury of your peers.
- Decisions about you are derived from asking what would a "reasonable" person do in such circumstances?
- The accident caused by swerving to avoid an oncoming vehicle, for example, is excusable; falling asleep or being intoxicated and causing an accident is not.

These examples merely illustrate the practical wisdom integrated into the common law that most Americans would agree represents "common sense."

To enlarge on one of the examples, it was out of the common law that the jury system was developed—a group of peers who would together be expected to make a "reasonable" judgment as to a defendant's guilt or innocence. The most important standard in the common law is what a reasonable person would do in this particular situation. More than anything else, this idea of a reasonable person is held in the highest regard. The backbone of tort law codifies the common law with respect to negligence. It uses the notion of reasonableness to assess the degree of negligence in a particular case.

The common law is the opposite of ironclad rules that supposedly guarantee certain results. The guideposts that common law lays down are to be influenced by circumstances under investigation. This makes common law inherently flexible and progressive. By nature, it evolves with new court decisions and with changing times. Therein lies one of its powers.

> Supreme Court Justice Benjamin Cardozo, considered the greatest common law judge of the twentieth century, said that the common law "is at bottom the philosophy of pragmatism."

Our argument is really a simple one. You could achieve more reliable classroom teaching quality for your school-age children if the process of continuous improvement were clearly seen, adopted, and internalized as an everyday approach in your school. Not only would the common-sense protections for teachers be strengthened, but better learning for all customers of education—including students, their parents, and their future employers—would result. The following enlarges this premise as it applies to classrooms.

A PARENTAL GUIDE TO DUE CARE

You are your student's most important advocate and mentor. As an actively interested and involved parent, you have a valuable job. Remember, it is also your school and you have a constructive role to play in helping the school achieve reliable quality in classroom teaching. Don't let anyone try to convince you otherwise. Among your tasks is to see to it that through the application of American *Kaizen*:

Each teacher makes it clear to everybody just what the end product, skill, or knowledge will be (KOE Knowledge of Expectations).

- If teachers want students to be able to repair an automobile part or sail a steady course, they need to show them how and make sure that they have the "end product" well in mind.
- The same is true when teaching students how to solve equations, write grammatical sentences, or design experiments.
- Show and tell the students exactly what it is they want them to be able to do. Teachers often won't need to tell them anything else. Many a school class has changed direction when the objectives were hammered out carefully between teachers and students in clear terms.

Each teacher lets everybody know how each objective is going to be tested.

- The more information the teacher gives the students about how they are to be tested, the more easily and quickly students develop the required skills.
- Teachers sometimes are hesitant to let the student know what the test is. The teacher may be worried about "giving away" the test. These teachers are in a *teach-about* mode rather than a *teach-how* mode.
- There are very few skills that are taught where a teacher can't let the student know what the skills are and how they are to be tested.
- It is only when they are teaching *about* (and using the test as a sample of what the student can say about the subject) that they have to guard the nature of the test.
- With American *Kaizen*, teachers eliminate the opponent relationship between student and instructor. The quickest way to do that is to be as direct and open about the nature of the test as a teacher can be.

Each teacher takes advantage of what students know and can do when they come in.

- This important readiness factor can be determined by encouraging students to respond to expectations. This is one of the aspects of

American *Kaizen* that almost everybody will agree with, but it's one of the hardest to implement.

- Teachers find out what students can already do, then they productively use that information.
- Once the instruction is divided into the expectations (skills and knowledge, objectives, the means of testing each skill and knowledge), the students can look at both the objective and test, and decide if they have the skill or not. Here is where assistance comes in.

Each teacher gives his or her students as many choices or paths through the instruction as possible, with Knowledge of Assistance (KOA).

- If students are going to build a table, they proceed in a certain order from cutting to assembling to finishing. But if they were to learn the skills of table building, they could learn sanding and finishing skills first, or last, or in the middle somewhere.
- The tendency to teach in the same order that steps are performed is strong, yet enthusiasm can be dampened when teachers force students to put off parts that seem interesting to learn less-interesting things first.
- One of the primary attributes of American *Kaizen* is one of wanting students to like the subject matter.

Each teacher provides a range of materials, approaches, and media whenever possible (Knowledge of Assistance).

- An instructor performs a certain number of functions — informs, shows how, provides feedback, counsels, and so on.
- Some of these functions are easier than others, and computer, book, tape recorder, TV, or movie can aid the instructor and student.
- It's desirable to use additional personnel. There should be no reluctance in raising the value of the instructor.

Each teacher allows enough time for any qualified individual to finish.

- A counterproductive aspect of public school is the fact that they are time-based rather than competency-based.

- Too often, the students are started, ready or not. After a period of time, the instruction ceases whether or not the students have mastered the skill.
- The folly of this practice becomes clear when students are made to move on to new skills that depend on mastery of the old.
- Instructors don't make mistakes like that when they teach someone to fly a plane. The students work on landings until they can do them. The students master navigation before instructors let them do cross-country flying. When teachers begin teaching *about* rather than *how,* they push and prod the slower student to keep up with a time schedule and then cut him or her off when time is up.
- With the exercise of American *Kaizen*, teachers give the student assurances. The student is given the time needed to read, ponder, practice, work out difficulties, look at other explanations, and talk to other students, whatever it takes to learn.
- The other side of the coin is just as important. Students need to know that they are in a system designed so that if their interest catches fire they won't have to sit around and wait for others to catch up.

Each teacher provides a "road map" to keep students informed about where they are in the curriculum.

- Teachers know this, yet not many take the simple step of providing and continuously updating a "course map."
- Teachers provide opportunity for practice of the skill being taught.
- There is strong temptation for teachers to tell students exactly how to perform a skill, what to watch out for, and how to tell when they are doing it right, but they need to provide space and time for actual practice under their guidance.

Each teacher needs to provide adequate feedback to their students on their practice sessions.

- Teachers not only provide practice of a skill, but ensure that students know directly if they are practicing correctly, or if not, why not (Knowledge of Results).

Each teacher "tests" and assesses often and in a nonthreatening way.

- When students dream of an ideal teacher, one of the things they often want to change is the brittle, enemy relationship between them and the instructor, driven by the way some teachers test and grade. They want a teacher who is fair and gives them respect, the essence of due regard.
- Two things help: first, each teacher needs to test often, so that students don't have to go too far before finding out if they're on the right track. Second, teachers need to test in a nonthreatening manner. This means cautioning students in advance what the test will be like, letting students pick their own time for testing when feasible, giving timely feedback on test results, and by letting students keep testing until the desired skill has been demonstrated.
- Under American *Kaizen*, teachers accept feedback from the students and from colleagues for self-correction. They know that no one or no system is perfect.

Each teacher compares each student to expected objectives. The teacher is interested in individual mastery, not solely some group average.

- Optimum acceptability of each student's achievement is what's necessary to flourish in the Information Age. Wherever the bar is set, the student's skill is compared to that standard.
- Teachers must avoid making the conventional mistake of changing standards based on what some other students did on the test. The most blatant example of out-of-date schooling is grading on a bell-shaped curve that guarantees that a certain number students does poorly or fails.

American *Kaizen* has several aliases that bear directly on school management and therefore on the improvement of learning and leadership.

From the framework of management, these form the best features of MBO (management by objectives). The basic practice strategy described here also matches *Direct Instruction,* which has been consistently found through careful research to be the most effective way to improve the learning of skills.

American *Kaizen* introduces into schools the neglected concept of quality control that is the foundation of accountability for results. It does this because the bottom line of quality control is feedback of results, directly followed by timely corrective action.

We give particular emphasis to learning in our analysis of American *Kaizen* because it is central to your student's success in the new economy. Learning is a before-and-after happening. You cannot define a word, or fix something, or solve a problem *before* you have learned. You can define it, or fix it, or solve it *after* you have learned. Try doing your own home plumbing or electrical repairs. The most crucial factor in all learning is the learning experience.

Although learning occurs from cradle to grave, if we do not focus on the experience from which it flows, we fail to give the learning process much thought. While you might recognize *what* you have learned, if you give little or no thought to *how* you learn, you eventually lose the key opportunity to continually learn more.

Trial and error help us relate to having learned some things firsthand, but an informed and practiced person in a proper setting provides the most effective learning experience. That person is a guide and comes with a variety of names—parent, teacher, coach, and doctor, just to name a few.

The principal places where these learning guides function are in the home, school, and workplace. You and your student's teacher can practice American *Kaizen*. With practices in partnership and alliances through a shared understanding of the process, American *Kaizen* provides the quantum leap to reliable classroom teaching and greatly improves our nation's competitive advantage in the new economy.

CHAPTER 8

Prescription for Healing the Chronic Illness of Public Schools

The clinical method must be based not solely on finding answers, but on finding the question-and-answer pair that is central to a particular situation. The clinical method is based on formulating detailed, particularized question–answer pairs. The question–answer method is applicable to every clinical setting and in every step of the clinical process. "Why is this person sick?" is a very different question in year 2000 than in 1980, and in Newark, New Jersey, than in San Francisco, California.

The need to know the patient requires that the doctor carefully nurture the bond with the patient as the primary avenue to necessary information. It is the love of the patient that binds the doctor to him and his fate, and it literally drives the doctor to find out what is the matter. Good physicians desire both knowledge and a desire for a well patient.

Similarly, the Baldrige and ISO 9000 criteria demand that school leadership wrestle with its operational and teaching processes. We cannot overstate the importance of rethinking the processes of the school from the ground up. Keep in mind, our major objective is getting dependable teaching into the classroom, every time.

We now know that a process is a repeated activity that changes something. Understanding and improving the classroom teaching processes is the goal of each element of the winning prescription. Managing all school processes well is the challenge in organizing and steadily achieving reliable classroom teaching. The six elements discussed below form the core of its success.

Almost every repeatable school activity is a process of events. Systems behavior shows us that problems are not the property of a single individual or the result of some special event. Most problems are neither isolated events nor special causes, and are often buried deep within the system. Problems that crop up are the result of system behavior. They are chronic flaws, not glitches in the system that in some way impair the desired end result.

Applying the winning prescription requires constant attention to the *how* of school processes. It means asking probing questions. Answers need to flow freely. They need to describe sequential activities, as well as comfortably discuss the tools, techniques, and methods being used during the schooling process. The winning prescription is a survey of processes intended to motivate, plan, and ensure classroom reliability.

Attention to process leads to continuous improvement. By its very nature, a process problem is never solved. These problems either become ingrained bad habits, leading to further deterioration, or become consciously improved. Once fully committed to taking the winning prescription, the school staff pulls away from solely playing the role of inspectors. They evolve into system designers. They seek to constantly improve the systems that achieve what school leadership and the customer require.

USING THE RIGHT TOOLS TO DO THE JOB

In recent years, the advent of online, computer-assisted communication between patient and physician databases has been heralded as a major step forward in the treatment of chronic illness. It holds the promise of replacing a great deal of the medical care now delivered in person. However, problems might occur, such as inaccurate information, varied opinions, and contradictory information.

This suggests that computers and information systems might create more knowledgeable patients who are active participants in their own care, but does not necessarily render the physician unnecessary. Sometimes the information itself will do the work of doctors. The major error of twentieth-century medicine is the belief that medicine only involves the application of facts to an objective problem that can be separated from the person.

In public schools, as in medicine, it is how to solve the problems that counts. To do so, you need to use the right tools to help uncover the underlying reasons for the illness. It wouldn't make much sense to put together a team of sharp people and then neglect to give them the right tools to do their jobs.

A bright executive would no more communicate with a colleague halfway around the world today with a third-class letter when he could use e-mail. Similarly, none of us would want to be treated in a health-care facility without the proper diagnostic tools. A high-reliability organization has and uses the right tools to do the quality job.

The tools used for mining, metalworking, and carpentry are different from those used for hunting, farming, cooking, and making clothes. The skills and knowledge needed to use these tools correctly are vastly different. The right tools are essential to doing a job well. In spite of these obvious facts, people are asked to do their jobs almost daily using the wrong tools or no tools at all. It's as though people in an organization are able to create and build value without tools at all, as though some sort of magic will yield something from nothing.

The fact is, good tools can make us smarter. We see evidence of this almost every day. There is only so much we can learn and remember, but we have the tools to extend our memories. We invent things that make us smarter.

Things that make us smart can also make us dumb. They can entrap us with their seductive powers. Television captures us with thousands of hours of commercials each year, and news is capsulated into easy-to-swallow dosages. But do we know any more about what is going on in the world? Tools must fit the task. If we need to learn, we need to use the right tools.

We humans are thinking, interpreting creatures. The mind tends to seek explanations, to interpret, and to make suggestions. We are active and creative. We seek interaction with others. We change our behavior as we attempt to understand what others expect of us.

Efficient, routine operations are okay for machines but not for people. The body shows wear and tear with such repetitive stress as *carpal tunnel* syndrome, which afflicts the wrists of thousands of computer users. The mind can wear out with a syndrome called *burnout,* which causes the loss of ability to create, innovate, or simply even care about our work.

A worn-out teacher can become demoralized, someone who no longer cares about the job or the quality of teaching work being produced. Worse yet, the improper design of a job can lead to an uninspired staff, where mental activity is much reduced. None of this was planned—it is an accidental by-product of this age of increased stress.

This goes a long way toward explaining the angst people feel as they struggle to do the best they can in often trying circumstances. The experiences prey on people's fears and self-doubts. Teachers are being told that they're inadequate, that they need to become something else or to be something better. This advice may be well meaning, but then the road to hell is paved with good intentions. Do teachers want to improve classroom performance by becoming someone else? Or do they want to improve their professionalism by improving what they know? We show how the right tools that lie within the winning prescription can help.

The power in using the right tools is that they don't ask you to become someone else. They help create an extension of yourself. With a little time and skill, using the right tool helps you become more than what you are.

Marshall McLuhan in *Understanding Media* (1968) tells us that tools are a medium for self-expression. An appreciation of good tools offers us a way to influence the world. We learn to listen differently, to see differently, and to view with a different sense of proportion. The doctor and teacher see the world differently. Good tools expand our perceptual boundaries.

To only see technology and tools as a way to either reduce costs or speed up output is too simplistic. Technology is a medium for creating productive environments. In the high-reliability organization, technology is at its most expressive and powerful in the form of tools—tools that help build more productive and effective environments.

This leads directly to the conclusion that the only tools worth having are those that create and enhance value. Directly and indirectly, the tools people use—and organizations choose—reflect the sort of value they wish to create. Leaders must deal with an organizational reality—work is a place where people interact to create value.

The means now exist to transform and harden these ideals into a new organizational reality. Ironically, these ideas are modeled on traditions of excellence and innovation. They demand that people reexamine the way they look at tools—and themselves.

The Meaning of Tools

Accurate measurement underlies all of science. Without simple, reliable measurements, science would be denied the use of its most powerful tools. By this we mean precise measurement, repeatable experiments, under controlled conditions, and mathematical analyses. The problem is that when it comes to measuring human capabilities we are somewhat limited.

People are extremely complex to say the least, the most complex ever studied. Each of our actions is the result of multiple interactions, of a lifetime of experiences, knowledge, and subtle personal relationships. The scientific-measurement tools try to strip away the complexities by studying a single variable at a time. Much of what is of value to a person results from the interaction of the parts: when we measure simple, single variables, we miss the bigger point that we are "dealing with the elephant," as described in our chapter on systems thinking.

We choose tools to make our personal lives richer, more meaningful, and convenient. Tools can help create the values that we deem important. These same choices need to also be available for making our professional lives richer, more meaningful, and more productive.

TOOLS FOR TEAMWORK

From a practical point of view, tools force us to choose between two schools of thought—experiential and reflective thought. Tools for experiential thought provide us with a wide range of sensory stimulation, with enough information provided to minimize the need for logical deduction. The telephone extends our voice as well as letting us hear spoken words from hundreds or even thousands of miles away. Similarly, tools for reflective thought need to support the exploration of ideas. They need to make it easy for us to compare and evaluate, and to explore alternatives. The criteria given to us by Baldrige and ISO 9000 provide such guidance. In both cases, the tools must be invisible. In other words, they must not get in the way.

Look at the collection of tools in a typical school principal's office. The principal sits behind his desk with a chair for visitors. On the desk stand the ubiquitous tools of his trade—the phone, the calendar, in and out baskets, pencils and pens, paper clips, rubber bands, a stapler, a letter opener, and the personal computer with a collection of software packages. Not far away stands a family photo as a morale booster. Nearby is a file cabinet and reams of paper. The successful principal has ready access to a secretary and other tools, and can schedule a conference room when needed.

Individuals need tools to support their work, but there is nothing in the typical school, however, to support collaboration. Simple synchronization and cooperation do not necessarily call for much brainpower. Ants cooperate in an impressive variety of tasks and not through any conscious desire to work together. Similarly, birds flying in a V-shaped formation or schools of fish darting this way and that do not result from any knowledge, but rather individual responses to the situation. Still, it shows how hardwired behaviors can lead to sophisticated behavior.

True cooperative behavior calls for some sort of shared knowledge and a conscious desire to cooperate. Quality collaboration, the kinds of efforts that have resulted in breakthroughs in science, the arts, and technology, come about with neither frequency nor intensity. Organizations are simply not structured for collaboration.

It is now self-evident that tools play a significant role in shaping the way work gets done. It is not unreasonable to assume that using the proper tools that are designed to encourage collaborative work could similarly motivate people.

Language is a collaborative tool. Indeed, language is at the core of virtually all the tools one finds in the typical office—the phone, the copier, the dictating machine, and the word processor. Without language, these tools are mute. Most people can speak a language fluently, but it takes care, craftsmanship, and sincerity to speak in a way that consistently evokes understanding and commitment. Most people aspire to a high level of expression, and they need tools to help them achieve their aspiration.

Under these circumstances, language is more than a medium of communication. It needs to be the main tool for collaboration. Language augments collaborative relationships. To understand and appreciate that, one needs to better understand and appreciate the role of language.

The virtue of good tools is that they don't ask you to become someone else. They invite you to create an extension of yourself. With a little time and skill, good tools let you be more than what you are. Tools are a medium for self-expression.

Tools designed to support collaboration, as personified in the winning prescription, are qualitatively different. Application of such award-winning collaborative tools as total quality management (TQM), Baldrige quality education criteria, and ISO 9000 education standards are qualitatively different. They are vastly different from the array of tools provided to support individuals in a school building, and as well they should be.

Developing a School Quality Accountability Program

In recent years, total quality management (TQM), Koality Kids (KK), and Baldrige took center stage as a popular means of achieving school organizational transformation of the HRO. While the TQM and Baldrige models are sound in theory, they fall short and are at risk in long-term practice. Each relies on good management intentions for achievement and follow-through. TQM, KK, and Baldrige fail to provide the HRO with the internal and independent external auditing necessary to meet the measures for continuous quality improvement. The accountability program for schools based on implementing the winning prescription of Baldrige *and* ISO criteria combined brings a solid set of "tools" to achieve measurable quality objectives:

- to help educators achieve measurable quality in schools;
- to help school districts build capacity to assess progress and involve its educational stakeholders in the process;
- to motivate policymakers and the public to support measurable quality;
- to reach beyond assessment standards; to view accountability as a reciprocal path rather than a one-way street (for example, the second grade teacher who sees herself as accountable for results to the third grade teacher);
- to foster collaborative work, to rethink measurable quality, to build capacity for continuous improvement, to actively involve the public;
- to initiate and conduct research, analyze and spread findings on best practices;
- to join forces with the organizations working to improve quality in learning and to apply such knowledge to the local school; and
- to link these efforts, to multiply results to produce better quality schools and school districts.

The accountability program that is built into the winning prescription uses applied research and best-practices benchmarking for schools. It applies proven planning standards and quality processes to identify the knowledge, skills, and tools needed to teach more effectively. Our message is about the means to achieve measurable quality for continuous improvement in schools. The focus of the accountability program includes:

Visioning. The program builds awareness of school results improvement by practical examples. It stirs up the dormant skills in teachers and parents. It combines these with the practical needs of employers. The winning prescription accountability program does not try to solve all school problems. It builds a healing process based on needs, and does so one school at a time.

Goal setting. The program focuses the educational stakeholder on what they need to know about school quality, the facts related to classroom practice, and sets priorities to match classroom needs. The program shows how to shape state and local policies to achieve reliable classroom quality. This process uses proven tools to help the school's teachers and district leaders raise its sights.

Using the ISO Organizing System and Baldrige Quality Criteria. The program trains educators in using tools to bridge the gap between policy and practice. The program offers the means for training internal peer auditors and bringing an independent ISO registrar to the school. The program organizes the links between businesses and schools through a partnership to better deliver a "fully prepared" graduate to the workplace. The winning prescription encourages partner schools to apply ISO methods for meeting Baldrige criteria.

The HRO comes about through the proper use of the winning prescription, including the tools of ISO 9000 and Baldrige Quality criteria. When we look at applicants for the Baldrige National Quality Award or one of the forty-four state quality awards based on Baldrige criteria, we quickly find that a surprising number of them eventually apply for ISO certification. There are two reasons for this. First, they need to be world-ready as suppliers of products and services. Second, they recognize that ISO 9000 standards and the Baldrige Quality Award criteria are two nonduplicating ends to the same goal that can be called a total quality commitment. The HRO framework for adopting and applying Baldrige and ISO standards uses the following input:

1. An HRO school will communicate a clear mission and achievable goals to its staff and stakeholders, and passionately focus on seeing that they are actually achieved.

2. Staff in HRO schools show a strong sense that their main mission is helping all students achieve the standards reflected by the objectives.
3. High reliability in classroom teaching is literally built on the use of good practice as standard operating practice.
4. High-reliability organizations obsess over the quality of their workplace processes and insist on taking steps to continuously improve them.
5. HROs use a standard operating practice in dealing with employees, utilizing both procedural and substantive due process.
6. HROs pay strict attention to daily functioning. They are alert to small failures and lapses.

Our objective in applying the winning prescription is not to discover defects. We want to uncover the processes that lead to defects. Using our prescription helps uncover and prevent problems before they lead to undesirable consequences. Applying the winning prescription criteria through Baldrige and ISO 9000 ensures school and classroom reliability.

The education criteria of the winning prescription are built upon a set of core values and concepts. These values and concepts are the foundation for developing and integrating all requirements. Quoting an important core value from the Baldrige Criteria for Education:

Learning-centered education places the focus of education on learning and the real needs of students. Such needs derive from the requirements of the marketplace and the responsibilities of citizenship. Changes in technology and in the national and world economies are creating increasing demands on employees to become knowledge workers and problem solvers, keeping pace with the rapid changes in the marketplace. Most analysts conclude that schools of all types need to focus more on students' active learning and on the development of problem-solving skills.

Schools exist primarily to develop the fullest potential of all students, affording them opportunities to pursue a variety of avenues to success. A learning-centered school needs to fully understand and translate marketplace and citizenship requirements into appropriate curricula. Education offerings need to be built around learning effectiveness. Teaching effectiveness needs to stress promotion of learning and achievement.

The Baldrige Criteria for Education lay out the importance of the *how* word in the following manner:

> Items requesting information on approach include areas that begin with the word "how." Responses should outline key process information such as methods, measures, deployment, and evaluation/improvement/learning factors. Responses lacking such information, or merely providing an example, are referred to in the Scoring Guidelines as *anecdotal information*.
>
> It is important to give basic information about what the key processes are and how they work. Although it is helpful to include who performs the work, merely stating who does not permit feedback. For example, stating that "student satisfaction data are analyzed by the student advisors" does not permit feedback, because from this information, strengths and weaknesses in the analysis cannot be given.
>
> Does the response show a systematic approach, or does it merely provide an example (an anecdote)?

THE WINNING PRESCRIPTION IS BASED ON SOLUTION TALK

Problems such as conflicts, symptoms, or difficulties are often problems in language. By this we mean they are caught, retained, and maintained through communications formulae that seal off alternatives, block the way out, and rob authorship.

The riddle of the problem is most often solved not from within its formulation, but through a back door that opens to new ways of describing it. This also opens the doorway to exploring novel solutions.

Conversations take place in a shared time/space of the common language-in-action. This is the locus of consensus. Solution talk is sharply different from problem talk. Sometimes problems are maintained simply by the fact that people think and talk about them excessively—and incessantly.

Even though solution talk tends to focus on the future rather than the past, this does not mean that the talking about the past should become a forbidden or even an undesirable topic. The past does not need to be discussed as a source of troubles, but it needs to be looked upon as a resource. One can learn to see past misfortunes as ideals that, in addition to having caused suffering, have also brought about something valuable and worthwhile.

Adverse life events (even victimization) can later, in hindsight, be seen as valuable leaning experiences, but it should be emphasized that this does not in any way justify violence, abuse, or neglect. The metaphor of the healing of bones is useful here. Even if fractured bones may sometimes become stronger after healing, it does not justify fracturing bones. However strong a bone may become from recovering from an accidental fracture, we do all in our power to protect others and ourselves from such injury.

The act of connecting problems to one another or seeing them as causing each other often interferes with a person's ability to maintain his or her optimism or creativity. When multiple difficulties exist, seeing each problem as an independent element with a life of its own allows people to consider the possibility that progress in dealing with one problem may help to solve another.

The way we explain problems and the actions we take to solve them are tightly interconnected. It is not only that a particular explanation leads to certain kinds of solutions, but also that particular solutions reflect certain types of explanations. A change in the way we explain a problem tends to result in a change in the way in which we attempt to solve it and vice versa.

Explanations differ in the extent to which they attribute blame and elicit shame. Therefore, some explanations are better than others in fostering collaboration and creativity. When it appears that current explanations impede finding solutions, the replacement of those explanations with new ones can be useful. There are multiple ways of explaining a particular piece of behavior.

Rather than instructing people what to think about the cause of their problem, it is better to tell them a story that portrays the idea, or to invite them to become a partner in the search for more fruitful explanations. Bringing out several explanations rather than suggesting only one reminds a colleague (as well as ourselves) about the importance of keeping an open mind.

IS SCHOOL REALLY SO DIFFERENT FROM BUSINESS?

The Baldrige Award for Education identifies the subjects of competitive factors and strategic context as issues for school planning. How can an institution that is a legislatively mandated monopoly have any competition? In what way does the school have strategic context? It's clear that no business would survive without comprehensively answering these questions. What about the school?

The public school has been under attack for more than two decades. During Allen's tenure as a board member in Plainfield, N.J., one out of five school-age children living in the city was enrolled in private or parochial school, at parental expense. In recent years, the national political agenda has promoted the debate over school vouchers for alternate schooling.

The vouchers approach was started to bring about competitive pressure on the public school monopoly, and to force improvement on the public schools. Another competitive proposal is charter schools, which are intended to promote innovation and experimentation in public schools. Home schooling, available more and more through distance learning, is beginning to be advocated by parents unhappy with the experiences of their students in the local public school district.

These are just a few of the changes influencing school competition. Each new situation is certain to squeeze the public school for improved results. Concentrated programs are the mainstay of alternative education. By veering away from the "general curriculum," the alternative school offers real competition to the public entities. The school district needs to assess these needs with an open mind, and face the facts of why this is happening. Only then can the public schools determine how to improve their offering to students.

More than ever, school administrators and teachers need to put their collective thoughts together. The strategic context for the public school is a new agenda, and for this, the public school needs new thinking. The school needs to identify and enter new markets and market segments. In school language, this means adding such programs that may include internships and apprenticeships.

First, the school must accept the fact that the ultimate customer of the school is the employer. Next, the teacher needs firsthand experience in the world of work for which they are preparing their students. The sooner this can happen in a teacher's working life cycle, the better prepared they can be. The student learns the values of the work ethic in the early grades. By high school, these habits are set, both good and poor.

Admittedly, private and parochial schools have more chance to introduce and work with new technologies. They can practice service innovation in order to attract new students to their enrollment. The nonpublic school has greater freedom to form strategic alliances and cooperative efforts with employers, but this need not be the only way.

Every community has employers, both large and small, who are involved in some way with quality awards, including the state quality standards, Baldrige, and ISO 9000. In one mostly rural county, the authors found more than a half-dozen employers of all sizes who had already complied with ISO 9000 standards. In fact, one company proudly displayed a large banner on their fence reading ISO 9001. The more you venture into this subject, the more you'll discover that this quality stuff is no longer any great mystery.

STICKING TO THE WINNING PRESCRIPTION

Prescription #1: Continuous Dosages of Leadership

If there is one ingredient essential to the success of any organization, it is leadership. Drucker reminds us "If an enterprise fails to perform, we rightly hire not different workers, but a new president" (Drucker 1973).

The leadership of the public school district is placed with a board of education. The board has ultimate responsibility, by law, for the conduct of the school organization in its dealings with employees, suppliers, customers, and the public. The most important board responsibility is to ensure the quality of the active management. In any discussion of school leadership, the board is included as part of top management. Over the long run, and because they choose to support or thwart the school operating executives, the board ultimately determines the success or failure of the school organization.

The process of changing an organization begins with those who make policy and financial decisions. It begins at the top. The first criterion of the winning prescription—leadership—is an outline of how the top transforms itself and how a school system thinks about and performs its services to meet customer needs.

The quality of classroom teaching isn't unreliable because of Murphy's Law. Quality experts remind us that only 6 percent of the problems in an organization's performance can be blamed on isolated problems or poor workers. Fully 94 percent is a direct consequence of a poorly performing system, controlled and maintained by the top leadership. Teachers and principals, the frontline employees and midlevel managers in the public schools, working alone, do not have much chance to make changes against a stubborn and tradition-encrusted organization.

This first criterion addresses this dimension of the David-and-Goliath scenario. It brings frontline and midlevel persons around to a common theme of reaching reliable classroom quality in pursuit of satisfying customer needs. Achieving reliable quality in classroom teaching is a radical shift from a defensive to an offensive strategy. To manage that shift requires top leadership with courage and security.

This transformation in the school requires leaders who are facilitators. They must encourage the flow of improvement knowledge from the bottom as well as from the top. New skills have to be learned by all. Major financial decisions need to be made. Old habits need to be broken and new ways mastered.

Such a change can safely be predicted to result in a period of turmoil. Change of this sort demands a steady and enlightened hand at the wheel of this sailing ship to keep everyone in the boat and on course. Leaders must demonstrate that they are in control, and that they have the vision of where the school organization is headed.

The winning prescription calls for leadership qualities to be developed by anyone at any level in the school. One of the major roles of senior administrators needs to be directed at this very thing. The criteria are directed at exploring the actions of the highest-ranking officials in the district through an inquiry centered on four dimensions:

1. Personal involvement
2. The leadership system for promoting reliable quality
3. Integrating staff into the vision and use of good practices
4. How leadership performs in the world of the stakeholders

These criteria recognize that management behavior and actions register a far greater impact on employee behavior than policies, memos, rules, and suggestions. The winning prescription asks school leadership to look critically at how and if senior administrators are actively and personally involved in quality-related activities. To satisfy this criterion, a school leader must be out front as a role model for motivating people, problem solving, and helping improve processes. Optimism is a necessity, not an option.

Employees need to be shown, not just told, that reliable classroom teaching time comes first. The challenge to school leaders is to find ways to make clear this highest priority so that it influences all school operating procedures and the traditional habits that school employees normally count on.

Quality activities are time consuming and they require shifts in personal priorities. The problem is not one of finding more time, even though most leaders' schedules are already fully loaded. The challenge is reallocating time to pursue the central purposes of quality.

Senior school administrators play a major role outside the organization. They have the task of making sure that all those in their organization understand the important needs of school stakeholders. Schools need support from the larger constituencies of public interests to allow the district to prosper.

The winning prescription not only asks how leaders communicate reliable quality to employees. It wants to know the other half of the story as well. How do the employees accept and perform the quality message? These criteria seek more than words and promises; they expect hard data. The school must show that it has created a working feedback loop for quality control to measure its progress in meeting their own goals.

Prescription #2: Looking Forward with Strategic Planning

The strategic planning standard asks school leadership and staff to examine how goals and plans are formulated. How are these strategies used throughout the school and school system? The questions to be answered run along these lines:

- By what process and methods do you develop the improvement strategies and the action plans to fulfill them?
- What specific action steps do you need to take to achieve dependable and durable (that is, reliable) quality in teaching time?
- How do you get the participation of all administrators, staff, and support persons involved in quality planning and working together on the same broad objectives? How do you involve the board and other stakeholders?

- Specifically, what are the short-term goals? The long-term goals? The plans to ensure reliable quality in classroom teaching performance?

In response to this criterion, school leadership must demonstrate a disciplined, process-oriented, customer-driven approach to quality planning. The ideal school organization fuses together their financial, operational, and quality planning to identify and measure reliable teaching time objectives. Financial planning and classroom quality planning are two faces of the same coin.

Quality planning demands rigor and detail, much like that in a budgeting process. Everyone in the school organization from superintendent and principals to teachers and custodians need to be involved. When this approach is taken, the school and school system take the necessary actions. It directly links strategic plans (what to improve) with process capabilities (how to improve).

Schools know their strategic plans are useful when:

- Employees know the school's short- and long-term quality initiatives thoroughly and where their objectives fit in;
- Valuable data is collected and then used;
- Plans confront and root out failure in all functional areas, including classroom teaching support;
- The school consciously plans for continuous improvement through understanding and use of measurable approaches to quality; and
- Episodic and narrowly focused plans are replaced by bold quality initiatives.

Prescription #3: Focus on Student and Stakeholder Needs

This element examines how the school determines requirements, expectations, and preferences of its students and stakeholders. Also examined is how the school builds relationships with students and stakeholders and determines their satisfaction. (Baldrige Education Criteria 1998)

The student and parent are the school's customer. The school must focus on creating a learning organization that understands, cares about, and works for the student and parent. In the school, where this customer-centered mission becomes a clear and continuous purpose, the standards are known and the teachers work together to form an aligned instructional program.

Teachers are skilled in the classroom processes. These processes enable teachers to predict in advance and act quickly on the impact of their methods. This increases student achievement. Victoria Bernhardt (1994) makes a case for the power of this winning prescription criterion to defeat the tyranny of chance when she writes:

> Until teachers are able to predict the impact of their actions on students, change their actions based on these predictions, corroborate the effect of these actions with students, and work with peers to build a comprehensive learning organization, any increases in student achievement and changes in the classroom will be temporary. (Bernhardt 1994)

Through the information and analysis criterion, the school leadership assembles the data to better understand the student population. The student and stakeholder element excites the commitment of the entire school to find out and act on:

- the identification of students in terms of their needs and how they learn best;
- the impact of processes both those used and those that should be used; and,
- the essential student achievements.

Essential student achievements. These achievements are the classroom teacher targets. Essential student achievements come from asking such questions as: What will these students eventually face? What is it going to be like when they get there in the real world? What must we make sure the students can do by the time they get there? Students need objectives for future successful careers and a quality of life.

For a specific career, the learning objectives come from a model of the situation in which the graduate will use the performances he has learned. This is the model of the trade or professional school, but elementary and secondary school education is not employment. Here we find a different situation. The behaviors to be learned are someday to be applied in a wide variety of life situations. Trying to identify and analyze all possible life situations in which students may find themselves is an enormous and impractical task. Therefore, it is necessary for us to turn to a different type of model—a developmental model.

A developmental model. The new model is a developmental one. It assumes that there are six areas of human behavior capable of being developed. These are not always independent from each other, but at times they may overlap or interrelate. The six areas are (1) intellectual, (2) communicative, (3) social, (4) emotional, (5) learning, and (6) physical. The school needs to be concerned with organizing learning situations that develop these six behaviors in various ways that also permit them to be used in life outside the school.

Intellectual development. Aptitude and ability testing have identified a large number of talents. Some educators suggest that there are as many as 120 different intellectual abilities. A smaller set of seven or eight have been identified for many years. Among these are the commonly referred to verbal, comprehension, word fluency, numerical, reasoning, spatial visualization, spatial orientation, and perceptual speed.

We are suggesting that the school can design explicit methods, materials, and procedures for deliberately practicing the abilities required for intellectual development. There is persuasive evidence that this is now feasible.

Communication skills development. What distinguishes the student from the pet dog or cat is the ability to communicate in a variety of ways. The skills he needs to develop are those of sending (or transmitting) and receiving in a variety of media. The school must develop students who can write correctly and clearly, in a form appropriate to the communication, and if need be, with art and beauty.

The school should try to develop students who can read with high speed, who can read as fast as those who have taken speed-reading courses. The student should be able to read graphs, charts, and tables of data. The student should be able to speak his or her mind clearly and with clarity, without becoming nervous or getting stage fright. He should be able to communicate with both verbal and quantitative symbols.

Social development. There is an enormous range of social skills that could be developed into a ladder of objectives. Teachers might begin with the simplest forms of cooperation and peaceful competition between children, move on to forms of courtesy and politeness desirable in social life, to skills of leadership and followership, up to the skills required to be effective American citizens. Much of what is now taught in social studies could be taught here.

Emotional development. We all know people who bear the scars of emotional injuries or inadequate emotional development. The amount of time and energy devoted to try and heal these scars is enormous. Instead of investing vast amounts of effort in attempts to set right what has gone wrong, we need to try not to let it go wrong in the first place.

The student can be taught such skills as the socially acceptable ways for releasing aggression, ways of dealing with fear, how to recognize when another person is having an emotional problem, and how to help that person overcome his difficulty.

Skill development. We live in anything but stable times. In a stable society, there is little need for a high degree of skill in learning. There is a finite amount of material to be learned and it does not change. However, you and the student both know that this is not the kind of world in which we are living, nor is it the kind of world in which anyone is likely to be living for a long period of time. We have repeatedly stressed that technological change is occurring at such a pace that many people will have to learn at least two different occupations during their working life. It probably goes without saying that the person who can learn most rapidly will have an enormous advantage.

It is possible for the school to teach the student the skills of effective learning and problem solving. There are self-instructional programs that teach students to ask questions. These students make higher scores than other students on a science achievement test and, in turn, are rated higher in classroom participation.

Physical development. Physical development is the final area with which we are concerned. Athletic performance should emphasize using skills to achieve significant purposes. For example, students should be taught sports, such as swimming or tennis, which they could pursue through most of their life. They should be taught exercises which could be used to build up or slim down specific parts of the body. The more active forms of dancing could serve as both athletic and social performances. Of course, there should be instruction in knowledge about the body, its functions, and how to stay healthy.

Prescription #4: Using Information and Analysis to Improve Decision Making

The winning prescription looks to appropriate and reliable data as the lifeblood of the school's pursuit of its objectives. Absent an effective system of data collection and analysis, school leadership simply cannot know how their teaching time (their time in front of students) is performing, what progress has been made on their vision, and what needs improving.

Currently, data collection and analysis is the weakest link in public education. It is the rare school or school system that gathers and analyzes relevant data about its processes, complaints, and results for the purpose of fostering change and continuous improvement. Most often, data is collected in response to state or legal mandates. Schools need to collect performance data that can be aggregated and looked at over time to spot important trends. It is important to also look for patterns in the data, not just data at fixed points in time.

The school that collects and uses reliable data can soon perform frequent evaluations. It can continually validate its data and information bases. It will then actively analyze and use the data to improve its planning, its day-to-day decision making, and its improvement processes. In short, this winning prescription element helps foster a school or school district that manages by fact, not by assumption or bias. It is a school and school district that is well on its way to meeting or exceeding world-class benchmarks.

Schools that fall short or would fail on this criterion are easily identified and are found everywhere. They neither adequately collect nor analyze data. They do not even attempt to benchmark those schools that perform better within their same school system. They lack the most rudimentary statistical orientation for quality. Their leadership and management style is strongly reactive. They are on top of things and engaged full-time in "stamping out fires." The tyranny of chance feeds on such a situation.

Once again, in the school, the primary focus of data collection and analysis should be on prevention of student failure and the enhancement of student and teacher mastery. Spending time early on prevention reduces the amount of time, effort, and expense that comes later. For each process—from teaching to safety to school climate—data collection efforts need to focus on key control points. It is up to staff to define those control points as crucial junctures where something is likely to go wrong, or where factors exist that usually are fraught with variation.

The prevention-based approach to data collection means designing and implementing a measurement control device at the earliest monitoring point. It can provide an early alert so that teachers, parents, and administrators can take corrective action swiftly.

Prescription #5: Focusing on Faculty and Staff Needs

A healthy and happy employee is more apt to be a productive employee. This credo could well serve as the catchphrase on a winning prescription banner. It suitably describes the spirit behind this prescription. It is the school system that defines employee satisfaction. How the school system uses this definition in practice determines the quality of work life.

Fair-treatment procedures, for example, are generally recognized as a key factor. Fairness affirms the employee's right to appeal an issue through a review by higher administrative levels. It provides feedback to administrators and the school board regarding policies and operations as well as statistics for trend analysis.

Proper recognition of employee achievements is essential to the quality process. Recognition reinforces reliable quality objectives. It encourages staff to cultivate creativity above and beyond the expectations of their typical job performance. It is hard to develop fair systems that balance individual and group recognition. Quality winners have approached performance in a variety of ways. Chief among these is employee involvement and empowerment. The employee needs interest and sense of ownership in his job in order to improve performance. Indeed, this is the best way to ensure that school employees perceive the approach to be fair and meaningful.

Involvement and a sense of ownership are effective tools. First of all, it is superb training. It creates a pool of talent by training the frontline staff of teachers and principals in problem solving and decision making. Empowerment does not mean employees run the show. A good system requires tracking and evaluation based on measurement. Questionnaires and interviews that get at such topics include "listening to my ideas" and "decision-making authority on the job."

Baldrige judges and ISO auditors look for evidence of process and continuous improvement in a systematic effort by the school and school system. They search for increased staff participation in reliable quality-improvement efforts. Every method should have its own set of indicators and be tracked to ensure that stated objectives and benchmarks are met. The idea is to monitor the system and measure its effectiveness. In work team formation, for example, the school should know how many teams have been implemented. With a suggestion system, there should be a measure of the number of suggestions per year and how many got implemented.

Employee involvement is a major buzz phrase in education, but how one gets beyond the slogan is challenging. There are many methods for getting faculty and staff to participate. One of the best is to involve them in teams. The team concept gives groups of workers the chance and authority to identify problems and opportunities. It helps uncover where and why processes go wrong. It collectively develops and tests proposed solutions. It seeks to implement those improvements that show promise of working. Teams give individuals the opportunities to help solve problems they could not solve on their own.

The underlying spirit of this winning prescription is optimism with experience. Optimism is not naïve, but practical. It shows that all employees want to contribute to the school's success and do good work. Further, optimism confirms that given the tools, the training, and responsibility, employees will respond with intelligence and innovation. Optimism is not an option.

Prescription #6: Actively Pursue Performance Results

The relentless focus on continually improving processes is directly related to the solid research-based knowledge that processes are the "royal road" to excellent results. If the first five criteria of the winning prescription are functioning correctly, the school is exhibiting the expected quality characteristics. The school is now a reliable school. It is prevention-based; uses appropriate tools, techniques, and methods; and is systematic in its attention to process improvement. Each system—from classroom instruction to transportation and budgeting to logistical support of teaching—is aligned. The school is now thoroughly process-oriented.

Results are the bottom line of the sixth criteria. Results neatly summarize the passage from the approach taken to approach execution to final outcomes. A well-documented set of results is the sure sign that the school is ready for continuous improvement.

To assess progress, results are compared against goals. Since quality control is a foundational pillar of the winning prescription. If there are gaps in the trend of results, then school staff learns why and goes on to devise corrective actions to be taken.

If measurement data show progress and evidence of classroom reliability, the systems are in control and producing the desired compliance with state and local standards. The spirit of the winning prescription is now invoked to set even more ambitious improvement plans and goals.

Schools using the winning prescription want to be selective in presenting data to customers and stakeholders. Data needs to show comparisons, be clear and specific, and explain promising as well as adverse trends. In brief:

Be Selective: Explain clearly which key measures are being used. Narrow the number down to the vital few and summarize the rest.

Provide Comparisons: Without comparisons, there are few ways to understand how well or how poorly the school is performing. Use competitive data, benchmarks, and goals as a frame of reference.

Be Clear and Specific: Information should be plainly and concisely presented. Explanations should relate to the data. The data do not all have to be numeric. Awards and recommendations are also appropriate.

Explain Both Positive and Negative Trends: Nobody expects everything to be positive. Adverse trends in results need to be explained and corrective actions taken detailed. Carefully documented results s[ ] telligent planning and action.

A FINAL WORD

How we arrive at our conclusions has a great deal to do with how we eventually create quality schools and the classroom teaching reliability we can count on. A major part of the problem of educating students concerns not only our view of students or teachers or schools or programs, but also more critically our all-but-outdated assumptions about school organization. We continue to argue that all students can learn, all schools can teach them, and that all barriers to reform can be dealt with, but first, we argue that what is needed is to organize ourselves to make that happen.

In our fieldwork, we found many pockets of remarkable children, teachers, schools, and programs that have chalked up success in the face of formidable odds. But to date, we have been unable to produce examples of school systems in which all children learn. If we are to address the learning needs of all children, then entire school buildings and respective systems must achieve levels of quality that exceed the broad-based experiences to date.

Relying on chance is a form of cruelty in education. It is a tyranny that sentences great numbers of students to painful deficiency in what they must learn to be successful. It wastes scarce resources that are solely committed to education. It blocks the path of both systematic and organized efforts to improve quality. In this respect, education continues to stand in its own way.

Today, too much of educational practice in U.S. classrooms is subject to the tyranny of chance, but the good news is that we know a great deal about the theory and the practice of teaching, learning, and management. We are better able to realistically and practically come closer to the ideal of making every student a winner. We have explored the philosophies, the effective tools, and the methods for waging a war on the tyranny of chance in classroom teaching. It applies what has worked ll for more than a decade in business to achieving the winning pre-ption in the public schools tomorrow.

Special Message to the Parents

Children have a natural tendency to explore their environment and to do things for themselves. When parents encourage a child to explore the environment, the child develops a strong sense of competency or self-efficacy and a sense of control. Parents can discourage this sense of competency by not allowing children to do things for themselves. The world-renowned psychologist Rudolf Dreikers said, "Every time you do something for a child that he can do for himself, you are discouraging the child. If you dress children when they can dress themselves, or clean up for them when they can clean up for themselves, you are sending messages of incompetence."

The principal characteristics of the parents of successful children can be classified as "nurturing caregivers" and "teachers." Nurturing caregivers give love, encourage independence, and support the child's goals in school, sports, and hobbies. The emphasis of their nurturing is on commitment, control, and challenge. In that kind of home support setting, the child can experience the world as meaningful, interesting, and challenging.

Loving, caring parents provide the basic conditions for the development of the healthy, hardy person. But love is not enough; parents must also be teachers for their children as witnessed by the following.

Petra Kelly, founder of the West German Green political party, states:

> I was raised until age thirteen by my grandmother, Omi. An anti-fascist both prior to and during the time of Hitler, she has always been a very courageous woman who, as a war widow, learned to live without men supporting her. She took care of both my mother and me during the hardest times. When I was six years old, she began reading newspapers and newsmagazines to me, going through them page by page. (Berman 1986)

One of two black female neurosurgeons in the United States in 1986, M. Deborah Hyde-Rowan states:

> My grandmother has been the most influential person in my life. Articulate and dynamic, she became a leader in both church and community. I am convinced that had opportunities for furthering her education been available, she would have been a powerful force in our society. Fortunately for me, she was not only my mentor but my best friend. She constantly told me that I was somebody and could be or do anything on this earth if I would only study hard and keep faith in God. (Berman 1986)

Children learn through the examples of parents, teachers, peers, television heroes, and even fairy-tale characters, but parents play the primary role. Through what they say and what they do, parents teach children how to adapt to the world. It is no surprise to find that robust people have robust parents. Parents of hardy people view life changes as natural and challenging.

Parents of strong people also teach their children to view change as challenge by teaching them skills for confronting new challenges. Many parents of successful executives taught their children how to read a map and get around in a city. Others emphasized learning new activities, such as music, sports, or crafts.

Nurture and healthy modeling from parents are the foundations of psychological health in the child. When absent, the child is at risk. Fortunately, another adult can provide the support. The school is a natural setting for the development of healthy personality characteristics because many of the child's challenges and triumphs are experienced at school. The classroom teacher provides nurture and instruction. By promoting programs that help children develop social skills, stress-management skills, and values, the school system can be a force for health and wellness.

Afterword:
Details of the Achievement of America's First Certified ISO 9000 School System

It takes a village to educate a child, and it took the entire Lancaster community to implement our quality system. To be the first school district in the world to implement the ISO 9001 quality standard required the dedication and support of all our administrators, professional staff, and service staff. In the early stages of our implementation process, it became abundantly clear that quality was everyone's work.

Any successful enterprise must begin with the "end in mind," with what is intended to be accomplished and what results are to be obtained. This simple approach has worked from General Electric to Auntie Anne's Pretzels. Whether it is wanting to be number one in market share for a company's products or to make the best soft pretzel, it is the tenacity and persistence to focus all corporate effort and energy on the intended outcome that has driven success in corporate America.

So it is with education and schools. Clearly, the results that schools are looking for take place in the classroom. The issue of school quality for parents is quite simple. For parents, a school system is only as good "as the teacher my child has this school year." Therefore, the strategic focus for educational quality must be on the parent/student/teacher relationship and on the teaching and learning events and activities of the classroom. Beginning with the "end in mind," successful schools nurture student academic achievement. The instructional processes, support services, and leadership focus must support the classroom teacher, for it is in this environment that students learn and grow into successful adults.

THE CHALLENGE OF BRINGING QUALITY INTO SCHOOLS

Schools are complex social organizations that have many stakeholders and many competing agendas. Within such an environment, it is easy to lose one's focus and apply resources, effort, and energy on planning and programs that do not add value to student success. No matter how great the ability to fund education, no matter how robust the curriculum, no matter how prepared the students are upon arrival, if the system and processes do not focus on students' academic success, schools will fail to meet the learning potential of all students.

For schools to be successful, they must keep focused on their intended result. Schools must remain steadfast in sticking to the important learning and support activities that will result in student success. Powerful entities with new ideas for education can easily take schools off track and move resources, effort, and energy on to activities that may compete with those activities that contribute to the success of students. Charismatic gurus, trendy literature, special interests, and popular rhetoric, though well intended, can lead to school failure. A focus on measuring quality of performance makes districts less susceptible to chasing every whim.

Schools must promote and reward fundamentally sound pedagogical practices. It is an easy trap for school leaders to press for better standardized test scores and not provide the support and resources needed to improve student instruction. Pressuring for higher test scores will merely add to the tension of the school and classroom if principals and teachers are berated. This tension is counterproductive, and although it may result in short-term gains, these gains will not be sustained. By focusing effort on continuous improvement, schools will help ensure student success in the long term. This is what Lessinger and Salowe refer to as "praxis" (what reliably works). The school district of Lancaster utilized research-based "standards in practices" and "content institutes" to ensure the best methods are consistently applied across the entire system. Moreover, the classroom teachers have become the "internal customers," where the school site and central administration serve and support their needs to provide quality instruction.

It was clear to the school district of Lancaster that we needed a quality system that would help us monitor our vision, seek continuous improvement, and endure as personnel change. Within this philosophical framework, the school district of Lancaster implemented and achieved certification to the ISO 9001 quality standard. The structure and discipline of the

ISO quality standard has provided the framework to focus our resources, effort, and energy on our most important clients—America's youth.

WHY WE NEEDED A QUALITY MANAGEMENT SYSTEM

Why Did the School District of Lancaster Choose to Implement a Quality Management System?

While there is no one simple answer, an exploration of the issues the district was facing in 1995 will help the reader understand the very complex answer. School leaders considering the implementation of a quality-management system will find it instructive to understand the circumstances that led Lancaster to choose a quality system never before implemented in a public school system.

Revolution does not occur during a time of comfort and serenity. The need for significant change comes when tension develops and the organization begins questioning the conventional paradigm. In the early to mid-1990s, the school district of Lancaster had all the obvious indicators of tension.

Some prominent sources of tension included the lack of student achievement, significant demographic changes, rapid personnel changes, and a crucial decline in available resources. More specifically:

- Student achievement scores on state-mandated tests and nationally normed exams showed no improvement from year to year, and far too many students were achieving in the lowest quartile.
- Developmental tests of pre-kindergarten and kindergarten children indicated that children entering school were in the thirteenth percentile.
- The number of students with disabilities increased from 1,754 in 1994 to 2,189 in 1998.
- Families of students who qualified for free or reduced lunch increased by 18 percent between 1973 and 1999.
- Non-English-speaking students increased by 42 percent between 1990 and 1999.
- In 1999, twelve of our thirteen elementary schools and two of our four middle schools qualified for Title I federal support.
- District enrollment increased by 812 students from 1990 to 1999.

To make the challenges of increasing enrollment worse, our school buildings averaged sixty-six years old and did not have the infrastructure to support technology and curricular improvements. In the personnel area:

- Negotiated contracts with our bargaining units needed to be competitive to attract and retain quality staff.
- Salaries increased by 73 percent between 1987 and 1994.
- As the district moved from a skills-based curriculum and from an isolated classroom structure to teams of teachers teaching groups of students, there was a significant need to invest in professional training.

Moreover, legislative requirements to support special needs students and additional curricular requirements in health, environment, and technology meant increased investment in staff training. From a resources perspective, the capacity of the district to generate revenue became more restrictive:

- The portion of state funding for public education declined from 42.74 percent to 40.78 percent in 1994.
- The school board and administration recognized that the tax burden the Lancaster community had to shoulder had become a growing factor for people on fixed incomes.
- Private businesses that supported the district tax base moved away as their business needs changed.
- Buildings vacated by relocating businesses were converted to tax-exempt status to support much-needed community services.

The school district of Lancaster has been undergoing major restructuring, driven by the development of our strategic plan. The plan mandates, among other actions, school readiness for our youngest children, improved attendance in school and classes, increased achievement in core subjects, increased achievement in higher-level and externally benchmarked courses, increased rate of graduation, and successful post-high school transition.

Actions Taken

In the process of addressing these issues, we initiated some significant changes in the way we do business. For example, we:

- reconfigured our traditional six-year elementary, three-year junior high, and three-year high school structure to a three-year primary and two-year intermediate program in elementary schools, a three-year middle school program, and a four-year high school program, which included two years of specialized preparation for post-high school choices,
- added an International Baccalaureate program,
- created partnerships with the community college to provide motivated students an opportunity to earn early college credit,
- expanded kindergarten from half-day to full day,
- revised the core curriculum and adopted content and performance standards,
- transitioned from centralized decision making to site-based decision making,
- replaced traditional summer school make-up and enrichment programs with extended learning time for students who had not mastered required core curriculum and standards during the regular school year,
- shifted focus from administrators as supervisors of teachers to supporters of teachers,
- restructured Office of Curriculum and Instruction to the Office of Teaching and Learning,
- replaced content area supervisors with instructional facilitators,
- established teams of teachers responsible for student learning,
- eliminated social promotion, and
- implemented new teaching strategies to improve teacher effectiveness and student achievement.

All of these research-based changes are being implemented as a means of keeping the promise of our strategic plan—that all students will achieve at high levels—a promise we made to all stakeholders in the school district of Lancaster. With so many major changes occurring simultaneously in the short span of a few years and with so many people involved or affected, addressing the question of bringing on line a quality management system seemed reasonable if not imperative.

Other external factors also influenced our decision to institute a quality management system. The school district of Lancaster, comprised of Lancaster City and Lancaster Township, has a static tax base, a fact that demands quality assurance of operating efficiencies within our financial limitations. Lancaster's population is increasingly diverse and our demographics are ever changing. Currently, Lancaster school enrollment is 45 percent Hispanic, 30 percent Caucasian, 22 percent African American, and 3 percent Asian.

Fifty-one percent of Lancaster students receive free or reduced lunches, and 50 percent of our schools receive schoolwide support from the Title I allocation because poverty, an increasing trend, is concentrated in certain areas of the district. These factors challenge us to provide the same high-quality education for all, and to have in place standards to ensure high-quality teaching and learning.

What Changed?

Once a monopoly, public schools can no longer rely on compulsory education laws and government funding to justify their existence and to guarantee their survival. We must compete for students and for dollars with private schools, home schools, and charter schools, and vouchers have become a concern to many supporters of public school education. To survive in this competitive environment, public schools must demonstrate that students exit their systems as well prepared as or better than students exiting other schools.

Leon Lessinger and Allen Salowe observed in *Game Time: The Educator's Playbook for the New Global Economy* (1997) that after the family, schools are the most important institution and potential influence on the future of students in the workforce. It falls on the schools, then, to teach the skills and knowledge necessary to continue leading the global economy. Producing competent thinkers, problem solvers, and decision makers is in our best national interest. The most wealthy and powerful nations of the world are transitioning from an industrial economy to a knowledge economy, one in which wealth and power are determined by the optimal use of human skill and intellect. As the knowledge economy emerges, the number of well-paying, lower-skill jobs will decline; the need for increased skills and knowledge for higher-paying jobs will increase. The long-term value of any current store of knowledge will decline, and the need to learn how to learn will become the number one job priority (Lessinger and Salowe 1997). These are compelling reasons for us to set high standards for student achievement and to ensure that the standards are met through a system of quality processes. The confluence of all of these issues made the need for efficiency and accountability mandatory. The school district of Lancaster needed a quality system.

WHY WE OPTED FOR ISO 9001 AS OUR QUALITY MANAGEMENT SYSTEM

ISO 9001 is a series of process-oriented standards developed by the International Organization for Standards based in Geneva, Switzerland, and used in more than 130 countries worldwide for the past twenty years. Although ISO 9001 originated as a business-oriented model, its recent expansion into the service sector demonstrates that the quality-management and quality-awareness issues facing businesses are similar to those facing schools. Lancaster is the proving ground where the ISO standards were tested and found to be effective.

Strength of Independent Auditing

ISO 9001 requires that accredited third-party independent auditors maintain standards of quality through periodic, usually yearly, surveillance audits. The third-party independent registrar can withdraw certification if continuous improvement is not demonstrated. To maintain registration compliance to the established processes, measurement of goals and objectives, and demonstrated continuous improvement are necessary. Clearly, the quality system needs to be fully institutionalized to be effective. The senior leadership must actively promote and support participation in the compliance and corrective action aspects of the system. In implementing corrective actions, we had difficulty convincing staff to analyze the "root cause" of system problems. As an organization, we had become so proficient at "putting out fires" that we collectively resisted root cause analysis. Putting out fires was a part of our work culture; and we were good at it. Up to this point, no one considered if our comfort with "putting out fires" led to improving our system or processes.

The ISO 9001 quality standard has many elements that help ensure schools achieve compliance and vibrancy.

- The Internal Audit element defines a process for the system to monitor itself through periodic internal audits.
- The Management Review element provides the district leadership with feedback on the continuing suitability and effectiveness of the quality system.
- The Corrective and Preventive Action element ensures that a continuous feedback loop is maintained.

This continuous feedback loop encourages every employee to complete a corrective action if he or she sees a function within the system is not working. The request for corrective action, whether it comes from a custodian, a groundskeeper, a secretary, a principal, or a teacher, must be answered. The loop is always closed. Therein lies another value of ISO 9001. The quality system must be sustained and improved through leadership changes, staff changes, and community changes. Adhering to procedures can change the processes but the requirements to keep the integrity of the standards must be maintained.

Staff turnover and the atrophy of quality system skills provide a challenge for the system to keep all employees at the required levels of competence. This means quality training must continue after the system has been established. The school district of Lancaster countered these challenges by planning new employee induction presentations, introductory quality system workshops, initial internal auditor training, and intermediate internal auditor training. Additionally, all district schools and departments requested quality system familiarization presentations for on-site staff development. These formal methods of training provided forums for discussion regarding system changes and improvements.

ISO 9001 does not prescribe the design and delivery of instruction. Decisions regarding these are left to the professional educators. It does provide the framework for appropriate design and adoption criteria to ensure decisions are well researched and representative of the school community. In addition, it provides a framework that disciplines the school system to meet certain requirements in processes and accountability. It is an ongoing process, not a product. For example, our school district has designed core content standards identifying the essential components of our curriculum. Additionally, schools adopted *New Standards* for reading and writing instruction, *Everyday Math* for math instruction; *New Standards Reference Exams* for assessing student progress, and locally designed on-demand assessments for assessing instruction. Essentially, the ISO 9001 standard provides the discipline to ensure established procedures are solidly focused on student needs.

By earning the right to fly the ISO 9001 flag, we improved rapport and credibility with the business community. The business community values the discipline and accountability we have established to meet our responsibilities as a world-class learning institution. However, the notion of school as a business is a difficult concept for many educators who passionately believe public education is not a business. When confronted with many excellent arguments as to why we are not a business, we indicated that the school district of Lancaster operated with a $90 million annual budget, maintained twenty school plants, served more meals than the largest restaurant in the county, and is the eighth largest employer in the county. Whether you view public education as a business or not, few will disagree that quality business practices are an important component of any effective organization.

HOW WE GOT STAKEHOLDERS TO BUY INTO THE PROCESS

Convincing the board of school directors to approve our adoption of ISO proved to be no problem. They recognized the benefits of improved management, improved teaching and learning, and improved accountability. Among their membership were two executives of ISO-certified private manufacturing companies who contributed their expertise to promote ISO 9001.

Parents, once they understood the benefits of ISO certification to their children, offered no resistance; and taxpayers, who saw it as a step toward fiscal responsibility, were elated. The business community, the Chamber of Commerce, and service organizations such as Kiwanis and Rotary clubs applauded our initiative.

Employees Were the Toughest Challenge

Acceptance was most difficult among employees who voiced legitimate concerns. How can we manage another major initiative on top of all the other major changes we're already making? Our plates are piled too high! The task was clear—convince the naysayers that the ISO process would make their jobs more manageable and ultimately take some of the pile off the plate.

After a few false starts, our strategy moved from a philosophy of ideas to implementing practical tasks that people could do, for example, housecleaning obsolete documents. We believed that helping skeptics understand how ISO 9001 relates specifically to their jobs would make them more likely to embrace the framework. To this end, we scheduled a series of meetings with small groups of personnel with similar responsibilities, for example, the dozen or so people responsible for curriculum development. We posed the question, "What is the process by which you develop curriculum in the district?" As they answered the question, we documented and analyzed the process. What can be improved? Does everything pass the "common sense test?" Does the process add value to the curriculum? The analysis helped to identify weaknesses in the process and areas we needed to change.

The review and approval procedure, for example, was found to be overly cumbersome, so the curriculum experts changed it. The result of this small group strategy was that the participants saw themselves empowered to make critical decisions about their areas of responsibility. More importantly, in the first year of our curriculum reform initiative, the ISO model for 4.4 Design Control began to pay dividends. Our feedback loops from teachers indicated that changes were necessary to improve the value and use of our curriculum.

Teachers Show Leadership

A series of teacher-initiated corrective action requests led to adjustments to our curriculum procedures. These corrective actions provided the input for planning important curriculum changes. The ISO model provided the framework for the changes and improvements to our curriculum. Additionally, the process of involving the staff in the curriculum restructuring required staff development training in the most current research and literature on curriculum and instruction. This effort provided the rich and deep curriculum and the foundation for building staff capacity in quality pedagogy. Meetings with other small groups had the same positive outcome.

We knew that gaining the support of the leadership of the unions representing teachers and service staff was imperative if the quality systems initiative was to succeed. It was important to involve them early on, but we learned this more by chance than by design. The first internal quality audit conducted was at the elementary school where the president of the teachers' union taught. As luck would have it, he was first on the list prepared by the principal of staff members to be interviewed. Realizing that his support could be gained or lost in this interview, we approached it with some trepidation. Fortunately, the interview went well; he saw the quality-assurance framework as an opportunity for greater teacher empowerment and he became an advocate of the initiative. We learned later that he got to all the other teachers on the list to be interviewed before we did and told them, "It's okay!"

As our team of internal auditors became more proficient, our staff became more and more comfortable with the audit process. Staff soon learned that the internal audit process is not intended to audit people. It is focused on auditing the system and seeking methods to improve our processes and effectiveness. With this important understanding, trust and confidence grew in the audit process. This resulted in more valuable and focused internal quality audits. Our auditors began looking for consistency and reliability in our system across the entire district. When we began the internal audit process, compliance to the ISO 9001 standard was observed. With improvements and maturity of the quality system, we looked for compliance to our district quality manual and procedures. We have now reached the stage where our internal auditors will observe our progress in implementing our strategic plan.

It is important to point out that I disagreed with our ISO consultant, who was adamant that we begin our internal audits immediately. I wondered how he could suggest that we begin auditing before we had fully implemented our quality system. He assured me it would be okay and I reluctantly complied saying, "The internal audits would not work at this early stage of our implementation process."

Needless to say, I ate my words. Audits turned out to be the best way to implement the quality system. The internal audits energized our quality system, involved more people in a meaningful way, and provided our school leadership with feedback on the extent of the implementation and areas where more training was needed. While I was certainly wrong about the internal audits, these consultant and quality manager debates about the implementation process were important for subjecting each implementation step to thorough scrutiny before rolling it out to the staff.

The interpretation of the ISO standard gave rise to many delays and more confusion about what was required for the successful implementation of quality. While our staff was learning about quality, our leadership was learning at the same time. Many times, the quality manager was trying to figure out the requirements at the same time the staff needed the information. This was clearly a new way of doing business, and often we were compelled to pause and interpret our needs. This slowed down the implementation process considerably. We had to keep asking ourselves three important questions: (1) how each element of the ISO standard applied to public education, (2) how to interpret and implement the quality requirements in a public education setting, and (3) what will make sense to our staff.

The Quality Systems Office

Within this environment of uneasiness, the quality systems office made a conscious decision to be actively involved with the staff as they worked to develop their quality-improvement plans. We committed to leading them through the process, to working hand in hand with them, rather than merely dictating to them what they had to do and allowing them to find out how to do it. As the date approached for a site's first internal quality audit, many sites complained that they were not ready. We developed a strategy, which came to be known as a *find-and-fix session*. Find-and-fix sessions turned out to have the highest payoff in stakeholder buy-in. Prior to the internal quality audit, we scheduled an "assistance visit," where we asked questions similar to those asked in an actual audit. As we discovered the causes of their unreadiness, we rolled up our sleeves and worked with them to resolve the problems.

A common problem was meeting the element 4.5 Document Control. We could have told them to refer to the *Standards*, which states, "The supplier shall establish and maintain documented procedures to control all documents and data that relate to requirements of American National Standards including to the extent applicable." Instead we said to them, "What that means is you need to have in one place, available to everyone who needs to use them, the most current documents on how things are done around here. You need the *Board Policy Manual*, *Student Discipline Guidelines*, *Core Curriculum Documents*, the *New Standards*, the *Health Services Manual*, etc. Now, let's see what you have."

In every find-and-fix session on document control, we uncovered reams of obsolete documents, some of which had been obsolete for decades, and scattered throughout the site. We never threw anything away. Old copies of documents were routinely kept after new ones had been issued. The first step was housecleaning, discarding everything obsolete or irrelevant. The second step was to identify all the documents the site needed and to determine that only the most recent edition of each was on hand. Third, we prepared a master list of the documents indicating title, distribution, and date, and established procedures for accommodating any updates to documents. Finally, we helped them organize the documents on a single bookshelf. The typical reaction was, "Wow! So that's what document control means. Everything I need is right here in one place." We were successful because the experience showed them the value that the discipline of the quality system imposes.

This value was reinforced by the experiences of principals meeting with teachers new to the district to instruct them in policies and procedures. One new teacher observed that it would have taken her two weeks in her previous district to find all this information, and here it was all in one place on one shelf. Assuming her observation about time to be true, two weeks multiplied by the number of new teachers in our district (100 plus in 1999–2000) equals considerable hours of non-teaching time. Factor in a teacher's hourly rate of pay, and you have a considerable waste of money. As principals came to this realization, they were able to relate compliance with the document control standard to increased teaching/learning time and to dollars and cents for their sites.

HOW THE PROCESS EVOLVED

The process began with informal discussions between a board member familiar with ISO standards and the superintendent about whether application of business standards to the district's operation could help solve some of our problems. These discussions resulted in their inviting a consultant to present the ISO story to the full board. The board agreed that quality assurance was something we should explore further. From this point on the process evolved through four major stages, the first of which was a baseline audit in May 1994.

Baseline Audit

A team of ISO auditors, working with myself as the designated quality manager, made lists of things to look for in our organization to preliminarily determine whether ISO 9001 would work. Within twenty-four hours, they concluded that there were enough similarities between a business and a school system that we should pursue ISO 9001. For the remainder of the week, the auditors visited departments and school sites to identify ways in which ISO 9001 could serve the district in terms of bringing continuous improvement and process control to our work processes. Following the baseline audit, we moved into the implementation stage.

The baseline audit convinced us that ISO 9001 would work for us. During the early months of implementation, we questioned whether or not we could make it work. For more than six months, we struggled to understand ISO's methodology, implementation techniques, and business-oriented language. Many work sessions ended on a note of frustration and disillusionment. At some point, what should have been obvious from the beginning dawned on us. If it's not applicable to a school system, don't try to do it. If the business language doesn't translate into educational language, don't try to translate it. If the concept does translate, translate it into language educators understand. If there's no match between business and education, don't try to force one.

This line of thinking led us to discard some of the conventional ISO implementation strategies and to reinterpret some of the ISO standards into what we do in a school system. But before doing this, we had to be sure we were at the point where we understood ISO methodology and language well enough to make the leap from business to education. Once we felt we were there, our implementation got a renewed start. First, we wrote goals in language understandable within an educational community.

- Establish a quality system that focuses on teaching and learning.
- Establish a quality system that focuses on student and community needs.

- Establish an institutional framework that focuses on quality processes throughout the district.
- Establish consistent quality processes and standards throughout the system.
- Develop systematic processes for best practice and managed change.
- Establish a methodology for measurement and accountability.
- Improve support and communication to all school sites.

Proceeding Further into the Process

Next, we began the process of understanding and interpreting the twenty elements of the ISO 9001 standard. This process required us to analyze the "shall" statements in each of the twenty elements.

The "shall" statements are the requirements that must be met for the district to successfully complete the document review phase of a rigorous third-party independent audit. For example, Element 4.1 Management Responsibility states, "The supplier's management with executive responsibility shall define and document its policy for quality." This element of the standard does not direct what our quality policy should be but clearly indicates the requirement that we define and document our policy for quality.

The quality policy requirement is straightforward and easily interpreted because of its universal understanding and application to any organization. However, many of the other elements of the ISO standard required much more effort and energy to understand, interpret and define for use in our school district. For example, the 4.4 Design Control element includes nineteen "shall" statements regarding planning, interfaces, input, output, review, verification, validation, and changes.

To a manufacturing plant, design control is easily interpreted to be product design. For planning the school district response to the design element, we had to ask the questions, "Do we design anything? Does design control add value to our process? Can our processes be enhanced with the discipline of the design control element?" After much analyzing and interpreting the design control element, our educational experts agreed that we design curriculum and, perhaps most importantly, subjecting it to the same rigorous requirements as corporate product design would enhance our curriculum-development process.

This careful analysis and interpretation became the basis for writing school district of Lancaster procedures for each element of the ISO standard. This writing process was intellectually hard work that required many revisions in consideration of each "shall" statement, and significant changes to our current practices and implementation procedures. Each procedure had to make sense for the user and at the same time meet the requirements of the ISO standard. We soon realized a valuable by-product of our hard work. Our systematic plan for understanding, interpreting, defining, and documenting our processes led us to seek quality benchmarks and improvements in our business practices.

After months of work on each element, the process yielded the following ISO 9001 procedures:

- Leadership
- System structure
- Parent/student/teacher agreements
- Curriculum
- Document control
- Purchasing
- Student materials
- Cumulative folders
- Teaching and learning
- Assignments
- Academic standards
- Student progress
- Learning assistance
- Corrective action
- Handling procedures
- Record keeping
- Internal audits
- Staff development
- Transcripts
- Measurement

Standard operating procedures (SOPs) were established for each element and increased consistency and reliability emerged across the entire district. We have utilized our strategic plan to identify the areas where we want to improve, the ISO 9001 element "statistical techniques" to identify how we measure the areas identified in our strategic plan, and our SOPs to describe the process of how we will improve. This is what Lessinger and Salowe refer to as "the dependable and durable management system."

Having crossed this hurdle, we began to address the challenge of referencing the standards to district operations. Although the process about to be described is presented as a linear sequence, it was anything but linear. We developed, tested, revised, retested, and revised again. Various groups were developing various parts of the process simultaneously. Sometimes the left hand didn't know what the right hand was doing.

Building the Structure

One thing that focused us was the adoption of our quality policy: "The school district of Lancaster will deliver excellent teaching and learning as evidenced by high student achievement." With this as our policy, we recognized the need to revise the strategic plan to reflect the means of measuring how we implement the policy. A totally revised strategic plan was developed with input from individuals representing the entire school community. The revised strategic plan addressed high expectations and support for student learning. Six main ideas provided the foundation for our strategic focus.

1. Commit to an audacious plan, goal, and vital signs of progress to mobilize all stakeholders.
2. Articulate coherent core beliefs to guide the journey.
3. Build trust in the goals and strategies to provide the foundation for accomplishment.
4. Promote excellence in teaching to accelerate student success.
5. Build empowering relationships with stakeholders to enroll the whole community.
6. Provide essential supports to facilitate sustained student and staff performance at all levels.

Building on these six main ideas were also six vital signs for measuring progress toward our long-term goals. The six vital signs include: (1) Readiness for school, (2) Attendance in school and class, (3) Achievement in core subjects, (4) Achievement in higher-level and externally benchmarked courses, (5) Persistence of the ninth-grade class to high school graduation, and (6) Successful post-high school transition.

These six ideas and vital signs led to fifteen core strategies that provided the framework for the significant work of the district. In many respects, our strategic plan became the district's "balanced scorecard," which is used in business to build the capabilities and acquire the capacity needed for future growth. Communicating the balanced scorecard promotes commitment and accountability to the business's long-term strategy (Kaplan and Norton 1993).

With the strategic plan in place, schools worked on school-improvement plans to target specific areas for improvement. The school-improvement plans gave the superintendent a process for ensuring that all schools aligned their site objectives and resources to meet the vision, goals, and vital signs outlined in our strategic plan. Using our quality policy and strategic plan to guide their work, school-site councils developed and presented their school-improvement plans to the superintendent and board of school directors.

Each school-improvement plan reported data on the current school status with regard to the strategic plan, vital signs, and their plans to improve the data during the school year. The process of measuring, tracking, and analyzing school data became a routine business practice for our schools. Most importantly, the school-improvement plans linked the district strategic vision to the day-to-day actions of the people who would make the vision a reality. New attention and precision were given to student instruction. Every school ensured that student learning came first.

Support services, such as facilities, health services, food and transportation services, and the business office developed to ISO 9001 standards department manuals on how they serve teaching and learning. Within the office of planning and quality systems, the *Quality Manual* was being written along with *Standard Operating Procedures* and *Work Instructions*. Bringing all of this together in time for the registration audit at times seemed an almost impossible task. Last-minute changes in the *Quality Manual* had a ripple effect on site and department documents, adding to the frustration and pressure. To complicate the matter further, people were trying to learn the process as they were using it.

Toward the Audit—Support Tools

To help people cope with these pressures and with the added pressures of the imminent registration audit, we prepared a *Survival Guide for the ISO 9000 Audit*, a kind of everything-you-need-to-know pamphlet. We felt that by providing the answers, people would feel more comfortable with the auditors' questions. Although it served its purpose at the time, it also set up a dependency that made it unnecessary for people to think about the questions and internalize the answers. It became a crutch for many. For the first surveillance audit, we reformatted the publication to *Are You Audit Ready?* Essentially this was a self-help check of "I understand . . .," "I have located and reviewed . . . ," and "I have located and read . . ." statements that require the user to think about quality in terms of his or her operation.

Many publications, presentations, and notices were produced to keep our quality system in the forefront of the staff activities. Each activity became a commercial user-friendly "sound bite" to provide energy and maintain district focus on the implementation of our quality system. A few examples included: large posters promoting the quality of district staff reading simply, "best teachers, best students, best staff"; a "quality system newsletter" providing background information, upcoming events, and best practices around the district; a *Quality Handbook* answering frequently asked questions such as "What is ISO 9001? Why is ISO 9001 important? What does this mean to you? What does it take to meet ISO standards? etc."; quality alerts were e-mailed to all staff indicating notices for implementation strategies, reminders of key elements of our quality system, frequently observed problems, and a " 3-2-1 countdown" calendar was produced to remind everyone of the school days left to the third-party independent audit.

The time period from June 1996 when we began the implementation stage until our registration audit in February 1999 was surely one of the most work-intensive three years in the history of the district. As the date for the registration audit grew nearer, the work intensified even more as schools and departments finalized their preparations. The questions we kept asking ourselves were, "Have we said what we do? Are we doing what we say? Can we prove that we're doing it?"

Independent auditors from Bureau Veritas Quality International (BVQI) of Jamestown, New York, began their five-day audit on February

1, 1999. The BVQI auditors visited seven of our schools and all central office functions, carefully scrutinizing every aspect within the organization. They interviewed scores of staff and tracked our processes from beginning to end. At the end of each day of auditing, our central office administrators met with the audit team to answer any questions from the day's activities and to finalize the next day's plans. While the auditors had reviewed our *Quality Manual* and *Standard Operating Procedures* before the on-site visit, it was impressive how quickly they gained full understanding of the district's organization and system. No one on our staff knew what to expect from the auditors. To our delight, they were intelligent, knowledgeable, and courteous people whose interpersonal skills and positive demeanor provided a productive and professional business atmosphere.

To our relief and credit, the auditors found no major noncompliances and only a few minor noncompliances that were corrected on the spot. They also included in their report a few observations or suggestions for improvement before the next audit. In recommending our registration, they observed that we were "a solid quality-management system" resulting from "a team effort like none I've ever seen."

ISO 9001 safeguards the integrity of its registration through an annual surveillance audit, the fourth stage in the process. BVQI auditors returned on January 31, 2000, to observe not only our compliance with the standards but also to look for evidence of continuous improvement. During this visit, they found only three minor noncompliances that we had ninety days to address and report back to the auditors. Earning ISO certification and maintaining and improving our level of excellence throughout the first year convinced skeptics that ISO 9001 can and does work in a public school system.

Our ISO 9001 certification and pursuit of continuous improvement ensures that a quality-assured educational process has academically prepared our students.

HOW WE BENEFITED FROM THE PROCESS AND CERTIFICATION

The initial excitement and publicity that accompanied our becoming the first school district in the world to be registered with ISO 9001 did not last long. Those who had worked so hard to develop our quality-improvement plans and documents were eager to relax from the pressures of the previous four years and to focus on making the system work. Staff members who joined the district after February 1999 were largely unaware of how the district operated pre-ISO registration, and accepted how we do business now without much question.

Although many stakeholders understood bits and pieces of ISO's impact on their specific roles in the district, a relatively small number understood its strategic importance to the district as a whole, and this is as it should be. An effective quality-management system should not hover over an organization as a watchdog. It should not stand out as an entity unto itself. It must become one with the organization. Ultimately, it does not matter whether most stakeholders can articulate what being ISO 9001 registered means. What matters is that they can articulate within their spheres of responsibility what they do, that they do it, and prove that they've done it.

Therefore, it must be from the perspectives of those with the "big picture" that we assess the benefits of having persevered through the registration process. Some of these benefits are documented; some are anticipated. Some are tangible; some are intangible. In no particular order, these are some of the benefits we can point to:

- A clear sense of direction
- A framework for implementing the strategic plan
- A sense of unity—school board, administrators, teachers, and service staff working together for the common good
- A renewed focus on student achievement and on best practices in teaching
- Affirmation that the teacher is the most important person in the child's school life, that we must give teachers all the support they need, and that to support the teacher is the only reason the rest of the organization exists
- Commitment to ongoing review and continuous improvement
- Uniformity and consistency throughout the district
- Increased teaching/learning time through more efficient use of time
- Cost savings and revenue increases through streamlined business office procedures
- Greater efficiency through data-driven decision making and feedback loops

- Empowerment of all employees as agents of change
- Greater credibility with the business community and taxpayers

What we ultimately expect to see are increased student achievement, improved attendance rates, fewer dropouts, and improved post-high school success. These changes will materialize over time as our commitment to quality assurance continues.

Perhaps the most valuable benefit of our quality initiative was the discipline applied to making decisions. ISO 9001 requires measurement and data analysis when making decisions for improving the processes of our quality system. Clearly, schools are in the people business and decisions can easily be made based on emotion, special interest, perceptions, or feelings such as "that's the way it's always been done around here." An excellent illustration of drawing conclusions without evidence was observed in the school district of Lancaster regarding the achievement of students who transferred in and out of our schools. There was a widely held belief that our student-achievement scores were pulled down by our transient population. However, when we analyzed the data, a different picture emerged. In fact, at some sites, students who moved into the district raised the average achievement scores.

WHAT WE LEARNED

Had we not been the first school district to test the applicability of ISO 9001 to a public school system, common sense would have dictated that we learn from the experiences of others who had tried before. But there were no others to learn from. We had to learn from our own mistakes and false starts, and rely on our own best judgment on how to proceed. Our lessons learned will make it far easier for other school districts to embark on their quality systems initiatives.

- Put someone in charge of the process full time from the beginning.
  —This is not a part-time job. Be prepared to add staff as needed.
  —This is not a one-person job.
- Identify centers of influence inside and outside the district early in the process—union leaders, businessmen and women, civic leaders, service organizations, elected officials.

—Explain to them what you're doing and why you're doing it.
—Buy-in from a wide audience of stakeholders is critical to success.

- Establish documentation formats early.
  —Productivity is dependent on everyone's knowing what to do and how to do it.
- Work at pieces of the system; work from the parts to the whole;
  —Don't try to bite off too much at a time.
- Work with those responsible for developing the system.
  —Coach, don't dictate; support, don't criticize.
- Begin internal quality audits early.
  —Do find-and-fix sessions to prepare school sites and departments for audits.
- Ensure all feedback obtained during internal audits is kept confidential.
- Identify school sites that are well ahead in the process and target them for a "quality blitz."
  —Concentrate assistance on them for extended periods of time to capitalize on their momentum.
- Remain aware of the human aspects of internal quality audits. People tend to become defensive when they're protecting their turf.
  —Stress that noncompliances are not reflections on people but on the system and the process.
- Work with small groups to develop the process.
  —Help them understand how ISO 9001 relates to their areas of responsibility.
- Recognize that competing agendas may interfere with your time line and progress.
  —District priorities can change, for example, in a difficult budget year or a difficult union negotiations year.
  —Prepare to put some matters on the back burner temporarily.

STAYING THE COURSE

During the course of becoming ISO 9001 registered, there were times when the excitement and energy were so high as to be almost palpable. There were times when the stress and frustration were so intense as to be unhealthy. At times, the momentum was so great that we could hardly control it. At other times, we experienced total inertia. Some people thrived in this roller-coaster working condition; others had a hard time coping. Some had the work styles, personalities, and tools to persist; others wanted to give up. During the best of times, we believed we would succeed. During the worst of times, we asked ourselves why we ever attempted this. But we stayed the course. Our best advice to other school systems interested in applying for ISO 9001 certification is to expect the worst of times along with the best of times but stay the course. You will be rewarded in the long term.

There are many indications that public education must change to meet the growing public clamor for accountability. The public is questioning education's processes and results. Government entities are growing intolerant of failing inner-city schools that graduate high school seniors who cannot read, write, or compute. States are establishing statewide testing programs, teacher exams, and district takeover initiatives to leverage high standards demands in student performance. The federal government intends to fund programs to replace decaying public school infrastructure and reduce class size. All this interest is not an accident; it is intended to keep America competitive in a global marketplace where quality and competitive price equal market share and higher living standards.

No one has a crystal ball to predict the future, but clearly, there are trends that point to the need for accountability in public education. Futurists track trends to make intelligent predictions. Our prediction is the first decade of the new millennium will see growing support for formal quality systems in public education.

DR. WILLIAM N. KIEFER

Epilogue

WHAT HAPPENED TO OUR PUBLIC SCHOOLS?

An unparalleled series of events, reports, and forums, convinced elected representatives that America's public schools were in desperate need of improvement. Legislatures went ahead and passed hundreds of laws aimed at bettering education. In 2001, the President made education his number one priority. Support for this issue was achieved in a bipartisan agreement. Like business and industry in the 1980s, our schools need to be transformed if America is to prosper in a technology-driven and fast-paced global economy.

Since World War II, the history of failed attempts to improve public schools is awash with "innovations" taken up with great enthusiasm. They last for a brief period but fail to take root, like rejected transplant surgery. Such good intentions involve a small number of interested parties that *temporarily* subsidize programs with heavy outside funding. The attitude of teachers that "this too shall pass" or "here we go again" speaks loudly to such "educational faddism."

EDUCATION'S CHRONIC DISEASE: UNRELIABLE QUALITY IN CLASSROOM TEACHING

Every semester in every school, parents question the quality of teacher that their child will be assigned to *this* time. Parents know that a teacher's knowledge is the most important ingredient in their child's success in school. But what parents may not realize is that the system within which that teacher works is, in large part, responsible for the outcome. Parents with the time and skills ensure, by hook or by crook, that their child is assigned to the best teachers.

Thus, it might not come as much surprise to learn that today's public schools operate under a tyranny of chance. A missing factor that helps explain much of the shortcoming in school improvement to date. What is missing is an acceptance that for dependable quality classroom teaching to consistently be there the *system* that leads, manages, and administers that school must both mandate and support reliable quality classroom teaching.

The major lessons learned from the successful quality revolution in American business and industry has, to date, either been unknown or ignored. That is why the odds of getting a good teacher in every school classroom are akin to the chance one has in a Las Vegas or Atlantic City casino. Reliable quality classroom teaching can only be ensured in a system that is specifically designed *and* managed to achieve that result. Further, putting a qualified teacher into an unreliable system only increases the probability that the teacher will not stay long or, worse yet, be severely hindered in achieving his or her full teaching potential.

WHY TRYING TO CHANGE SCHOOLS IS SO DIFFICULT

We still have an agricultural calendar and industrial model in a digital age. Most people have shared common public school experiences, so changing schools causes both educators and the public to experience some sense of loss. Today's challenge is to identify quality management processes to help public school leaders and teachers better meet their 21st century demands.

All organizations have a culture. The school's culture is the shared understanding about how to treat one another, what the organization really values, and what the rules are for getting the job done. These shared understandings are what holds the school system together and gives it a distinctive identity. It is what is meant by "that's the way we do things around here."

WHY CALLS FOR CHANGE ARE NOW MORE POWERFU

The traditional school culture is now challenged by the growing realization among the general public that:

Learning and earning are inseparable.

- People know that a quality educational system is absolutely essential to the economic, political, and social well being of the United States. Today's public school classroom sentences too many students to a future low standard of living and a neglect of civic responsibility.
- Without systemic change, the public schools will continue sentencing more students to future low-pay or no-pay jobs. This is a tough truth to face. We can gnash our teeth, rage, point fingers and blame, and wish it were not so. But we all bear witness to job and career obsolescence and we know that although unskilled jobs are disappearing, those that are still available no longer pay a living wage.
- To make a decent living, all workers must have more knowledge and skills than they currently get in school. Even our so-called best schools do not generally provide this level of quality schooling now.

It's now time to think and work smarter.

- Asking or demanding that people work harder and do more of what has always been done in the way it has always been done cannot produce needed changes or results.
- Today's public schools are structured, organized, and managed to meet the needs of yesterday; an age and society that no longer exists.

Make "this is the way we've always done it around here" famous last words.

- Educators need help to make the needed changes in the public schools. Education is government. The "public" nature of the school makes every citizen and business the legitimate partner of the school.
- To change the public schools requires a long-term commitment to improvement. It is unrealistic and misleading to think in terms of a quick fix.

In light of the new and more demanding societal expectations for school improvement, every aspect of the educational process and school system must be reconsidered, step-by-step.

WHAT NEEDS TO BE DONE IN ORDER TO LEAVE NO STUDENT BEHIND?

The answer lies in reengineering a system of public education to bring every student to high standards, regardless of where they start so that no student is left behind. Currently, and for some time now, schools have sorted students into academic types and then proceeded, often unintentionally, to educate those students judged to be most capable.

We propose a winning prescription comprised of two proven formulas, both widely used in the private sector today. One is nationally recognized and can lead to the prestigious Presidential Award, the Baldrige; the other is both nationally and internationally recognized, and can lead to world-class certification, ISO 9000-04. Each makes its unique contribution to improving school management; both have been found, when working in concert, to bring about reliable quality teaching in every school classroom.

Through continuous doses of the winning prescription, education stakeholders can start to observe marked changes in all classroom teachers, based on applying the following quality characteristics:

Good planning

- Effective communication of standards and lesson goals to students and parents
- Teacher agreement within the same school in choosing subject matter
- Elimination of inconsistency in effective use of classroom time for subject matter
- Stopping of all labeling of students and using different approaches to such groups
- The use of good classroom work-time management
- Effective managing of student discipline
- Effective motivation for learning and proper evaluation of students

- Mastery of quality control (feedback and corrective action) in classroom instruction
- Overcoming ignorance and apathy towards what works (solid educational research)

WHAT THE READER HAS GAINED

Healing Public Schools provides a winning prescription for building reliable quality into classroom teaching for all students. Applying the winning prescription formulas allows school leaders to eliminate the need for *The Dance of the Lemons*, the ritual performed each term when school administrators distribute their poorest teachers into those teaching spots least likely to generate parent criticism.

As recently as the mid-1990s, public schools would reward leaders who:

- Avoided risk
- Focused on the internal school environment
- Set standards for students and staff but not themselves
- Maintained the status quo, and
- Reacted to external pressures and politics.

The 21st century school leaders who operate a reliability-oriented quality management system:

- Take calculated risks, continuously
- Focus on the needs of internal and external customers, constantly
- Work with students and staff to jointly set standards, goals, and objectives
- Review current operations and commit to change and ongoing improvement
- Anticipate external pressures and plan to meet them.

These formulas are not magic. But they encourage a leadership and management style to produce greater student achievement, less failure and less need for remediation, more dedicated and satisfied teachers, and vastly happier parents. How?

- First, guesswork is minimized. From each stage of the schooling process, information is fed to the other stages, including good statistical data that allows everyone, including students and their parents, to easily understand.
- Second, administrators and teachers learn from each other and all learn from outside stakeholders and suppliers. Across all levels there is teamwork; private turf wars become a thing of the past.

Now, we have the tools to take the gamble out of the quality of classroom teaching. We can stop condemning school children to a poor future. We can recognize and build school quality upon step-by-step improvements. We know how to get even more qualified teachers into the system. We must use these tools to forge advances in the school system to assure optimal development and use of teachers. We now know why and we now understand how to do it.

Appendix A: Getting Public Schools Back to Health

The appendix is probably the most overlooked portion of a book. In these additional pages, the authors distill for the parent and educator the essence of those actions necessary to achieve reliable classroom teaching. These are:

- Learning standards
- Procedures for reliable classroom teaching
- Good practices
- The teacher
- What works
- Data collection
- Survey forms (student, parent, and district staff)

Taken together, the winning prescription can heal the chronic illness of the public schools. We can keep the classroom in the grip of caring teachers, parents, and educational leaders.

The central focus of a reliable school classroom is teaching and learning. Teaching without learning means little. A parent who claims, "I taught my child to ride a bike, but every time he gets on he falls over" has not taught the child to ride a bike.

We stress the need for a reliable school to use classroom learning standards that clearly establish what the student is expected to learn. These standards apply to every student enrolled in the school. This includes those who are non-English-speaking students as well as students in exceptional programs. In every case, the teacher is teaching to the same set of high standards and committed to helping each child reach those standards.

Teachers have many examples of student work that meet each of the standards. In this way, both the parent and the child can see exactly what high achievement looks like at the student's grade level or a particular course.

LEARNING STANDARDS

A standard is a clear description of what students should know and be able to do in a subject area. In language arts, for example, there are standards for reading; writing; speaking and listening; spelling, punctuation, grammar, and language; and literature.

As a parent, you can ask for work samples produced by students that meet the published standards at the school. As you review student products, you will immediately notice that the work becomes better and better as the student progresses through school. This is as it should be.

There are two kinds of learning standards to keep in mind, and they require each other. Content standards tell parents and teachers what the students should know and be able to do in each subject area. For example, they tell that the student must be able to write a report or know the causes of the Civil War. Performance standards tell you how good the student work must be to meet the content standards.

What We Know about Successful Students

We know that students have greater success when they clearly understand what it is they are expected to learn. We also know that students are more successful when the parents know what is expected, and when the parents are involved in helping their children learn. The teacher/student/parent partnership is essential to the winning prescription.

It is most important that each student knows the kind of work needed to reach the standards. In a reliable school, each teacher takes care of that part. It is also important for the parents to know what is expected so that they can help the student at home. A reliable school provides extensive information about the standards to the parents. This includes student work samples as well as suggestions for helping the child reach the standards.

This information tells you, the parents, the best places to get more information about standards. The school gives you a copy of the information that explains what a standards-based education system is. It tells how the content standards were developed. It also answers frequently asked questions you most likely have about standards, and provides a glossary of terms.

If you visit your student's classroom, you can see a wall chart that contains an overview of the school's performance standards. These are the things your student must know and be able to do by the end of their elementary, middle, and high school years. If you are interested in reading a more complete version of the school's performance standards, the teacher can show you a copy of the school system booklet. If you prefer, a copy of this summary can be requested for you. In this way, you and the teacher are on the same team with the student.

A reliable school actively encourages you to take time to read these standards documents. It looks for any chance to discuss the standards with others at the school. You are encouraged to talk with the principal and the teacher. They will show you by their actions a willingness to share the standards with you and to talk about student progress.

How Parents Can Help

The parent can:

- Talk with the teacher to determine the kind of help the student needs.
- Read the report card in areas identified for needed improvement.
- Talk with the student about his or her work.
- Ask the student how the work might be revised to meet the standards.
- Compare your student's portfolio with examples that meet standards.
- Go to the school. Ask questions of designated staff, such as:
  "How can I help my student meet the standards?"
  "Where can my student get help to meet the standards?"
  "What programs does the school have to help meet standards?"
  "Can I help the school support student progress toward the standards?"

A reliable school helps a parent do something constructive if his or her student is having trouble meeting the standards. The entire school community is aligned. It works to support student achievement of standards and assists each child. This is their top priority. The district is responsible for providing the resources and support to the student needing extra help to meet the standards. Keep in mind that each school is charged with developing an intervention plan for each student not meeting the standards.

PROCEDURES FOR RELIABLE CLASSROOM TEACHING

Here we summarize the steps necessary to implement the classroom standard operating procedures.

- Each student must know what he or she is expected to do, how to do it, and when each expectation will be judged. The student must have an opportunity to influence—but not decide—what is required to meet the expectations. This is the Knowledge of Expectations (KOE).
- Each student must be given assistance—when needed—in meeting each of the expectations. This is the Knowledge of Assistance (KOA).
- Each student must be given timely feedback on how well or how poorly he or she is meeting what is expected (KOE), and specifically if an expectation or expectations are not satisfactorily met. This is the Knowledge of Results (KOR).
- For each expectation not met satisfactorily, as expressed in KOR, specific corrective action must be developed with the student. Then the sequence of the first three principles is used again. This is the Knowledge of Corrective Action (KOCA).
- Each student must be given many chances to succeed before any final formal notice is served regarding any termination. Essentially, this is a repeat of all of the previous steps. This is the Knowledge of Repetition (KORep).

Through trial and error, successful schools have learned these principles. These are precisely what research has found to be the basic foundation of good teaching practice for reliable quality in classroom instruction. The eight-step principles of *Good Practice* for each teacher in working with the students follow.

GOOD PRACTICES

Step 1: Share expectations.
Communicate what the student is expected to know and be able to do to be successful.

Step 2: Listen carefully to concerns about expectations.
Let the student comment on each expectation. If feasible, adjust the expectation to fit a concern.

Step 3: Use "what works" as assistance in meeting each shared expectation.
Provide assistance in meeting each expectation by using good practice—what works—as the basis of your assistance. (See "What Works.")

Step 4: Let people know results.
Provide timely feedback through agreed-upon assessment methods. Show him or her how well or how poorly the expectations are being met.

Step 5: Plan again for success, not failure.
For each of the poorly met expectations, develop a plan for corrective action.

Step 6: Assist the student to successfully meet the new plan.
Repeat Steps 1 through 4 while he or she enacts the corrective action plan.

Step 7: Be patient and let him or her try again.
Give him or her many chances to be successful. Repeat the entire process if necessary.

Step 8: Maintain fundamental respect for each student with no reservations.
There can be no "disqualification" by reason of gender, race, ethnicity, alleged aptitude, physical handicap, or age.

THE TEACHER

Through the application of the eight-step principle, each teacher:

1. Makes it clear to everybody just what the end product skill or knowledge will be.

If teachers want students to be able to repair a computer or sail a steady course, they show them how and ensure that they have the end result well in mind. The same is true if they are teaching students how to solve equations, write grammatical sentences, or design experiments. In fact, many teachers report that if they tell and/or demonstrate to the students exactly what it is they want them to be able to do and how their work will be judged, they often won't have to tell them anything else.

Many a classroom course has changed direction when the objectives were hammered out (with student input) in clear performance terms.

2. Lets everybody know how each objective is going to be assessed (tested, measured, and evaluated).

The more information teachers give students about how they are to be tested, the more easily and quickly they can develop the required skills. Teachers understandably are sometimes reluctant to let the student know what the test is. Probably they find themselves worrying at the thought of "giving away" the test. They are probably in a *teach-about* mode rather than a *teach-how* mode. There are very few skills that are taught where a teacher can't let the student know what the skills are and how they are to be tested.

With these fundamental principles, teachers can eliminate much of the adversary relationship between student and instructor. The quickest way to do that is to be as direct and open about the nature of the test as a teacher can be.

3. Gives each student many chances to succeed before any final formal notice is served regarding any termination.

This is one of the aspects of American *Kaizen* (see chapter 7) that almost everybody agrees with, but it is also one of the hardest to implement given the time constraints and the need to "cover" the course materials. Teachers need to be both effective and efficient. They need to find out what students can already do. Then they can productively use that information in behalf of each student once they have it.

Once the instruction focuses on skills (the objectives) and the means of testing each skill is made known, the student can look at both the objective and the test, and decide if they have the skill or not.

4. Gives students as many choices or paths through the instruction as possible, through the implementation of American Kaizen.

For example, if students were going to build a table, they would proceed in a certain order, from cutting to assembling to finishing. If they were to learn the *skills* of table building, they could learn sanding and finishing skills first, or last, or in the middle somewhere. The tendency to teach in the same order as the instructions are performed is strong, yet a lot of enthusiasm can be dampened if teachers force students to put off parts that seem interesting in order to learn less interesting things first.

One of the main attributes of American *Kaizen* in action is the emotional one of always wanting students to like the subject matter.

5. Provides a range of technology (materials, approach, what works, and media) whenever possible.

The instructor performs a number of functions—informing, showing how, providing feedback, counseling, and so on. Some of these functions are easier than others. Computers, books, tape recorders, TVs, or videos can assist the teacher and student.

It is desirable to use a living human being to the highest purpose. There should be no reluctance in adding to the effectiveness of the instructor with "tools" and/or the technology that promotes their use.

6. Allows enough time for any qualified individual to finish.

One of the most counterproductive aspects of many traditional schools is the fact that they are most often time-based rather than performance-based. Too often, the students are started, ready or not, and after a period of time the instruction ceases, whether or not the students have mastered the skill. The loss in this poor practice (critics would argue malpractice) is made clear when attempts are then made to move the students on to new skills, which depend on the mastery of the old. Instructors do not and cannot make such mistakes when they teach someone to fly an airplane. The student works on landings until he can do them. The student masters navigation before the instructor allows him to fly cross-country.

It seems that as soon as teachers begin teaching *about* rather than *how,* they tend to push and prod the slower student to keep up with a time schedule and then cut him or her off when the time is up. The chronic problems of cumulative ignorance and learned helplessness stem from these poor practices.

With the exercise of the American *Kaizen* principles, teachers give students assurance that they have the time they need to read, ponder, practice, work out difficulties, look at other explanations, talk to other students—whatever they need to learn to do the skill.

The other side of the coin is just as important. Students need to know that they are in a system designed so that if their interest catches fire, they won't have to sit around and wait for others to catch up.

7. Provides a sort of "map" to keep students informed about where they are in the curriculum.

Teachers know this and should be encouraged to take the necessary steps of providing and continuously updating a course "map."

8. Provides opportunity for practice of the skill being taught.

Teachers are strongly tempted when designing instruction to tell students exactly how to perform a skill, what to watch out for, and how to tell when they are doing it right. Unfortunately, the teacher often does not provide space and time for the students to actually practice under their guidance. This again demonstrates the awesome pressure of restricted time.

9. Provides feedback to students on their practice.

Teachers provide practice at a skill. They ensure that students know immediately if they are practicing correctly or not, and if not, why not?

10. Tests and assess often and in as nonthreatening a way as possible.

When students dream of an ideal teacher, one of the things they most often want to change is any brittle, enemy relationship between them and the instructor. This is often brought about by the way the student may have encountered testing and grading. Two things could help considerably. First, teachers should test often. In this manner, students do not have to accumulate too much before they find out if they are on the right track. Second, teachers should test in a nonthreatening manner. They need to accurately forewarn students what the test will be like. They can let students pick their own time for testing when feasible. They can give timely and constructive feedback on the results of the test, and let the students keep testing until the desired skill has been demonstrated.

11. Accepts feedback from the students and from colleagues for self-correction.

They know that no one and no system is perfect.

12. Compares each student to expected objectives, through the discipline of caring.

Too much interest in competitive values can obscure a proper concern for the acceptable values required of the "prepared" student. This is why the winning prescription stresses the principle of competition as being of value.

Everyone knows that even in the most highly regarded classrooms, class time can be wasted, lessons can be vague, and students can be totally confused and unmotivated. The eight-step principles of good practice point clearly to the essential nature of the teacher's job. It is easy to forget that teaching is a job and that schools are workplaces where learning is to take place.

To perform the job with dependability, the teacher must accomplish a series of tasks. In the most fundamental sense, the mastery and execution of these tasks marks what is meant by quality teaching. The processes for executing these tasks form the content of the second major characteristic of the high-reliability organization.

WHAT WORKS

There is an inventory of good practice instruction to achieve reliable results. We also know a great deal about what works in education. We know the sets of authoritative practices that have been verified by actual tryout to ensure better results. The following thirty-three elements were drawn from the first-ever book of good practices published under the title *What Works* (1986) by the U.S. Department of Education.

1. *Curriculum of the Home Works*
   Parents are their children's first and most influential teachers. What parents do to help their children learn is more important to academic success than how well off the family is.
2. *Reading to Children Works*
   The best way for parents to help their children become readers is to read to them, even when they are very young. Children benefit most from reading aloud when they discuss stories, learn to identify letters and words, and talk about the meaning of words.
3. *Independent Reading Works*
   Children improve their reading ability by reading a lot. Reading achievement is directly related to the amount of reading children do in school and outside.
4. *Counting Works*
   A good way to teach children simple arithmetic is to build on their informal knowledge. This is why learning to count everyday objects is an effective basis for early arithmetic lessons.

5. *Early Writing Works*
Children who are encouraged to draw and scribble "stories" at an early age will later learn to compose more easily, more effectively, and with greater confidence than children who do not have this encouragement.

6. *Speaking and Listening Works*
A good foundation in speaking and listening helps children become better readers.

7. *Developing Talent Works*
Many highly successful individuals have above-average but not extraordinary intelligence. Accomplishment in a particular activity is often more dependent upon hard work and self-discipline than on innate ability.

8. *Ideals Work*
Belief in the value of hard work, the importance of personal responsibility, and the importance of education itself contribute to greater success in school.

9. *Getting Parents Involved Works*
Parental involvement helps children learn more effectively. Teachers who are successful at involving parents in their children's schoolwork are successful because they work at it.

10. *Phonics Works*
Children get a better start in reading if they are taught phonics. Learning phonics helps them to understand the relationship between letters and sounds and to "break the code" that links the words they hear with the words they see in print.

11. *Reading Comprehension Works*
Children get more out of a reading assignment when the teacher precedes the lesson with background information and follows it with discussion.

12. *Science Experiments Work*
Children learn science best when they are able to do experiments so that they can witness "science in action."

13. *Storytelling Works*
Telling young children stories can motivate them to read. Storytelling also introduces them to cultural values and literary traditions before they can read, write, and talk about stories by themselves.

14. *Teaching Writing Works*
    The most effective way to teach writing is to teach it as a process of brainstorming, composing, revising, and editing.
15. *Learning Mathematics Works*
    Children in early grades learn mathematics more effectively when they use physical objects in their lessons.
16. *Estimating Works*
    Although students need to learn how to find exact answers to arithmetic problems, good math students also learn the helpful skill of estimating answers. This skill can be taught.
17. *Teacher Expectations Work*
    Teachers who set and communicate high expectations to all their students obtain greater academic performance from those students than teachers who set low expectations.
18. *Student Ability and Effort Works*
    A student's understanding of the relationship between being smart and hard work changes as they grow.
19. *Managing Classroom Time Works*
    How much time students are actively engaged in learning contributes strongly to their achievement. The amount of time available for learning is determined by the instructional and management skills of the teacher and the priorities set by the school administration.
20. *Direct Instruction Works*
    When teachers explain exactly what students are expected to learn and demonstrate the steps needed to accomplish a particular academic task, students learn more.
21. *Tutoring Works*
    Students tutoring other students can lead to improved academic achievement for both student and tutor, and to positive attitudes toward coursework.
22. *Memorization Works*
    Memorizing can help students absorb and retain the factual information on which understanding and crucial thought are based.
23. *Questioning Works*
    Student achievement rises when teachers ask questions that require students to apply, analyze, synthesize, and evaluate information, in addition to simply recalling facts.

24. *Study Skills Work*

The ways in which children study influence strongly how much they learn. Teachers can often help children develop better study skills.

25. *Homework Quantity Works*

Student achievement rises significantly when teachers regularly assign homework and students conscientiously do it.

26. *Homework Quality Works*

Well-designed homework assignments relate directly to class work and extend students' learning beyond the classroom. Homework is most useful when teachers carefully prepare the assignment, thoroughly explain it, and give prompt comments and criticism when the work is completed.

27. *Assessment Works*

Frequent and systematic monitoring of students' progress helps students, parents, teachers, administrators, and policymakers identify strengths and weaknesses in learning and instruction.

28. *Effective Schools Work*

The most important characteristics of effective schools are strong instructional leadership, a safe and orderly climate, schoolwide emphasis on basic skills, high teacher expectations for student achievement, and continuous assessment of pupil progress.

29. *Discipline Works*

Schools contribute to their students' academic achievement by establishing, communicating, and enforcing fair and consistent discipline policies.

30. *Unexcused Absences Work*

Unexcused absences decrease when parents are promptly informed that their children are not attending school.

31. *Effective Principals Work*

Successful principals establish policies that create an orderly environment and support effective instruction.

32. *Teacher Supervision Works*

Teachers welcome professional suggestions about improving their work, but they rarely receive them.

33. *Rigorous Courses Work*

The stronger the emphasis on academic courses, the more advanced the subject matter, and the more rigorous the textbooks, the more high school students learn.

DATA COLLECTION

Quality information fuels the quality-improvement process. Among the key customers surveyed annually by quality teams are parents, professional and support staff, high school and middle school students, and high school alumni. The objective is to determine if their needs and expectations have been exceeded. High school graduates are surveyed to determine the extent to which their high school education has met their college and career needs. The site-based and districtwide quality teams generate surveys and conduct focus groups as needed. All survey and focus group data are incorporated into the continuous quality-improvement process.

A series of sample survey forms used to collect data from students, parents, and district opinions and expectations was drawn from the Long Beach (Calif.) Unified School District. It serves as a starting point for developing your own survey data.

THE LONG BEACH UNIFIED SCHOOL DISTRICT STUDENT SURVEY FORM

1. Leadership (Student)
   - Who is in charge of your educational program?
   - From whom do you learn of changes in your education program?
   - Where would you like to learn about changes in education?
   - Do you understand what behavior is expected of you in school?
   - Do you know what your teacher expects of you in school?
   - Do you know what your school is trying to do in educating you?
   - If you have a problem at school, can you get an answer easily?
   - Do you believe your school does its best to educate you?
   - Who is the leader in your school?
2. Planning (Student)
   - Education plans for students include these kinds of items: achievement, safety, instruction, special programs, activities, behavior, school maintenance, learning resources and materials, parent education, testing and curriculum.
   - Is there a plan for your education?
   - What does the plan prepare you for upon graduation?
   - Were you asked to help develop the plan?
   - Do you contribute to the content of the plan?

- If you offer opinions on the plan, are they considered?
- Underline the items in the statement under "Planning" included in your educational plan.

3. Focus (Student)
- Do you know what is expected of you at school?
- When is that communicated to you?
- Is it communicated to you early enough?
- How is it communicated to you?
- Do those expectations agree with your goals and objectives in school?
- Do you have a plan for your future?
- Does your school work fit into your plans for the future?
- Is the school interested in your plans for the future?

4. Information and Analysis (Student)
- Does your school gather information on your educational progress?
- How does your school obtain information on your educational progress?
- Do you understand the meaning of the information gathered on your progress?
- Does that information accurately reflect your educational progress?
- Has your teacher discussed your Academic Profile with you?

5. Educational Process (Student)
- Do you understand the standards required of you to be promoted to the next grade?
- Is the subject matter taught the same as that on the tests that apply to it?
- Underline the school facilities that are adequate: cleanliness, school temperature, paper, pencils, books computers, playgrounds, classrooms.

THE LONG BEACH UNIFIED SCHOOL DISTRICT PARENT SURVEY FORM

1. Leadership (Parent)
- Who is in charge of your child's educational program?

- Who communicates changes in your child's education program to you?
- Where would you like to learn about changes in education?
- Do you understand the school's expectations of your child's behavior?
- Do you understand what your child's teachers expect of him or her in schoolwork?
- Do you understand the various levels of "success" in your child's education?
- Is the school system's leadership easily accessible to you?
- Do they respond to you in a reasonable amount of time?
- Do you know the school district's or your child's school's mission?
- If so, do you agree with it?
- Do you know how to reach the leaders in the school system and your child's school?
- Do you get information from them?
- Have changes you have seen in education affected you or your family?
- Do you know whom to contact for educational concerns you may have?

2. Planning (Parent)
   - Do you contribute to the content of the plan?
   - If you offer opinions on the plan, are they considered?
   - Education plans for students include these kinds of items: achievement, safety, instruction, special programs, activities, behavior, school maintenance, learning resources and materials, parent education, testing, and curriculum.
   - Is there a plan for your child's education?
   - Where does the plan lead for your child upon graduation?
   - Were you asked to help develop the plan?

3. Focus (Parent)
   - Do you know what is expected of your child at school?
   - When is that communicated to you?
   - Is it communicated to you early enough?
   - How is it communicated to you?
   - Do those expectations agree with your goals and objectives in school?

- Do you have a plan for your child's future?
- Does your child's schoolwork fit into your plans for his or her future?
- Is the school interested in your child's plans for the future?

4. Information and Analysis (Parent)
   - Does your child's school gather information on his or her educational progress?
   - How does your child's school obtain information on his or her educational progress?
   - Do you understand the meaning of the information gathered on your child's progress?
   - Does that information accurately reflect your child's educational progress?
   - Has your child's teacher discussed his or her Academic Profile with you?

5. Educational Process (Parent)
   - Do you understand the standards required of your child for him or her to be promoted to the next grade?
   - Is the subject matter taught in your child's classes the same as that on the tests that apply to it?
   - Underline the school facilities that are adequate: cleanliness, school temperature, paper, pencils, books computers, playgrounds, and classrooms.

THE LONG BEACH (CA) UNIFIED SCHOOL DISTRICT DISTRICT STAFF SURVEY FORM

1. Leadership (District Staff)
   - Who is in charge of the District's student educational program?
   - Who communicates changes in the District's education program to you?
   - Where would you like to learn about changes in the District education program?
   - Is the District's leadership clear in its expectations of the staff?
   - Do you understand the leadership's goals and objectives for the District this year?
   - Do you understand how the District leadership will measure "success" in meeting goals and objectives for this year?

- Is the school system's leadership easily accessible to you?
- Do they respond to you in a reasonable amount of time?
- Do you know the school district's or our individual schools' missions?
- If so, do you agree with the District's? Do you agree with the schools' you know?
- Do you know how to reach the leaders in the District and the individual schools?
- Do you get useful information from the District? How about the schools?
- Have changes you have seen in education affected you positively or negatively?

2. Planning (District Staff)
   - Education plans for District students include these kinds of items: achievement, safety, instruction, special programs, activities, behavior, school maintenance, learning resources and materials, parent education, testing, and curriculum.
   - Is there an education plan for the District students?
   - Is there a strategic plan for the District?
   - Where does the education plan for students lead upon graduation?
   - Were you asked to help develop the student education plan?
   - Were you asked to help develop the District strategic plan?
   - Do you contribute to the content of the student education plan?
   - Do you contribute to the District strategic plan?
   - If you offer opinions on the student education plan, are they considered?
   - If you offer opinions on the District strategic plan are they considered?
   - Underline items in the "Planning" statement included in the student educational plan.
   - Similarly, circle the items in the statement included in the District strategic plan.
   - List the items in the statement that need special attention to improve educational effectiveness.

3. Focus (District Staff)
   - Do you know what is expected of you in your work at the District?
   - When is that communicated to you?
   - Is it communicated to you early enough?

- How is it communicated to you?
- Do those expectations agree with your goals and objectives?
- Do those expectations agree with the District's goals and objectives?
- Do you have a plan for your future at the District?
- Do you know of plans within the District for your future?
- Does your work at the District fit into the District's plans for the future?
- Is the District really interested in your plan for the future?

4. Information and Analysis (District Staff)
   - Does your child's school gather information on your job progress and effectiveness?
   - How does the District obtain information on your job progress and effectiveness?
   - Do you understand the meaning of the information gathered on your job progress?
   - Does that information accurately reflect your job progress and effectiveness?
   - Has your supervisor discussed your job progress and effectiveness with you?

5. Staff Focus (District Staff)
   - Is it clear who is responsible at the District for getting work tasks completed?
   - Underline the support systems that need to be improved: Facilities, Accounting.
   - Specify briefly what area of each needs to be improved.
   - Underline which of the following needs to be improved: Compensation, employee recognition, benefits, job definition, and work description.
   - Specify briefly what area of each needs to be improved.
   - Is your work environment pleasant?
   - Specify briefly any improvements you would suggest.
   - Are staff development programs available to you?
   - How are they communicated to you?
   - Do you take advantage of staff development programs?

6. Education Process (District Staff)
   - Do you understand the standards required of you in your job to be successful in it?

- Do you understand the standards required to be promoted to the next level in your job?
- Does the training you receive at the District help you to fulfill the standards required of your job?
- Underline the District facilities that are adequate: cleanliness, office temperature, supplies, computers, office equipment, office furniture, parking, and transportation.
- Are there personnel issues at the District that need to be addressed?
- Are there remuneration issues at the District that need to be addressed?
- Are there sufficient supplies and equipment readily available for you to do your job effectively?
- Are financial resources available for you to do your job effectively?

INSTALLING THE WINNING PRESCRIPTION

Installing the winning prescription achieves reliable quality in classroom teaching.

Phase 1 outlines the steps you can take to get senior management to commit to change.

Phase 2 describes what you can do to determine your customers' perceptions of your school and the condition of your system.

Phase 3 focuses on how you can institutionalize a customer focus.

Phase 4 places the focus on your system in the areas of strategic planning, employee involvement, process management, and your measurement system.

Phase 5 addresses the alignment of activities to meet and exceed customer expectations.

Phase 6, the final step, uses Baldrige criteria to assess your system and initiate the next round of improvements.

Phase 1: Commit to Change

Senior managers are the system's gatekeepers. If, and only if, they open the gates to cultural change will the transition begin. The leaders of world-class companies and schools not only open the gates, they lead the transformation, putting their minds, hearts, and souls into this new management model.

Action plan for committing to change

Goal: Gain commitment
Participants: Senior management and staff.
Steps:

- Assess your school's performance compared to your perception of how much better it could be and to industry and world-class leaders.
- Learn about the new model through reading, attending conferences and seminars, and training.
- Study the management styles of the Baldrige Award winners.
- Look at your school and school district from your customers' perspectives based on surveys.
- As a staff, brainstorm what the school would look like with the new management model in place.
- Identify the benefits, drawbacks, and obstacles of such a change.
- Develop a new vision, mission, policies, and values that capture the school you wish to be.
- Commit as the school's leaders to the long-term, permanent transition to management by quality.
- Communicate this commitment throughout the school and district.
- Begin work on a system of measures of senior administrators and school performance based on the new management model.

Phase 2: Assess Your System

By the time your school turns to a new approach to management, it seems as though it does not have much time left for assessments. Schools, like people, resist dramatic change until they run out of options. However, even a quick assessment is better than going with the first quality program that catches your eye.

The assessment needs to be both external and internal. Determine what your school customers think of your school and what your own measures tell you. The more thorough the assessments, the easier it will be to establish baselines by which to gauge progress and to identify and prioritize areas for improvement.

Action plan for assessing your system

Goal: Determine customer perceptions of your school.

Participants: Board members, administrators, teachers, staff support, and other employees who have direct contact with customers, particularly members of teaching, office, counselors, bus drivers, and community relations.

Steps:

- Identify the primary markets and customer groupings your system will target.
- Gather information from every possible source about these customers' requirements, their expectations, and their needs. How is your school and district doing at fulfilling these?
- Aggregate and analyze this information. Determine the customers' requirements and their view of your school and school system.
- Run your findings past key customers to confirm the accuracy of your findings.
- Document and present these findings to senior administrators and the board.

Goal: Performance system assessment.

Participants: Employees needed to conduct the assessment.

Steps:

- Establish the assessment teams. Train and assign responsibilities.
- Collect data and information.
- Document and present findings to senior administrators.

Goal: Develop action plan.

Participants: Senior administrators, their staffs, and other employees.

Steps: Compare findings with vision of where company needs to be to identify strengths and areas for improvement.

- Prioritize areas for improvement and assign to the responsible executive-owners.

- Determine how progress will be measured.
- Formalize a process for periodic system assessments. Act on what it tells you.
- Many of the steps that make this possible need to be taken again and again throughout all phases of the transition.

Phase 3: Institutionalize a Customer Focus

Since the new school management model is customer-driven, there is no time like the present to put the customer behind the wheel. Unfortunately, it is not as easy as slipping the customer into the driver's seat and handing over the keys. Institutionalizing a customer focus requires getting close to customers.

Action plan for institutionalizing a customer focus

Goals: Establish listening posts.
Participants: All employees, teachers, support staffs, administrators, and community services.
Steps:

- Identify all possible sources of information about present and future customers.
- Formalize processes for gathering information from these sources.
- Assess tools used to determine customer satisfaction.
- Improve the quality of information gathered, its timeliness, and its usefulness.

Goals: Aggregate and analyze customer information.
Participants: All employees, teachers, support staffs, administrators, and community services.
Steps:

- Formalize a process for collecting customer information from various listening posts.
- Formalize processes for passing on findings needing immediate action to appropriate units/individuals.
- Formalize processes for analyzing the collected information.

- Formalize processes for communicating this information to appropriate units/individuals.

Goals: Use customer requirements to drive internal processes.
Participants: All employees.
Steps:

- Determine links between those who satisfy customers and internal processes and measures.
- Focus on these key processes and measures in phase 4.

Phase 4: Institutionalize the New Management Model

The transition to the new school model will remain a transition until the model is institutionalized. Schools need to avoid jumping from quality program to quality program. What is called for is a process for weaving the quality program into the fabric of their school organization. Absent that tight connection, the school will never stray far from its old management model.

Schools convert to the new model in one of four ways: (1) strategic planning, (2) employee involvement, (3) process management, and (4) their measurement system. The avenues your school chooses will depend on which match best with your school and district. One does not seem to be better or more effective than another. Keep in mind that you can work toward all four of the goals at once. The steps toward each are often overlapping and complementary. And remember, many successful schools test everything before implementing it across the school district. Use pilot projects liberally to test and fine-tune your approaches.

Action plan for institutionalizing the new management model

Goal: Align all activities through the strategic planning process.
Participants: All levels of employees, customers, and suppliers.
Steps:

- Define a single strategic planning process by adapting the "best practices" of world-class schools to your school organization. Best practices are determined by "benchmarking" your school.

- Identify whom to involve in the quality process, including all levels of employees, key customer representatives, and key suppliers.
- Establish communication channels that feed vital data and information into the planning process.
- Determine those vital few long- and short-term goals necessary to improve customer satisfaction and operational performance.
- Assign executive ownership for each goal.
- Decide on measures for each goal.
- Deploy the plan to all employees, verifying that the activities of the district, departments, teams, and individuals are aligned with district objectives.
- Formalize processes for assessing progress and helping groups not performing to plan.

Goal: Involve all employees in continuous improvement.
Participants: All employees.
Steps:

- Communicate mission statement and vision statement to all district employees.
- Formalize processes for ongoing communication of district values to all levels of employees.
- Clarify management's role in the new system. Provide training and support to assist the transition.
- Train employees in the needed skills. Assume responsibility for their processes and results.
- Formalize feedback processes needed to assess and improve performance.
- Train employees in the skills they need to participate in quality teams.
- Initiate the use of quality teams to manage and improve processes and solve problems.

Goal: Manage and improve all key processes.
Participants: All employees.
Steps:

- Identify core processes that link directly to customer requirements.
- Train employees in process management and improvement.

- Assemble cross-functional quality teams to analyze processes that cross departmental boundaries.
- Formalize processes for using quality team findings to manage and improve processes.
- Reorganize the school around its core processes.
- Formalize processes for managing and improving processes involving suppliers.
- Assign responsibility for concentrating on processes within departments.
- Formalize processes for managing and improving these processes.
- Establish methods of communicating feedback to quality teams and results to the whole school.

Goal: Establish a system of measurement.
Participants: All employees.
Steps:

- Use information about customer and school requirements to identify key measures.
- Measure only what you can control.
- Make sure all measures are easy to collect, report, and understand.
- Train employees in taking, analyzing, and using measures to improve.
- Formalize processes for collecting and reporting data.
- Formalize processes for reviewing, analyzing, and using the data to improve.

Phase 5: Align and Extend Your Management Goals

One of the primary goals of the new model is to align every department, team, individual, function, process, plan, product, and service to meeting and exceeding your customers' requirements and your school's performance goals. Once the fundamentals needed to do this are in place, you can turn your attention to less urgent, though equally important, areas of your system.

The transition to the new school model begins with the areas that have the greatest impact on customers and the school. It then spreads out to include all that the school does. Now is a good time to remind yourself of the implications of managing the system, to place everything that is going on in your school in a holistic context.

Think of it as staging a play. You have chosen the play, assigned parts, begun practice, and booked theaters. Your attention now expands to include creating a set, designing costumes, and publicizing the events. You still work hard to fine-tune the performances, but you understand that the performances are only the most visible part of the production and that any area you neglect has the potential to detract from or undermine your efforts.

Phase 5 focuses attention on four areas that have had to wait: rewards and recognition, employee health and well-being, benchmarking, and school citizenship.

Action plan for aligning the system

Goal: Align compensation and recognition programs with the new management model.

Participants: All employees, particularly human resources professionals.

Steps:

- Survey employees. Understand their expectations, compensation, and recognition requirements.
- Form cross-functional quality teams that represent your employee base to assess and improve existing programs and to develop and implement new ones.
- Work with the quality teams to clarify the purpose of such programs. Focus on doing no harm first. Then promote the district's mission and vision second.
- Establish measurable program performance to meet the district's mission and vision.
- Study the issues affecting compensation to determine the best course of action for your district.
- Involve employees in running the district's recognition programs.
- Make at-risk pay and formal recognition dependent on measurable results, preferably team results.
- Formalize regular review and improvement processes for compensation and recognition programs.

Goal: Treat employees as the company's most important asset.

Participants: All employees, particularly senior executives and human resources staff.

Steps:

- Use employee feedback to determine their workplace requirements and expectations.
- Align employee health, well-being, and satisfaction goals with the district's mission and vision.
- Develop ongoing measures of employee health, well-being, and satisfaction.
- Formalize processes for reviewing and improving employee health, well-being, and satisfaction.

Goal: Establish a benchmarking program.

Participants: All employees.

Steps:

- Benchmarking is defined as "the continuous process of measuring and comparing the services and practices of your district's schools in relation to peers in those school districts recognized as leaders."
- Involve senior administrators, board members, and other key decision makers in learning about what benchmarking is and what benefits it offers.
- Formalize your school's benchmarking process, including defining who is involved, the steps in the process, and the expected results.
- Train employees in the benchmarking process.
- Use input from customers, suppliers, and employees to identify benchmarking opportunities, then prioritize those opportunities and assign responsibility.
- Empower benchmarking teams to organize and conduct the studies and present their recommendations.
- Formalize processes for translating recommendations into action plans, and for evaluating and improving the benchmarking process.

Goal: Provide leadership and support for publicly important purposes.

Participants: All employees, particularly senior administrators.
Steps:

- Establish your school district's mission, vision, and values in public responsibility and citizenship.
- Communicate these values throughout the organization, orally, through involvement in relevant activities, and by supporting employee participation in community affairs.
- Develop measures for employee and school involvement in such areas as waste minimization, environmental responsibility, volunteerism, charitable contributions, and community service.
- Formalize processes for reviewing and improving performance in these areas.

Phase 6: Refine Your System

The new school management model focuses on continuous improvement. The only way to continuously improve is to periodically look at where you are, compare it to where you want to be, and change course, speed up, or leap ahead. System assessments give you the information you need to decide what to do next.

They also help you develop the discipline of "refinement." Most schools fail to close the loop on their processes by leaving out the refinement cycle. They develop a terrific approach, deploy it throughout the district, then move on without leaving behind a process for regularly evaluating and improving the approach. The same concept applies to the entire system; the approaches you are taking need to be evaluated and improved on a regular basis.

We recommend an annual assessment based on the Baldrige criteria. No other tool is better at helping you explore, understand, and improve your entire school system.

Appendix B: Understanding Processes in Schools

There is almost a pathological competitiveness of medical students that acts as a barrier to the development of team approaches to the care of patients. Changes in relationships among medical specialists cannot come about if it must depend on friendship between individual physicians. In some areas of the United States, large multispecialty practices have been the mode for years. The growth of locations across the United States of such eminent medical practices as the Mayo Clinics, Cleveland Clinics, and Scripps Clinics have set the pace for a new era of medical practice and process.

The winning prescription for healing the illnesses of public schools requires all school personnel to wrestle with the nature of processes. The primary importance of processes for achieving dependable and durable teaching time in every classroom is a major stumbling block for many educators. Most people are in the habit of thinking solely in terms of things. We tend to think about the specific elements of products and the need for services. We need to think about the methods that underlie the creation and duration of the things.

A process is simply a repeated activity that changes something. Coming to grips with the importance of understanding and continually improving the school processes that underlie each of the six elements of the winning prescription is central to successful healing. Managing and improving processes is the critical challenge. It allows the school to approach, organize, and continually improve the reliability of classroom teaching time.

Here are some examples of processes needing study for continuous improvement.

- Determining student readiness for teaching when starting a class.
- Informing the teacher of earlier student performance to build continuity into instruction.

- Resolving customer complaints, and recruiting, orientating, training, and developing staff to handle problems.

Examining virtually every repeatable activity in a school and its school system needs to be viewed as a process of events. Indeed, processes are the system.

Schools need to stop thinking of problems as the property of an individual or some special event. Systems thinking shows us that most problems are not isolated events or special causes. They are built into the system, and they are a consequence of the system. These are flaws in the system that in some way impair the desired end result.

Deming shares an interesting statistic from his vast experience on the importance of the processes that make up the system. Deming teaches us that fully 94 percent of the troubles an organization has can be attributed to system. Only 6 percent are due to what he terms "special causes" (Deming 1986, 315). The bottom line for quality experts is simple and direct. Fix the processes and the end result you want will take care of itself.

The winning prescription for healing requires constant attention to the *how* of processes. It asks users to describe the sequence of activities, to discuss tools, and to define the techniques and methods at work during the process. Implementers are urged to think of the Baldrige/ISO criteria as a "census of processes" for motivating employees, planning for needs, and ensuring results.

Understanding and paying close attention to the processes at work inevitably lead us to the value of continuous improvement. Processes by their very nature can never be solved. Processes can only become a bad habit and deteriorate, or we become conscious of them and improve. Once fully involved in Baldrige/ISO, school staff cease playing the role of inspectors. They evolve into architects and engineers, seeking to improve the systems that create and sustain what internal and external customers require.

The heart and soul of the constant focus on improving processes is its road to prevention of failure and the need for remediation. Practicing good fire prevention helps reduce the need to fight as many fires. The target is not defect discovery, per se. We are looking at the processes that lead to defects. The goal is the elimination of problems before they lead to undesirable consequences.

Appendix C: Resources for Healing Public Schools

The Malcolm Baldrige National Quality Award
The Education Criteria for Performance Excellence*
Baldrige Quality Program
Contact:
  National Institute of Standards and Technology
  100 Bureau Drive, Stop 3460
  Gaithersburg, MD 20899-3460
  Phone: 1-301-975-NIST (6478)
  Fax: 1-301-975-8295
*For paper copy of document, e-mail *nqp@nist.gov*
*For online version, *http://www.quality.nist.gov/bcpg.pdf.htm*

ISO Standards
Contact:
  American National Standards Institute
  11 East 42nd Street
  New York, NY 10036
  Phone: 1-212-642-4900
  Fax: 1-212-302-1286
Email: *info@doccenter.com*

Copies of ISO 9000 Family of Standards
American Society for Quality
Contact:
  ASQ Quality Press
  611East Wisconsin Avenue
  PO Box 3005
  Milwaukee, WI 53201-3005
  Phone: 1-800-248-1946 or 414-272-8575
Email: *http://www.asq.org*

The 32nd Annual Phi Delta Kappa/Gallup POLL of the Public's Attitudes toward the Public Schools
Contact:
  Phi Delta Kappa International
  PO Box 789
  Bloomington, IN 47402-0789
  Phone: 1-800-766-1156
URL: *http://www.pdkintl.org*

Appendix D: Healthy Schools with Systems Thinking

A disease is not an object, a thing to be found. It is a process inextricably bound up with the unfolding story of a particular patient. In medical practice, the doctor is trained to rely on objective data. If the doctor wants to retain his bias in his personal life, that is purely a personal matter.

The most powerful intellectual technology for planning a reliable quality school is systems thinking. It is also the major tool for understanding the relationship of technology to the professional practice of education. In its simplest language, the systems thinker says: "It's better to see the whole problem than just a part of it."

Systems thinking is an aid to clear thinking about good teaching practice as standard or prevailing school classroom practice. It clearly shows that technology is the embodiment of what works.

A system is a group of components, integrated or coordinated to accomplish a purpose. There are many examples of purposes served by the idea of systems. The purpose can be to produce a car, to produce a computer program, to produce a caring environment, or to produce an educated citizen. The notion of a system is a very general one—that is what gives it such great practical power.

Two main ideas form the fabric of the systems concept. The first idea is the purpose or result. The second idea is coordination or management of the elements that make up the system. Schools have purposes, and there are elements and functions that form the school system. These various elements must be carefully managed to see that the school's purposes are realized.

The school system is also made up of many subsystems. There is, generally, a transportation system to get the kids to school and home safely and on time, a food services system to feed them, a communication system that gets information to and from the children and their parents, a policymaking and implementation system governs the school, and a teaching system that carries out the objectives of the adopted curriculum.

The principal task of school administration is to keep each system functioning efficiently and effectively. It means keeping them supporting each other on behalf of the overall purpose of the enterprise, rather than clashing. The systems can and do often operate quite independently. Effectiveness is improved when they act in synchrony and assist and reinforce one another.

The heart of the educational system is the instructional system. A good definition of this system in classrooms is *an integrated set of technology (media, equipment, methods, materials), and persons (teachers, students, parents, and administrators giving logistical support) to efficiently and effectively perform the functions required to accomplish the standards.*

System thinking can cause a remarkable improvement in teacher and administrator attitudes toward the process of instruction. It is an attitude directly opposite the mind-set that exists under a tyranny of chance. It is an attitude of professional responsibility for getting hold of what works.

The spirit represented by this attitude may be the single most important change to help heal the illness afflicting our schools. System thinking has the most direct bearing on school system effectiveness. Through the winning prescription, all school partners share a healing attitude. This new attitude translates into actions. If the instructional system (the teachers, materials, equipment, methods, time, or any other components that make it up) is not effective and the students do not learn what is expected or required, the system is redesigned until it does. Neither parents nor teachers nor students are blamed.

The functions that make up an effective instructional system have been identified and well documented in the educational research. At a minimum, the following five functions must be present and taught well.

1. Specification of the Desired Learning Outcomes

Until we can derive some adequate physiological indicators, learning is a concept that can only be inferred. We can't really see any learning directly. What we see is a change in two states. First, the person can now do something that he or she could not do before the learning experience. Second, that something is the target or purpose of the classroom learning experience.

It has been a long struggle to persuade educators to spell out the learning targets in ways that can be objectively recognized. There remains a common practice of stating the desired targets in terms that are themselves highly abstract. Thus, we hear of such targets as the development of understandings, beliefs, and knowledge. We need descriptions of how we will reasonably estimate the extent to which the learner understands, appreciates, knows, accepts, or believes what the classroom learning experience intended.

A technology for the adequate description of learning targets, both of training and education, does exist by describing the targets in ways that can be reasonably verified by both the school and the customer of the learning experience. We can then harness the power of system thinking.

2. The Presentation of Knowledge and Performance

Teachers can employ a variety of teaching technologies, such as reading, lectures, graphic aids, television, films, tape recorders, computers, videotapes, and CD-ROMs.

In the past, presentations traveled one way, from teacher to learner. Now, there are readily available more effective two-way or interactive modes. It is in the learning system function, the presentation of knowledge and performance, that classroom learning experiences can be shared with students in a cost-effective and efficient manner.

3. The Practice of Knowledge and Performance

The targets of education consist of the skilled performances to be learned, and the enabling skills and knowledge components that are essential for mastering the performances. Think of any budding musician or athlete.

To be effective, learners must practice both the end performance and the enabling skill and knowledge components. While it is necessary for the mastery of full task performance to provide the practice on the full performance, it is also more effective to provide practice of the enabling skills and knowledge. Here we see the catching and throwing of a ball.

This can materially reduce the amount of time and expense required to master the full performance.

4. The Management of the Learning Experience

This function refers to those classroom activities designed to keep the learner actively interacting with the elements of the learning experience. Several modern developments have emerged to move this process along. Cooperative learning, new forms of individualized instruction, and providing incentives tied directly to progress are among some of the most important.

5. Quality Control

The measurement of the actual learner performance is the source of the information that serves as the cornerstone of quality control. Because this information is the feedback that leads to corrective action, the data on the learner's performance must be valid, reliable, objective, and detailed in a given classroom learning situation.

Quality control is the function that measures how well the target has been achieved. It identifies the need for corrective action and activates the corrective action. It is feedback plus corrective action. This is the basic advance over common classroom evaluation that merely identifies a gap between what was intended and what was achieved.

Quality control can produce the remarkable change in attitude of those providing the education described earlier. It is the attitude of mutual accountability for results. If the learning experience provided the learners does not achieve what was expected, the learning experience is redesigned. The learner is provided additional opportunities to be successful. Nobody is blamed. It is the system's job to deliver the achievement of standards.

Appendix E: Draft State Reliability Legislation

Simple examples of preventive medicine include helping patients stop smoking, eating a healthier diet, or starting an exercise program. The active participation of the patient with the doctor as teacher goes a long way toward helping the patient. It requires greater understanding of human development and extends the entire range of potential for change into later years.

The following sample legislation may enable you to partner with your legislative body to form a healthier school.

DRAFT LEGISLATION

An Act concerning the institution of continual improvement through quality assurance in the public school systems

BE IT Enacted by the Senate and General Assembly of the State of _____.

1. The Legislature finds and declares that:
   a. It is the goal of the State of _____ to prepare its students to be internationally competitive and to meet world-class standards through our system of public education.
   b. In order to achieve this State priority, leaders from government, education, business, and our local communities must work collaboratively to promote quality, creativity, and accountability in the delivery of educational services.
   c. An alternative program of continual improvement and quality assurance of schools may be used to promote the goals of quality and excellence in our schools and to effectuate educational improvement in this State.

    d. The utilization of an alternative program of continual improvement and quality assurance of schools could effectuate educational improvement by promoting greater use of quality management principles, increasing the exchange of information concerning best practices and the achievement of excellence in education, and promoting partnerships between the public and private sectors in pursuit of educational excellence.

    e. The State of _____ would benefit from the use of an alternate program of continual improvement and quality assurance of schools because:

        (1) The alternate program stimulates increased cooperation among internal and external stakeholders in a school system;

        (2) The program mobilizes the business community to assist school districts by sharing its expertise in total quality management principles;

        (3) The program fosters consensus in establishing district goals, clear values, high standards, and organizational excellence;

        (4) The ongoing nature of the district's self assessment process shall result in continuous improvement and increased accountability for public schools; and

        (5) The application of quality management principles and a self-assessment process shall more efficiently utilize State and local resources.

2. a. Notwithstanding any law to the contrary, a school district may apply to participate in an alternative program of continual improvement and quality assurance for the purpose of certification. Prior to the application of the school district to the State Superintendent of Education for participation in the alternative program of continual improvement and quality assurance, there shall be consensus between the school districts and the majority representative of the school employees in the district concerning the district's participation in the program.

    b. A school district approved to participate in the alternative program of continual improvement and quality assurance shall conduct ongoing continual improvement and quality assurance according to the criteria established by the State Superintendent of Education, in consultation with the State's Industry–Education Council. The criteria shall include, but not be limited to, the criteria used in the education eligibility category of the Malcolm Baldrige National Quality Award, established pursuant to the proper subsection of Public Law such as: (1) leadership; (2) information and analysis; (3) strategic and operational planning; (4) human resource development and management; (5) educational and business process management; (6) school performance results; and (7) student focus and stakeholder satisfaction.

   c. Instructional design criteria from ISO 9000 provisions for education and training may be used to augment the Baldrige criteria.

   d. The State Superintendent may eliminate a school district from participation in the alternative program of continual improvement and quality assurance, if the State Superintendent deems it to be advisable. The State Superintendent shall inform the school district of its elimination from the alternative program of continual improvement and quality assurance provided for in the proper sections.

3. The State Superintendent shall promulgate rules and regulations pursuant to the _____ Act, P.L. ____, necessary to effectuate the provisions of this act.

4. This act shall take effect immediately and the State Superintendent of Education shall make the alternative program of continual improvement and quality assurance available to eligible school districts in the 2001–2002 school year.

STATEMENT

This bill provides for an alternative program of continual improvement and quality assurance for school districts for the purpose of certification pursuant to section ___of P.L. ____. The alternative program of continual improvement and quality assurance shall be based on the district's continuous process of self-assessment according to criteria established pursuant to this act.

A school district that participates in the alternative program of continual improvement and quality assurance shall conduct ongoing continual improvement and quality assurance according to criteria established by the State Superintendent of Education, in consultation with the State Industry–Education Council.

The criteria shall include, but not be limited to, the criteria used in the education eligibility category of the Malcolm Baldrige National Quality Award, augmented by the instructional design sections of ISO 9000 for education and training established pursuant to subsection of Section ___ of Public Law ____ and the State Quality Achievement Award established pursuant to Order No. ____ which focus on key requirements for organizational excellence.

The criteria shall address leadership, information and analysis, strategic and operational planning, human resource development and management, educational and business process management, school performance results, and student focus and stakeholder satisfaction.

The bill provides that the State Superintendent of Education may eliminate a school district from participation in the alternative program of continual improvement and quality assurance, if the State Superintendent deems it to be advisable. The State Superintendent of Education shall make the alternative program of continual improvement and quality assurance available to eligible school districts in the 2001–2002 school year.

Appendix F: Articles and Books

There are several good resources for continuing your search into the subject of implementing quality principles in public schools. Some focus on the mechanics of the subject. Others provide guidance in leadership. Still others are listed because they provide unique insights into quality thinking.

A book should be a valuable resource, and we are fortunate that we have so many publications that offer us keen insights into the subject of quality. Do not be fooled by a "how to" approach to the subject of quality. Quality is a frame of mind. This frame of mind determines your eventual success in pursuing and implementing quality principles in the public school classroom.

Alexander, William F., and Serfass, Richard W., *Futuring Tools for Strategic Quality Planning in Education,* American Society for Quality, 1999.

Bonsting, John Jay, *Schools of Quality: An Introduction to Total Quality Management in Education,* ASCD, 1996.

Burt, Samuel M., and Lessinger, Leon M., *Volunteer Industry Involvement in Public Education,* D. C. Heath Lexington Books, 1970.

Cassell, M.D., Eric J., *Doctoring: The Nature of Primary Care Medicine,* Oxford University Press, 1997.

Cousins, Norman, *Head First: The Biology of Hope,* E. W. P. Dutton, 1989.

Hills, James A., *Total Quality Management in the Classroom: Blue Ribbon Standards for Teaching,* Fairplay Publishing Co., 1999.

Hoy, Charles Colin, Bayne-Jarine, Charles, Wood, Margaret, and Brody, Celeste M., *Improving Quality in Education,* Palmer Press, 2000.

Goonan, M.D., Kathleen Jennison, *The Juran Prescription: Clinical Quality Management,* Juran Institute, 1995.

Kiefer, William N., and Krape Jr., Morris E., *I Like It When You Help Me Learn to Read.*

Kiefer, William N., *Putting Kids First with Quality: Implementing ISO 9001 in Public Education,* forthcoming.

Kossoff, Leslie L., *Executive Thinking: The Dream, The Vision, The Mission Achieved,* Davies-Black Publishing, 1999. [Cited as one of the top ten books of 1999 by Management General, and a main selection of the Doubleday Executive Program Book Club.]

Kossoff, Leslie L., *Managing for Quality: How to Implement and Manage a Business Strategy of Continuous Improvement,* 3rd edition, 1998.

Jenkins, Lee, *Improving Student Learning: Applying Deming's Quality Principles in Classrooms,* American Society for Quality, 1997.

Langford, David P., and Cleary, Barbara A., *Orchestrating Learning with Quality,* American Society for Quality, 1995.

Lezotte, Lawrence W., *Creating the Total Quality Effective School,* Effective School Products, 1992.

Lessinger, Leon M., *Every Kid a Winner: Accountability in Education,* Simon & Schuster, 1970.

Lessinger, Leon M., and Salowe, Allen E., *Game Time: The Educators' Playbook for the New Global Economy,* Technomic Publishing Co., 1997.

Lessinger, Leon M., and Tyler, Robert W., editors, *Accountability in Education,* Charles A. Jones, 1971.

Mergen, Erhan, "Quality Management Applied to Higher Education," *Total Quality Management,* May 2000, pp. 345–53.

Rose, Lowell C. and Gallup, Alec M. *The 32nd Annual Phi Delta Kappa/Gallup Poll of the Public's Attitudes toward the Public Schools,* August 2000, Phi Delta Kappa International, Bloomington, Ind.

Sallis, Edward, *Total Quality Management in Education,* Stylus Publishing, 1999.

Salowe, Allen, *Prostate Cancer: Overcoming Denial with Action: A Guide to Screening, Treatment, and Planning,* St. Martin's Press, 1997.

Shipley, Jim, and Collins, Chris, *Going to Scale with TQM: The Pinellas County Schools' Journal toward Quality,* SERVE, 1997.

Siegel, Petty and Byrne, Sandra, *Using Quality to Redesign School Systems,* American Society for Quality, 1994.

Wolverton, Mimi, *New Alliance: Continuous Quality and Classroom Effectiveness,* GWO School of Education and Human Development 1996.

References

Albrecht, Karl. 1992. *The Only Thing That Matters: Bring the Power of the Customer into the Center of Your Business.* 14.

American Institutes for Research. 1999. *An Educators' Guide To Schoolwide Reform.* Arlington, Va.: Education Research Service.

Avishai, Bernard. 1996. "Unemployables." *The Wall Street Journal,* 29 July. [1-19]

Baldrige Education Criteria. 1998.

Barlow, Jim. 1999. *The Houston Chronicle,* 23 July.

Bennett, William. 1986. *What Works.* U.S. Department of Education.

Berliner, David. 1979. Tempus Educare. In *Research in Teaching,* edited by P. L. Peterson and H. J. Walbert. Berkeley, Calif.: McCutcheon.

———. 1987. Simple Theories of Effective Teaching and a Simple Theory of Classroom Instruction. In *Talks to Teachers,* edited by D. C. Berliner and B. V. Rosenshine. New York: Random House.

Berman, Henry. 1986.

Bernhardt, Victoria. 1994. *The School Portfolio: A Comprehensive Framework for School Improvement.* Princeton Junction, N.J.: Eye on Education Publishers.

Broder, David. 1999. "Good Business in the Schools," *The Washington Post,* 14 July.

Cairnes, Herbert. 1949. "The Student Objective," *Lancet,* vol. 2: 665.

Clark, Don. Personal letter to Leon Lessinger, 5 June 1999.

Clowes, George A. 2000. Texas Academic Standards Upheld. *School Reform News* 4, March.

Connors, Eugene T. 1981. *Educational Tort Liability and Malpractice.* Bloomington, Ind.: Phi Delta Kappa.

Consumer Reports Annual Auto Issue. *Consumer Reports,* May 2000.

Dale, Edgar. 1967. "Historical Setting of Programmed Instruction." In *Sixty-Sixth Yearbook of the National Society for the Study of Education,* part 2, chapter 2.

Deming, W. Edwards. 1986. *Out of the Crisis.* Cambridge: Massachusetts Institute of Technology, Center for Advanced Engineering Study.

Drake, Telbert, and William Roe. 1986. The Principalship. 3rd ed. New York: Macmillan, 176–77.

Drucker, Peter. 1973. *Management: Tasks, Responsibilities, Practices.* New York: Harper and Row.

Gates, Bill. 1996. *The Road Ahead.* New York: Penguin.

Goodlad, John. 1984. *A Place Called School: Prospects for the Future.* New York: McGraw-Hill.

Green, Judith, and Robert Shellenberger. 1991. *The Dynamics of Health and Wellness: A Biopsychological Approach.* Fort Worth, Tex.: Holt, Rinehart and Winston, 567.

Hart, Christopher W. L., and Christopher E. Bogan. 1992. *The Baldrige: What It Is, How It's Won, How to Use It to Improve Quality in Your Company.* New York: McGraw-Hill.

Kaplan, Robert S., and Norton, David, P. 1993. Putting the Balanced Scorecard to Work. *Harvard Business Review* September–October, 134–47.

———. 1996. Using the Balanced Scorecard as a Strategic Management System. *Harvard Business Review* January–February, 75–85.

Law, James E. and Janis S. Law. 1994. *TQM in Education: A Guide to Survival.* Reston, Va: Association of School Business Officials International.

Leithwood, Ken. 1999. Personal letter to Leon Lessinger, 1 February.

Lessinger, Leon M. and Allen E. Salowe. 1997. *Game Time: The Educator's Playbook for the New Global Economy.* Lancaster, Pa: Technomic Publishing Company.

Mallak, L.A., L. S. Bringelson, and D. M. Lyth. 1997. A Cultural Study of ISO Certification. *International Journal of Quality and Rehability Management* 4 (4): 328–48.

Markle, Susan. 1967. Empirical Testing of Progress. In *Sixty-Sixth Yearbook of the National Society for the Study of Education,* part 2, chapter 5.

McLuhan, Marshall. 1994. *Understanding Media.* Cambridge, Mass: MIT Press.

Mayeroff, Milton. 1971. *On Caring.* New York: Harper and Row.

Miller, D. W. 1999. The Black Hole of Education Research. *The Chronicle of Higher Education*, August 6: A17–A18.

National Reading Panel Report: Teaching Children to Read. 2000. National Institute of Child Health and Human Development. Washington, DC: U.S. Government Printing Office.

Peters, Thomas J., and Robert H. Waterman Jr. 1982. In Search of Excellence. New York: Warner Books.

Rose, Lowell C., and Alec M. Gallup. 2000. *The 32nd Annual Phi Delta Kappa/Gallup Poll of the Public's Attitudes toward the Public Schools.* Bloomington, Ind.: Phi Delta Kappa International.

Sanders, William I., and June C. Rivers. 1998. Cumulative and Residual Effects of Teachers on Future Students Academic Achievement. *Thinking K–16* 3 (summer).

Sashkin, Marshall and Kenneth Kiser. 1993. *Putting Total Quality to Work.* San Francisco: Berrett-Koehler.

Senge, Peter. 1990. *The Fifth Discipline: The Art and Practice of the Learning Organization.* New York: Doubleday.

Spencer, Herbert. 1860. *Education: Intellectual, Moral, Physical.* London: Williams & Norgate.

Stewart, Don. 1971. *Educational Malpractices*. Westminister, CA: State Services Publisher 1971.

Stringfield, Sam. 1995. Attempting to Enhance Students' Learning through Innovative Programs: The Case for Schools Evolving into High Reliability Organizations. *School Effectiveness and School Improvement* 6 (1): 67–96.

Taylor, Frederick W. 1911. *The Principles of Scientific Management*. New York: Harper and Bros.

Zuckerman, Marilyn R., and Lewis J. Halata. 1992. *Incredibly American*. Milwaukee, Wis.: ASQC Press, 8.

About the Authors

Leon M. Lessinger is a senior fellow of the Florida Institute of Education (Type I State University System Education Improvement Center). He was the chairman of the Board of Governors, Florida Educational Research and Development Program. Dr. Lessinger was chosen by Vice President Hubert Humphrey to launch the National Teachers Corps. and served as president of the Aerospace Education Foundation.

Dr. Lessinger was associate commissioner of elementary and secondary schools in the U.S. Office of Education. He served as dean of the College of Education, University of South Carolina, clinical professor of medicine at UCLA, and superintendent of three California school districts. He is widely published and is a licensed California clinical psychologist.

A Florida eminent scholar of education policy and economic development, he holds a B.S. in mechanical engineering from North Carolina State University, a B.A. in psychology, and M.Ed. and Ed.D. in educational psychology and school administration from UCLA. He received an honorary doctorate in science from LaVerne College, California. He is the author of *Every Kid a Winner* and coauthored *Game Time: The Educator's Playbook for the New Global Economy* with Allen Salowe.

Allen E. Salowe, a consulting planner/educator, is a senior fellow of the Florida Institute of Education (Type I State University System Education Improvement Center) and senior fellow of the Florida Center for Electronic Communication (Type II Research Center at Florida Atlantic University). He served as president of the Plainfield (N.J.) school board and adjunct professor of management at Webster University.

Mr. Salowe is formerly senior vice president of planning for ITT Community Development Corporation, senior operations executive for ITT World Headquarters, group planning director for Champion International Products Group, and cofounder of Visualization Technologies, a computer animation firm. He serves as economic and financial adviser to Florida Community Development Special Taxing Districts.

Mr. Salowe holds a B.A. in economics from the University of Miami, an MBA in management from Nova Southeastern University, a member of the American Society for Quality and the American Planning Association, and a registered member of the American Institute of Certified Planners (AICP). He authored *Prostate Cancer: Overcoming Denial with Action* and coauthored *Game Time: The Educator's Playbook for the New Global Economy* with Leon Lessinger.

CONTRIBUTORS

Leslie L. Kossoff is a leading organizational thinker and consultant. Her firm, Kossoff Management Consulting, has been providing guidance in the areas of executive and management development, and organizational strategy and excellence since the mid-1980s. She has assisted a range of Fortune 100 clients, as well as nonprofit organizations in the public and private sectors.

Ms. Kossoff enjoys an outstanding reputation as an invited speaker at professional and educational conferences throughout the United States. During her long-term alliance with Dr. W. Edwards Deming, she assisted in his client consultations and presented at his seminars on implementation obstacles and strategies. Deming declared Kossoff "Quite simply, one of the best at implementation."

Dr. William N. Kiefer is an educator with over twenty-five years experience. He has been a teacher, school psychologist, program coordinator for early childhood education, elementary and secondary school principal, and central office administrator. Currently, he is the coordinator of planning and quality systems in the office of the superintendent of the school district of Lancaster, Pennsylvania.

Under Dr. Kiefer's leadership, Lancaster was the first U.S. school district to be registered to the ISO 9001 quality standard. Dr. Kiefer's books include *I Like It When You Help Me Learn to Read,* coauthored with Morris E. Krape Jr., and *Putting Kids First with Quality: Implementing ISO 9001 in Public Education,* forthcoming.

In addition to his work in school reform, Dr. Kiefer is a major general in the U.S. Army Reserve. His career with the Army has spanned thirty-four years of command and staff positions. He is a recognized speaker on leadership. Dr. Kiefer holds B.A. and M.S. degrees in psychology from Millersville University and an Ed.D. in educational administration from Walden University.